60 YEARS OF
PADDLE STEAMER PRESERVATION

THE PSPS STORY

COMPILED AND EDITED BY
RICHARD CLAMMER

FOR

THE PADDLE STEAMER
PRESERVATION SOCIETY

This book is dedicated to

Professor Alan Robinson
Founder of the PSPS

© Black Dwarf Publications, Richard Clammer and other contributors 2019
British Library Cataloguing-in-Publication Data. A catalogue record for this book
is available from the British Library
ISBN: 9781903599 27 3

BLACK DWARF PUBLICATIONS
Unit 144B, Harbour Road Trading Estate, Lydney, Gloucestershire GL15 4EJ
www.lightmoor.co.uk / info@lightmoor.co.uk
Black Dwarf Publications is an imprint of Black Dwarf Lightmoor Publications Ltd
Printed in Poland
www.lfbookservices.co.uk

CONTENTS

Forward by *Timothy West & Prunella Scales*

Introduction

This page and cover picture; Waverley *during a cruise around the Isle of Wight, 19th September 2015*
Roy Tait

Kingswear Castle *passing Greenway Quay during a harbour cruise on the afternoon of 21st May 2013*   Richard Clammer

FORWARD

A RESOLUTE-LOOKING couple, well wrapped-up, trudge their determined way along the promenade. They are obviously well into their eighties; where are they going? Church? An orchestral concert? A privately-owned railway?

No, they are en-route to board the paddle steamer *Waverley* and, on closer inspection, might be identified as Prunella Scales and Timothy West.

Pru's first memories of this vessel reach back to early professional days in Scotland; while my (Tim's) own paddle steamer history – mostly spent on board the six paddlers remaining of P & A Campbell's White Funnel Fleet – spans that brief Indian Summer between the end of the war and the beginning of universal ownership of the motor car.

We don't want to suggest that interest in paddle steamers is confined to octogenarians: the appeal is universal, thanks principally to the conception of the Paddle Steamer Preservation Society, whose 60th Anniversary Richard Clammer and his fellow contributors are celebrating in this beautiful and thoroughly-researched book.

As to the Society's origin, Pru and I knew nothing. I had never heard of Professor Alan Robinson who, while on holiday in 1959, became concerned that the lovely *Freshwater* was destined for the breaker's yard, and wrote to the Daily Telegraph about it. His letter was published, and enough public interest was generated to examine the possibility of forming an historical preservation society, looking after the memories of steamers of the past as well as the possibility of protecting those still afloat. After all, such societies already existed for railway locomotives, cars, buses, trams and even aeroplanes; why not for paddle steamers, who for decades had provided delighted families with the experience of a day's excursion to sea, sometimes without a promised destination.

The Society, of course, does not limit itself either to passenger craft or, indeed, their geography. *Paddle Wheels*, its quarterly journal, regularly reports on existing paddle-driven tugs, ferries and cargo boats from all over the globe, as well as the delectable lake-crossing passenger steamers of Switzerland and Italy.

After reading Richard Clammer's recital of the early days that gradually enabled the Society to become something to be reckoned with, we come to the significant purchase, restoration and return to service of *Kingswear Castle*, the beautiful 1924 river paddle steamer that went on to serve passengers in Thanet and the Medway for many years before being returned to her native Dartmouth. The purchase of this vessel and, of course, the later acquisition of *Waverley* for £1 from Caledonian MacBrayne has led to vigorous attempts to rescue some other existing vessels still in a condition of possible salvation: *Medway Queen, Ryde*, (no, surely!) and *Maid of the Loch* (in excellent condition, seaworthy and lacking but £1 million for a new boiler before being able to ply again between the various little piers of Loch Lomond.)

This book reports fully on these and other episodes in the history of the PSPS, and does so entertainingly and with something like two hundred photographs to jog our memories.

Characters in the story whom Prunella and I have become privileged to know as friends over the years include Douglas and Jean McGowan, Nick James, Ian Quinn, Nigel Coombes and Terry Sylvester. They have all in their different ways contributed to this present book and to the continuing success of the PSPS whose 60th Anniversary we joyfully celebrate this year. May this just be the beginning...

PSPS patrons Timothy West and Prunella Scales in Waverley's *wheelhouse, with Andy Dodds on the helm.* Douglas McGowan

Prunella Scales & Timothy West
April 2019

Typical of the many fine paddle steamers which went to the breaker's yard during the 1950s was P. & A. Campbell Ltd's Glen Gower seen here moored in St Augustine's Reach, Bristol City Centre, during May 1956. The large red Co-operative Wholesale Society building was erected in 1906 and demolished in 1973. Glen Gower was built in 1922 and fitted with engines from the Albion (ex Slieve Donard) of 1893. Based initially at Swansea, she spent many years on the South coast and reintroduced Campbell's cross-channel sailings to Boulogne in July 1954. After spending two years laid up she was towed away to the breakers in April 1960.
PSPS Collection

"Have you a cherished dream – a dream that just one great paddle steamer could stay operational far into the future, properly serviced, maintained and cared for? Have you?… This dream could now come true – let me tell you how."

INTRODUCTION

THESE visionary words, penned by Terry Sylvester early in 1974, formed the opening paragraph of a letter from the Chairman of the Paddle Steamer Preservation Society, announcing that *Waverley*, the last seagoing paddler in the World, had been offered as a gift to the Society by her owners Caledonian MacBrayne, and appealing for contributions towards the £50,000 which would be needed in order to return her to passenger service on the Clyde. The task seemed colossal and many doubted that the dream could possibly come true, but the letter was deeply persuasive and struck exactly the right notes of urgency, challenge and pride. Donors proved generous, a small band of dedicated individuals drove the project forward and the rest, as they say, is history.

Today, sitting on the deck of *Kingswear Castle* as she wends her leisurely way between the densely-wooded banks of the beautiful river Dart on her way upstream to Totnes; or watching *Waverley* come sweeping into a pier and go full astern in a welter of foam as the heaving lines snake ashore, I have to pinch myself to believe that it is actually happening. Is it really possible, that for 45 and 54 years respectively since they were withdrawn from service as outdated and uneconomical, these two gems of Britain's maritime history have still been earning their keep and giving pleasure to countless passengers on the very services for which they were designed?

That the public has indeed been able to view the British coast from the deck of an excursion paddle steamer; witness the timeless pageant of arrivals and departures; hear the hiss of live steam, the rhythmic thumping of paddle wheels, the clanging of engine room telegraphs or the clatter of gangways; and revel in the visual delights of subtle curves, colourful paintwork, shining varnish and polished brass is truly remarkable.

This unlikely miracle has been due to the continuing efforts of the Paddle Steamer Preservation Society and its associated charitable companies which own and operate the two steamers on its behalf. Arguably Britain's oldest and most successful maritime preservation society, the PSPS has exceeded its original aim of purchasing and preserving a single paddle steamer, has built up a superb collection of photographs, materials and objects associated with paddle steamers and does its very best to educate the public in the significance of these wonderful ships in the nation's maritime heritage.

Along the way it has raised almost £4million to support its two steamers which, quite rightly, are subject to stringent safety regulations and the consequent costly upgrades to structure or equipment. They also operate in a challenging marine environment, incurring corrosion and wear, and therefore require constant renewal and repair. Plans are in place for some major refurbishment of *Kingswear Castle* and, even as these words were being written, news was received that significant problems had been discovered in *Waverley's* 20 year-old boilers, which will now need to be replaced before the ship can sail again. A major fund-raising campaign has been launched and the need for the Society is greater than ever. PSPS has met major challenges in the past and, with public support, will strive to do so once again.

The aim of this book is to mark the 60th Anniversary of the PSPS by bringing its remarkable story to the widest possible audience. The first five chapters are broadly chronological and have drawn on the PSPS journal *Paddle Wheels*, the Society's extensive archive and the memories of a number of key, early members. The remaining chapters deal with key aspects of the Society's history and have been written by some of the people most closely involved. While the careers of our two steamers in preservation are covered in some detail, those wishing to learn more about their earlier history are recommended to follow the reading suggestions detailed in Appendix 3. The book is illustrated with a selection of rare and mostly unpublished colour images drawn from the Society's Archive and from the collections of individual members. They depict numerous fondly-remembered steamers as well as many important events and characters from the Society's history and will, I hope, prove to be a delight in their own right.

Having grown up in Weymouth and sailed regularly on board Cosens' paddler steamers *Consul*, *Embassy* and *Monarch*, I joined the PSPS at the age of eleven in 1962, at a time when my beloved ships seemed to be in imminent danger of extinction. In the 57 years since then, I have derived immense pleasure and stimulation from my membership, satisfaction from continuing to put to sea each summer on an operational paddler, and have made many lasting friends along the way. Being given the opportunity to compile this book has been a huge privilege and has reminded me of just how many individuals have given of their time, money and varied talents to make that "cherished dream" come true.

If you are an existing PSPS member, I hope that, in addition to stirring some happy memories, this book will amuse and inform you with some hitherto forgotten facts. If you are not, then I hope you will be deeply impressed by the remarkable achievements of the Society, and stimulated to join us. If a new generation of readers can be persuaded to step forward, join the PSPS, donate generously to fund-raising appeals, become actively involved and eventually take on the mantle of ensuring that *Waverley* and *Kingswear Castle* sail on for another 60 years, then the book will have succeeded in its aim.

Richard Clammer
Tutshill, Gloucestershire
May 2019.

Freshwater, the steamer which started the PSPS. During the early summer of 1959 she was renamed Freshwater II *to free her original name for her replacement, a double-ended car ferry. Having only been used on relief duties for several years, the paddler is seen here shifting berth at Lymington on a summer Saturday in readiness to help cope with the hoards who travelled by train and ferry to and from the Isle of Wight on "change-over" days.*

Keith Abraham

With her decks packed with holiday-makers returning from the Isle of Wight, Freshwater II *arrives at Lymington Pier on a Summer Saturday during 1959. The master has just rung down 'stop' on the telegraph and the seamen on the foredeck and sponson stand ready to throw their heaving lines ashore. Out of sight to the right of the photograph a train is standing ready at Lymington Pier Station to convey the passengers along the branch line to Brockenhurst where they will transfer to main-line trains for their onward journeys.*

Keith Abraham

CHAPTER ONE

THE FORMATION OF THE SOCIETY

With contributions from Victor Gray, Margaret Hutchinson, Pat Murrell & Alan Robinson

ALTHOUGH the large and colourful fleets of paddle steamers which graced our coastal waters in Victorian and Edwardian times were now but a fond memory, and the inter-war years had seen a further contraction of services, 1950s Britain still supported a wide and representative selection of paddle-powered vessels.

Despite the fact that a significant number were lost while serving as minesweepers, anti-aircraft ships or troop transports during the Second World War, and others were so worn out that by the end of hostilities they had been fit only for the breaker's yard, many well-loved excursion paddlers survived, were re-fitted and returned to their familiar, seasonal duties carrying crowds of happy passengers on day trips from piers and harbours on the South Coast, Bristol Channel, Thames and Clyde.

Paddle steamers were also well-represented on a number of regular ferry services. On the Clyde and on the three routes to the Isle of Wight from Lymington, Southampton and Portsmouth, the steamers had often been designed with a dual ferry/excursion role in mind, but on Britain's estuaries and rivers some far more specialised craft were to be found. The ferry fleets which carried cars and passengers across the Humber, Tay, Forth, Cleddau and the Thames at Woolwich were largely paddle powered and included some truly fascinating vessels, including the last paddle cargo ship which plied daily between Southampton and Cowes.

Finally, a substantial concentration of steam paddle tugs was still to be found in the north-East where the rivers Tyne, Tees and Wear together with the coastal coal ports of Seaham and Blyth formed a traditional stronghold. A few individual ships continued to operate on the Clyde, Mersey and Manchester Ship Canal, and the Admiralty maintained a small fleet of elderly but extremely powerful paddle tugs for specialised use in the Royal Dockyards. Indeed, the Admiralty was so convinced of the advantages of paddle power that between 1956 and 1958 it had commissioned a class of seven diesel-electric paddlers to replace some of the ageing steamers.

This diverse fleet provided a rich source of interest for paddle steamer enthusiasts, of whom there were many. Ever since the earliest days of competition and racing between rival fleets, some passengers had developed strong preferences and loyalties to particular ships or operators. For some the delight lay in sailing as often and on as many different routes as possible; others became avid photographers or collectors of postcards and memorabilia; and some began to research and record the history of the paddle steamer fleets. Captain Williamson had published his ground-breaking *The Clyde Passenger Steamer: Its Rise and Progress During the 19th Century* as long ago as 1904, Andrew McQueen had followed with his *Clyde River Steamers of the Last Fifty years* in 1923, and during the 1930s and 1940s a number of wonderful books by C.L.D. Duckworth & Graham Langmuir, Frank Burtt, Grahame Farr and, Geoffrey Grimshaw appeared. All resulting from countless hours spent delving in the archives in a pre-internet age, these invaluable histories did much to stimulate further research.

Strong friendships developed and many of these enthusiasts corresponded regularly, shared information and looked forward to summer meetings afloat on their favourite ships. In 1932 the Clyde River Steamer Club had been formed with the aim of creating opportunities for enthusiasts to meet, sail and talk together, and proved enormously popular. It thrives to this day, maintains an important photographic archive and produces regular publications which are noted for the high quality of their historical research. On the Bristol Channel a short-lived White Funnel Fleet Supporters' Association was set up in 1954 and within a year its newsletter had transformed itself into *Ship Ahoy* the excellent journal of The World Ship Society's South Wales Branch, which showed an intense interest in the steamers of P.& A. Campbell Ltd. and spawned a number of respected writers and historians.

As the decade progressed, however, the size of Britain's paddle steamer fleet began to dwindle. Between 1950 and 1959 changing fashions, rising fuel, wage and maintenance cost and sheer old age began to take their toll and a depressingly long list of ships departed for the breakers' yards. These included the Scottish steamers *Duchess of Fife*, *Marchioness of Lorne*, *Prince Edward*, and *Jupiter*; *Merstone*, *Solent Queen*, *Lorna Doone*, *Princess Helena*, *Bournemouth Queen*, *Victoria*, *Empress*, and *Emperor of India* from the South coast; and the Bristol Channel favourites *Ravenswood*, *Britannia* and *Glen Gower*. These were joined by the Tay car ferry *Sir William High* and no less than 38 civilian and Admiralty steam paddle tugs.

It was in this context that, during the summer of 1959 Dr Alan Robinson, a university lecturer from The University College of Wales, Aberystwyth was heading for a walking holiday on the Isle of Wight. He recorded in his diary that on Saturday 25th July he crossed from Yarmouth to Lymington "by the dear old paddle-steamer 'Freshwater', a pleasant contrast to the hideous car ferries" and learned from her crew that she was shortly to be taken out of service.

Dr Robinson had been born in Southampton on 3rd April 1920, the elder of two brothers. He was educated at Bitterne Park School and Taunton's School in Southampton before studying German and French at University College London, part of the time as an evacuee student at Aberystwyth during the war years. After a period of teaching at Merchant Taylors' and Haberdashers' schools and a year with the German section of the Foreign Office, he spent two years at the University of Edinburgh carrying out research for a PhD. In October 1950 he obtained a post as assistant lecturer at the University College of Wales, Aberystwyth and, since 1952, had been a full-time lecturer there.

Travelling on paddle steamers to the Isle of Wight and from Bournemouth along the south coast was a frequent leisure activity in his early years with his parents and later with his friend and next door neighbour who was also an enthusiast. He had developed a deep affection for these little ships and the news of *Freshwater's* imminent demise, coupled with the general decline of the British paddle steamer, set him thinking. Aware that groups of enthusiasts were successfully preserving cars, buses, trams and railway locomotives, he dared to wonder whether it might be possible to "preserve in running order an example of that once so familiar but now rapidly disappearing phenomenon of our seaside towns, the faithful old paddle steamer". He recognised that the task would be a difficult one but perceived that, due to her modest size and good condition, *Freshwater* might make the ideal candidate for an attempt.

His first step was to write to her owners, British Railways, urging them to add the old ship to their existing collection of historic vehicles but, unsurprisingly, they declined. He then contacted H.E. Moss & Co., the well known ship brokers, to seek

Dr. Alan Robinson, Founder of the Paddle Steamer Preservation Society, pictured in 1960.   Alan Robinson

Paddle Steamer's Passing

Sir—In this age of rapid change in the forms of public transport, it is heartening to read from time to time of small but determined groups of historically minded citizens (sometimes with official status but quite often without) who are striving to preserve representative specimens of older types of vehicle, such as veteran motor cars, early buses and trams, notable examples of the railway engine, and so on, in order that the solid achievements of the past may not be entirely forgotten.

But I have not so far read, to the best of my knowledge, of any move to preserve in running order an example of that, once so familiar but now rapidly disappearing phenomenon of our seaside towns, the faithful old paddle steamer.

Naturally, the preservation of such a vessel would involve a number of special difficulties, e.g. berthing, but it seems a thousand pities if this class of vessel were allowed to disappear from the British scene without any more tangible record than that of the photographer.

The disposal price at scrap rates of one of the smaller types of paddle steamer is by no means unreasonable, and I understand that there may very soon be an opportunity of acquiring a vessel of appropriate size and condition for historical preservation purposes.

Might I therefore ask, Sir, through the courtesy of your columns, any of your seafaring readers who have practical experience of the problems involved, anyone who might be able to help in the matter of berthing-space, or of course anyone who might be willing to contribute financially to such a preservation project, to write to me as soon as possible, c/o BM/RIAN, London, W.C.1, so that the formation of an historical preservation society may be discussed?

Yours faithfully,
Vienna.   A. R. ROBINSON

their advice and assistance, but they too were unable to help. Therefore, on September 4th 1959, while on a visit to Vienna, he wrote to the *Daily Telegraph* about the possible formation of a paddle steamer preservation society. His now-famous letter was published on September 17th, the day Alan returned from Vienna, and within a few days postal replies began to flow in, or appear in the letter pages of *the* Daily Telegraph.

By 28th September enough expressions of interest had been received to prepare and post a circular to potential members of the proposed society. During the next two days he travelled to Southampton to meet with Tony McGinnity and Eileen Pritchard, two very different characters who were both to play major parts in the preservation movement. Tony, aged 22, had spent some time as a trainee purser with the British India Line but had now come ashore to work as a journalist. Mrs Pritchard, a hairdresser by trade, had long connections with the Southampton shipping scene: Her late husband had worked in ship surveying and design at

Alan Robinson's letter to the Daily Telegraph, published on 17th September 1959 (left).

Below: One of the responses to Alan Robinson's appeal. C. Patrick Taylor became a founder member of the Society and served for many years on the London & Home Counties Branch committee.   PSPS Collection

PADDLE STEAMERS

Sir—I have read with great interest Mr. A. R. Robinson's letter about forming a society to preserve examples of our coastal paddle steamers.

There are two notable vessels that are worth consideration, namely the Medway Queen and the Consul. The Medway Queen, built in 1924, is the last surviving vessel of her class in the Thames Estuary, once the home of many fine paddle steamers. She played a considerable part in the Dunkirk evacuation, a fact which makes her preservation all the more desirable. The Consul, which was built in 1896 and which operates from Weymouth and Bournemouth, is probably the oldest paddle steamer still afloat.

It is to be hoped that it will be possible for the society to put these vessels into service on a non-profit-making basis, as they will lose their appeal if they become stationary museum pieces. Paddle steamers have a character and personality not found in the more modern vessels of to-day, and it would be a major tragedy if they were allowed to pass into oblivion.

Yours faithfully,
C. PATRICK TAYLOR,
Broadstairs, Kent.   *Sch 1050*

Day, Summers & Co. Ltd's shipyard; both of them had been active members of the local World Ship Society branch; and, along with shipping luminaries such as Bert Moody, H.A. Allen and Ron Adams, were deeply immersed in the local excursion steamer scene. As a result of their discussions Tony McGinnity spent 1st October visiting the offices of the *Echo* newspaper and Southern ITV to promote the idea of a preservation society, and much useful publicity resulted.

On Friday 30th October an initial meeting was held at Clwb y Cymru, in Oxford Circus, London and great enthusiasm was shown by the relatively small numbers of attendees, some of whom had travelled considerable distances to be there. A decision was reached to go ahead with the formation of the Paddle Steamer Preservation Society whose key objectives would be:

1. To stimulate and arouse interest in paddle steamers throughout the World and to bring together those who are interested in paddle steamers with the aim of purchasing and preserving an existing paddle steamer.
2. To encourage the retention and expansion of all paddle steamer services.
3. To form branches of the Society wherever practicable in order to effectively promote the above aims.

The inaugural formal meeting of the newly-constituted PSPS was held on Sunday 8th November 1959 at the Mission to Seamen in Southampton and the first committee elected. Dr. Alan Robinson became Chairman, Capt. George Thomas Vice Chair, Mr E.T. Randle Treasurer, Mr Tony McGinnity Secretary, Mr Bernard Cox Assistant Secretary, and Mr D.L. Dougan Auditor. Mr. J.H.P. Ellis and Mr S. Roberts were elected as ordinary committee members. With the formal business concluded, all present went into Southampton docks to visit the *Freshwater* that was laid up there awaiting her fate.

Needless to say, not all steamer enthusiasts were in complete sympathy with the aims of the new society. One highly-respected Clyde historian expressed the view that talk of

On board Consul *during the first-ever PSPS charter on the evening of 10th September 1960. Seated in the left foreground, clutching a glass of rum and a copy of Issue No 1 of the PSPS journal* Paddle Wheels, *is Capt. Harry Defrates, Master of Cosens'* Monarch. *Earlier that day Capt. Defrates had taken* Monarch *through Weymouth Town Bridge to her lay-up berth, on what proved to be her last ever voyage in steam. Next to him are Winston and Dorothy Megoran and Ethel Defrates. In the background sits John Megoran who in later life went on to be the highly-successful master and manager of Kingswear Castle. His brother Peter is leaning against the pillar.* R Clammer Collection

PADDLE STEAMER PRESERVATION SOCIETY
MEMBERSHIP CARD
VALID UNTIL.................. 3 1 DEC 1976
NAME.... *Capt. L.G.A. Thomas*
MEMBERSHIP No. *2*
№ 1233

I acknowledge receipt of annual subscription
of £.*1.75* *G V-W Gray* 2 MAR 1976
Treasurer ....Date

A membership card belonging to Capt George Thomas, who was PSPS member No.2. Mrs. Eileen Pritchard was member No 1.
PSPS Collection

preservation was premature as the surviving Clyde paddlers had many years of life left in them yet. A prominent member of the South Wales Branch of the World Ship Society, Donald Anderson, wrote to Alan Robinson in March 1960 wishing him well but stating "Perhaps I am a defeatist, a sceptic, a fatalist – call me what you will – but I fear that if the operating companies have proved that the paddle steamer in its conventional form is no longer an economical proposition, then nothing that any preservation society can do will keep them running." He pointed out that, despite an initial surge of support, the White Funnel Fleet Supporters Association had foundered after only one year and that, apart from its ultimate aim of purchasing a steamer, the PSPS was really not very different from the existing, 14 year old World Ship Society. However, he wished the new society every success and concluded "if the time should come when the Preservation Society's paddle steamer is one of the very few remaining ships in this class, I will no doubt be a regular traveller." Despite voicing the misgivings of many enthusiasts, in due course the writer went on to become an enthusiastic convert to the PSPS and served for many years as Chairman of the Bristol Channel Branch.

In July 1960 Tony McGinnity stepped down as National Secretary to be replaced by Victor Gray who, over the next 20 years, went on to serve as Membership Secretary, Treasurer and finally Chairman from 1976 to 1980. He is still an active member. Having grown up in Bournemouth Victor had a strong affection for the local steamers, sailed on Cosens' *Monarch* of 1888 during her final season and had clear childhood holiday memories of *Royal Eagle* and the screw vessels *Royal Daffodil* and *Empress Queen*. For two school holidays in the mid-fifties he had worked in Cosens' Bournemouth office as their office-boy which gave him an unusual insight into what happened behind the scenes. The pay was £2.50 per week but he says he would have done it for nothing! He recalls being introduced to Capt Shippick, then living in retirement in his birth town of Poole, who would come to the pier dispensing his advice which was always worth listening to as he had made a great success of the New Medway S. P. Co Ltd in the inter-war years.

The new committee lost no time in pressing ahead with developments. In March 1960 the first, slim edition of the society's quarterly journal *Paddle Wheels* was published, keeping members up to date with planned activities and news of the steamer fleets, of which there was plenty.

1960 saw the first two of four attempts by private individuals to purchase and operate well-known paddle steamers which had previously been owned by large, established companies. The two ships involved were Red Funnel's last Southampton-based paddle steamer *Princess Elizabeth* and British Railways' Lymington to Yarmouth ferry *Freshwater* whose withdrawal had prompted Alan Robinson to form the Society. These were to be followed a little later in the decade by Cosens' *Consul* and the Clyde favourite *Jeanie Deans*. None were ever owned by the PSPS, but the Society did all it could to support and promote the new ventures. The managing owners all became PSPS members, often attended meetings, and sought to involve and inform the broader membership, some of whom became shareholders or had other financial investments in the businesses. It is hoped that the full story of these four ships and their remarkable owners may form the subject of another book.

Princess Elizabeth, Red Funnel's last paddle steamer, had been withdrawn in February 1959 and replaced with a custom-built car ferry *Carisbrooke Castle*. Built in 1927, the paddler had been

maintained to a very high standard, and was quickly sold to Torbay Steamers Ltd., whose managing owner was Commander Edmund Rhodes. The ship was refitted at J.I. Thorneycroft's Southampton shipyard and on 26th April, at Commander Rhodes' invitation, a group of delighted PSPS members joined the ship for her acceptance trials. A fascinating day was spent admiring the sparkling paintwork, the freshly-decorated saloons and observing the ship's manoeuvres in the Solent and Southampton Water before she returned to moor alongside a bunkering barge and the PSPS party was taken ashore by launch after the Society's first official "outing".

Despite considerable opposition from local commercial boat owners, *Princess Elizabeth* entered service at Torquay on 1st June, offering cruises along the Devon coast. The Society sent a telegram to Commander Rhodes wishing his new venture every success and assuring him of its full support, while on at least one occasion during the summer members gathered at Torquay to enjoy an excursion on board. *Princess Elizabeth* was to operate under Commander Rhodes' management at various locations for the next six seasons and was arguably the most successful of all the privately-preserved paddle steamers.

The second ship to pass into private hands was the former *Freshwater*. She was purchased by Mr. Herbert Jennings of Budleigh Salterton who set up Brighton & South Coast Steamers Ltd., and moved the ship to spend the winter of 1959-60 at Topsham on the River Exe. Renamed *Sussex Queen* she spent the 1960 season attempting to revive sailings along the Sussex Coast from Brighton, but met with only limited success.

Princess Elizabeth alongside Haldon Pier, Torquay.   Keith Abraham

On board Princess Elizabeth *on a coastal cruise from Torquay.*

Keith Abraham

itinerary was chosen because it was relatively unusual, but some soul-searching was required as, equally unusually, *Glen Usk* was making an afternoon return sailing from Cardiff to Ilfracombe that same afternoon. Nevertheless, there were a good number of members and potential members on board *Cardiff Queen* that day, with those joining at Weston receiving a personal welcome from Campbell's Managing Director, Mr. Clifton Smith-Cox.

At the end of the season she returned to the River Exe while Mr Jennings considered his options.

The organised members' sailing on board *Princess Elizabeth* from Torquay was followed by a second nominated excursion on board *Cardiff Queen* on 14th August from Bristol, Clevedon and Weston to Barry, Mumbles and the Gower Coast. The

The success of this sailing contributed to the decision to form Bristol Channel Branch of the PSPS, the first of several local branches to be created. Of the fifty or so PSPS members who lived in the counties bordering the Channel, at least half attended the inaugural meeting which was held on 30th October 1960 in the Royal Hotel on College Green, Bristol. It is recorded that the hotel management stated that the Society would be welcome to gather there provided it could guarantee that there would be no marches or banner involved! The first committee elected consisted of the highly-respected Swansea maritime historian George Owen (Chair), Howard Davis (Vice-Chair), John Greed (Secretary) and Eric Procter (Treasurer), Patrick Murrell, Peter Southcombe and Duncan Edgell. Happily, several of these are still with us and one is forced to wonder whether members of the PSPS have a significantly higher life expectancy than the national average! Several more meetings were held at the hotel before the branch moved to a new venue on board the preserved lightship *John Sebastian*, which was moored in Bristol's Bathurst Basin as the headquarters of the Cabot Cruising Club.

Sussex Queen (*Ex* Freshwater) *struggling to berth at Palace Pier, Brighton, during the summer of 1960. A stern line has been secured ashore but a stiff south westerly wind is pushing the ship off the pier and her skipper is no doubt wondering how best to get her safely alongside.*

Medway Queen Preservation Society

Cosens & Co. Ltd's Consul *approaching Weymouth Pleasure Pier c. 1956.*   Richard Danielson Collection

Cardiff Queen *approaching Birnbeck Pier, Weston-super-Mare.*   PSPS Collection

Encouraged by the success of the two nominated sailings, the Society advertised its first ever charter to take place on the evening of 10th September 1960. The vessel chosen was Cosens & Co.'s veteran *Consul* of 1896, for an evening cruise in Weymouth Bay, departing at 7.30pm and returning at 9.30pm. As *Consul* offered occasional evening cruises as part of her normal timetable there was insufficient novelty value to attract PSPS members to travel from afar, and breaking even would therefore depend on whether effective advertising could draw in sufficient local passengers. The committee agreed to bear any losses out of their own pockets, a dance band was engaged and "games for the ladies" planned, all for a fare of 6/- (30p). All those who sailed enjoyed the occasion immensely but unfortunately public support did not come up to expectations and the charter made a modest but discouraging loss of £25.

The year ended on a high note, however, when the well-known poet, author and broadcaster John Betjeman accepted the position of Patron of the Society. As a founder member of the Victorian Society, a high-profile champion for the recording, conservation and celebration of Victorian architecture and engineering, and the subject of a recent Ken Russell film entitled "John Betjeman: A Poet in London" he was the ideal man for the job. In his acceptance letter dated 18th October 1960 he wrote "I am honoured that you should feel that my name is worth associating with your new society and I am glad to accept the title of Patron. I wish your efforts every success." Betjeman was Knighted in 1969, made Poet Laureate

in 1972, and was regarded as a "National Treasure" both for his distinctive poetry and for his memorable TV films such as the famous *Metroland*. He was to remain Patron of the PSPS until his death in 1984.

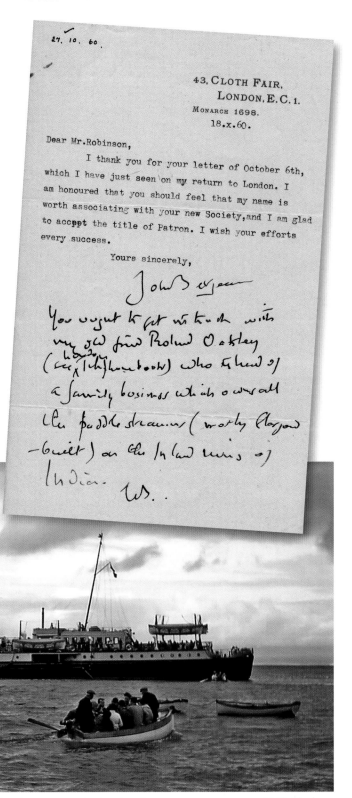

John Betjeman's letter of acceptance as Patron of the PSPS. The hand written afterthought reads "You ought to get in touch with my old friend Roland Oakley (see London telephone book) who is head of a family business which owns all of the paddle steamers (mostly Glasgow-built) on the inland rivers of India. PSPS Collection

Bristol Queen *lays quietly at anchor off Lynmouth while small local boats ferry her passengers back on board.* Keith Abraham

Cosens' coal-fired Monarch *of 1924 arriving at Bournemouth from Swanage.*　　　Fry/R.Clammer Collection

Monarch *embarking passengers at Bournmouth Pier fro another of her regular trips to Swanage*　　　PSPS Collection

CHAPTER TWO

THE EARLY YEARS, 1961-62

With Contributions by Victor Gray and Pat Murrell.

1961 OPENED with the depressing announcement that Cosens & Co. Ltd. of Weymouth's paddle steamer *Monarch* had been advertised for sale and would not be returning to her customary summer service between Bournemouth and Swanage. Built in 1924 as *Shanklin* she was the youngest of Cosens' steamers and had only joined their fleet in 1951, but the fact that she was coal-fired probably tipped the scales against her. Victor Gray immediately lobbied the local Chambers of Trade, councillors and the press but, apart from generating some useful publicity for the PSPS, was able to achieve little. On 1st March *Monarch* was towed away from Weymouth for scrapping at Haulbowline Industries' Cork yard, where the Admiralty paddle tug *Swarthy* was also to meet her end a few months later. PSPS members had, incidentally, paid a valedictory visit to *Swarthy* and her sister ship *Sprite* in Portsmouth dockyard just a few months earlier.

Cosens evidently did not resent the PSPS lobbying, for on 8th March 1961 they invited members to attend on board *Embassy* at her winter lay-up berth in Weymouth Backwater, where retired Managing Director Mr. C.H.J. "Charlie" Kaile presented the Society with the bell of their famous steamer *Monarch* of 1888. The 70lb bell was a beautiful object, supported by a pair of ornate metal dolphins, and remains a treasured part of the Society's collection today. After the presentation, members were given a tour of *Embassy* and then of *Consul* which was on the slipway before being entertained to tea in the board room.

Faced with the prospect of no paddle steamer on the Bournemouth-Swanage service, the Society encouraged Herbert Jennings, whose *Sussex Queen (ex. Freshwater)* had

Cosens' retired Managing Director Charles Kaile presents the bell of the 1888 Monarch *to PSPS member No 2, Capt. George Thomas, at the ceremony held on board* Embassy *in Weymouth Backwater on 8th March 1961. (Also below)*
R. Clammer Collection

experienced a rather unsuccessful season at Brighton during 1960, to base her at Poole during 1961 in order to fill the void left by *Monarch*. Renamed *Swanage Queen* and resplendent in a blue funnel, the ship duly entered service on 5th July, offering trips to the Isle of Wight alongside her regular "ferry" crossings.

PSPS members did their best to lend moral and practical support, but Mr Jennings' experience with the ship proved somewhat fraught. He had great difficulty recruiting suitably-experienced engine room staff and the ship suffered so many mechanical difficulties that he became convinced that she was being sabotaged. His brave venture made a financial loss and, despite some PSPS members making financial investments, the ship was withdrawn at the end of the season and departed for breaking up in Belgium on 8th May 1962. It was a great shame that the ship which had inspired the formation of the Society, and whose size and classic good looks made her an ideal candidate for preservation, should be lost in this way, but both her sale price and other circumstances ruled out a bid by the PSPS, and nothing more could be done.

The rules of the Society required the AGM to be held in November and this requirement was not changed until 1969. The 1961 AGM, held at Salisbury, was attended by 49 members, a remarkably high figure out of a membership of under 300. At this meeting the matter of the Society's name was raised. The minutes state: "On behalf of the Bristol Channel Branch Mr Southcombe told the meeting that in order to secure the goodwill of P & A Campbell Ltd in certain limited activities in which the Branch hope to engage with the Company and from which the Society would benefit financially it was desired to drop the word "Preservation" from the Society's title. It was emphasised that the Branch in all other dealings and connections would continue to use the full title of the Society." This motion was carried on a show of hands. The practical effect was that Campbells when mentioning the Society dropped the word, but the Society continued to use it in their dealings with Campbells! In defence of the Company, Mr Smith-Cox felt that as they were operating two relatively modern paddle-steamers, talk of preservation was regressive.

The spring of 1961 offered plenty to keep PSPS members interested. On 8th January members of the Bristol Channel Branch were given a guided tour of the paddlers *Bristol Queen, Cardiff Queen* and *Glen Usk* in Penarth Dock while on 5th March Campbell's Managing Director Mr Smith-Cox gave an entertaining and informative talk which left members in little doubt regarding the operational and economic difficulties of operating steamers in recent years.

On 18th March the inaugural meeting of the London & Home Counties Branch (L&HC) took place at Clwb y Cymru in London. Alan Robinson took the chair in a crowded room at 7.30pm. Ten minutes earlier a pre-recorded interview with him was broadcast on BBC Radio. Dr Robinson recounted what had been achieved in the first 16 months of the Society and praised the zeal which had been applied to getting the branch underway. In particular Russell Horwood, who became branch secretary, was mentioned and he in turn had given a detailed synopsis of the aspirations of the branch. There were 49 members eligible for inclusion in the branch area, including the recently retired Second Sea-Lord, Admiral Sir Alexander Madden, who sent his apologies. Offers of help for the Society came from many people both within and outside the shipping world. One of the attendees was Mr Philpott, a Director of the New Medway Steam Packet Co. Other members making up the

Swanage Queen *making a cautious approach to her overnight berth at Poole Quay on a sunny evening in early July 1961.* PSPS Collection

first Committee were Bill Prynne (later to become Chairman of the Society), Martin Henniker-Gotley, Collard Stone, Derek Wainwright, and John MacAfee (Lloyds Register of Shipping). The branch held its first meeting during April and a few days later, on 29th April, members were invited to visit *Medway Queen* during her winter refit at Rochester.

The summer season of 1961 saw a flurry of nominated excursions and other special events. On 11th June a group sailed on board *Totnes Castle* of the River Dart Steamboat Co.,

P. & A. Campbell's lovely Glen Usk, *pictured here passing Pill on the River Avon in the summer of 1959, was visited in winter lay-up by PSPS Bristol Channel Branch members in January 1961. She remained laid up throughout 1961 and 1962 and was eventually towed away to be scrapped in April 1963.*
PSPS Collection

British Railway's Isle of Wight ferry steamer Sandown alongside Portsmouth Harbour Station on 4th September 1960.

A.E. Bennett / Richard Clammer Collection

PSPS members look on as, trailing her characteristic plume of smoke, Wingfield Castle *departs from New Holland for Hull on 10th June 1973.*

Les Ring/PSPS Collection

whose Managing Director Mr Leslie Hobbs, in common with the operators of all Britain's other surviving paddle steamers except for Cosens & Co., had recently become a PSPS member. After their trip the party travelled to Torquay only to discover that the planned evening sailing on board *Princess Elizabeth* had been cancelled.

On 17th June members were invited to visit Plymouth Dockyard to view the Admiralty paddle tugs *Camel* and *Pert* . The 178ft, 637 gross tons Pert had been built in 1915 as the only one of her class and was the largest paddle tug ever built for the Admiralty. Having toured the tug and heard about her

extraordinary power and abilities, members transferred to the duty tug *Camel* which took them on a 70 minute cruise to seaward of the breakwater where she demonstrated the use of her independent paddle wheels. Both tugs were withdrawn and scrapped during 1962, so the trip was a huge privilege.

Whit Monday saw the Society's flag flying from the mast of *Sandown*, as another group enjoyed a morning light run from Portsmouth to Ryde from the vantage point of the ship's bridge. After spending a day on the Isle of Wight the group returned on another light run in the evening. During a heat wave on 24th June the L&HC branch sailed from Strood to Clacton on

Early on the morning of 7th September 1963, Medway Queen *lays alongside Strood Pier while her crew ready her to welcome passengers on board for another cruise. In this timeless scene local fishing boats lay on the mud, while Rochester Castle, Cathedral and Bridge are visible in the background*

A.E. Bennett / R. Clammer Collection

board *Medway Queen* and was permitted to mount an exhibition of paddle steamer memorabilia and PSPS advertising material in her saloons. On 30th June a group ventured north to join an excursion to Grimsby on board the Humber ferry *Wingfield Castle*, while on 2nd September London County Council hosted a visit to the vessels of the Woolwich Free Ferry. As well as sailing on the service vessels, members were allowed to walk round the *Will Crookes* which was under repair on the grid iron.

On 16th August Cosens' *Consul* was chartered for a second time. It was hoped that Wednesday evening in the peak holiday season would attract a good crowd, but a period of bad weather deterred casual passengers and another loss was made, leading the committee to ponder deeply on the planning of future events. The bad weather persisted for some time and a few days after the charter Victor Gray travelled from Bournemouth to Swanage and Weymouth on board *Consul*, which took four hours 40 minutes for a scheduled three hour voyage. Looking back, he wonders what the MCA would say if such a trip was attempted today with the ship pitching and rolling and the foredeck roped off!

Princess Elizabeth was still at Torquay offering cruises along the Devon coast, and gave great pleasure to many members. However, local boatmen and other vested interests remained hotly opposed to her presence and sought every opportunity to bring her into disrepute. Much was made of two short groundings at Lyme Regis, but things really came to a head when the ship continued to put to sea after the Harbourmaster had hoisted a flag warning smaller, locally-licensed passenger boats that it was too windy to leave Tor Bay. Eventually the

Passengers enjoy the brilliant late-afternoon sunshine as Consul *makes her approach to Weymouth Pleasure Pier during 1961. A seaman is hoisting her house flag and name pennant which, in line with Cosens' long-standing practice, were always lowered while the ship was at sea to save wear and tear! Note the wide steps leading down to the low foredeck, the elegant curved skylight, the canvas dodgers on the bridge wings and the oil navigation lamp hoisted on the funnel gantry.*

Keith Abraham

Made all the more beautiful by her unkempt surroundings, Bristol Queen *is pictured in Queen's Dock, Cardiff.*   Les Ring / PSPS Collection

Woolwich Free Ferry Will Crookes *under maintenance on the grid iron, where members visited her on 2nd September 1961. This view was taken on 2nd December 1962.* Bernard Dixon / PSPS Collection

H.M. Paddle Tug Camel *moored alongside the* Pert *in Plymouth dockyard on 17th June 1961, prior to taking a party of PSPS members on a trip to sea.* John Brown/Richard Clammer Collection

Council gave into local pressure and refused fuel tankers access to the paddler so, deprived of fuel, *Princess Elizabeth* was forced to make a premature retreat to winter lay-up in Weymouth.

A highlight of the season was a celebration to mark the Golden Jubilee of *Embassy*. On 27th August a large group joined the ship at Bournemouth for her afternoon sailing to Totland Bay. Whilst alongside Totland pier a champagne party was held, a specially made cake encircled with ribbons in Cosens' colours and bearing a small model of the ship was cut, and Dr Robinson proposed toasts to the ship, her owners, officers and crew. Capt. Haines replied and on the return trip to Bournemouth the Society's flag was flown at *Embassy's* masthead.

On 30th September 1961, the third branch of the Society came into being. The Wessex Branch covered the area south and east of the Bristol Channel and to the west of the Home Counties. Its first officers were R.L.P. Jowitt (Chair), the redoubtable Eileen Pritchard (Vice Chair), Mr R.J. White (Treasurer), Mr J.D. Bonsall (Secretary) together with the well-known enthusiasts Syd Roberts, Peter Ellis, Ted Randle and John Stay. The new branch immediately began organising meetings for the winter ahead. Thus, in less than a year, three branches of the Society had been formed.

By contrast with the previous year, 1962 was relatively quiet. The structure of the Society had been established and strong, co-operative relationships built with the various steamer operators. Winter visits were made to *Bristol Queen* and *Cardiff Queen* at Cardiff, *Medway Queen* at Rochester and the steam yacht *Norian* which was owned by L&HC Branch member Simon Sitwell. The sailing season saw another light run on board *Ryde* to the Isle of Wight, and a number of nominated excursions. On 24th June a group joined *Bristol Queen* for an unusual and very long day trip from Cardiff to Milford Haven, which encountered some very heavy swell near St Govan's Head. To coincide with this sailing and to mark the 75th anniversary of the arrival of Campbell's *Waverley* in the area, the

Bristol Channel Branch had organised an exhibition in Ilfracombe relating to the history of the Bristol Channel steamers. Some of the models for the exhibition were carried down Channel on board *Cardiff Queen* and, together with an array of bells, photos and ephemera, created great interest in the town. The exhibits were then taken back up channel by *Bristol Queen* and the exhibition re-opened at Bristol City Museum. Over 16,000 people visited the two exhibitions, which did much to raise awareness of the area's steamer heritage and the important work of PSPS.

At about the same time a suggestion was made that it might stimulate interest and boost passenger numbers if it was possible to arrange a fortnight's exchange between one of Campbell's *Queens* and a Clyde steamer such as *Caledonia* or

The paddle tug Eppleton Hall *which was visited by a PSPS group in September 1962. This photograph was taken in November 1967 and shows her steaming up the Tyne en route to the breaker's yard. In the event, having been burned out and partially dismantled, she was purchased by the San Francisco Maritime Museum, rebuilt, and set off during September 1969 on an epic voyage across the Atlantic and through the Panama Canal to her new home.*

Bernard Dixon / PSPS Collection

one of the turbine *Duchesses*. Although nothing came of this it was indicative of positive thinking and the Society's attempts to encourage operators to seek profitable new ways of employing their steamers.

On 8th July two nominated excursions took place; one on *Bristol Queen* to Ilfracombe from the up Channel ports, and the other to Clacton on board *Medway Queen*. Two of the most unusual and exciting visits of the season, however, involved paddle tugs. The first was a visit to Sunderland on 8th September to view France, Fenwick & Co.'s surviving paddle tugs *Eppleton Hall* and *Houghton* which had been retained for their unique ability to work in shallow water and manoeuvre in the tight confines of the local coal docks. Members were told that the company's third paddle tug *Roker* had recently been sold and was due to move north to join Scotland's last paddle tug *Elie* working on the Forth. They were given a fascinating talk and a tour of the tug fleet, and an open invitation was issued to any PSPS member who was in the area to call and arrange a visit at any convenient time. The second visit, on 2nd October, was to the diesel electric Admiralty tug *Forceful* in Portsmouth dockyard.

Princess Elizabeth, which had been forced out of Torquay at the end of 1961, sailed into the gap left by *Swanage Queen* and spent 1962 offering a Bournemouth to Swanage service together with short evening cruises. Despite concerns about her viability, for the second year running enthusiasts were able to enjoy the opportunity to sail on two competing paddle steamers from the same piers.

The joys of these wonderful sailing opportunities were somewhat clouded, however, by the news of more much-loved paddle steamers being withdrawn from service. The

Mary Cox and Capt. Haines cutting the celebratory cake during Embassy's Golden Jubilee *cruise on 27th August 1961. Note the model of the ship and the cake ribbon in the colours of Cosens' house flag.*
Bernard Cox.

magnificent but coal-hungry *Whippingham* which had latterly only been used on peak summer Saturdays, made her last sailings on the Portsmouth – Ryde service on 1st September. Down in Devon, the River Dart Steamboat Co.'s *Compton Castle* required too much work to pass her next survey so was withdrawn and replaced by a new motor ship, while on the River Cleddau in Pembrokeshire *Alumchine* had finished her days on the Hobbs Point to Neyland ferry.

The stately Whippingham *arriving at Ryde Pier during her last day in service at 11.20am on 1st September 1962.* A.E. Bennett / R. Clammer Collection.

Alumchine laid up on the foreshore at Neyland in July 1964, after the PSPS had abandoned its plans to buy her.

Richard Danielson Collection

CHAPTER THREE

ALUMCHINE – A FIRST ATTEMPT AT SHIP OWNING

DURING 1960 and 1961, amid all the other activity described in the previous chapter, there had been considerable discussion about how the fledgling society could best achieve its key aim of purchasing and preserving a paddle steamer. *Glen Gower, Jupiter* and *Monarch* had recently departed for the scrap yard and the fact that others including *Glen Usk, Whippingham, Medway Queen, Embassy* and *Swanage Queen* were not expected to remain in service for much longer lent a very real sense of urgency.

A Preservation Sub-Committee led by Tony McGinnity was set up, a preservation fund established, and an approach was made to the directors of Haulbowline Industries, the ship breaking company at Passage West, Cork. They advised the Society to make a direct approach to the owners of suitable ships before their final sale in the hope that generosity might be shown and a vessel offered at her written-down book price before a higher offer was received from a ship breaker. Most of the committee realised, however, that even if a large ship could be obtained by this means, restoring her and returning her to commercial operation would be far beyond the society's resources. The Admiralty paddle tugs *Pert* and *Camel* were also considered but rejected as far too large, complex and expensive to operate.

Thoughts therefore turned to the limited number of smaller, more economical ships. *Swanage Queen* which, as *Freshwater*, had sparked the formation of the society was nearing the end of an unsuccessful season on the Bournemouth to Swanage service but her owner was asking an unrealistically high price for her. On the River Dart three paddlers were still in service though *Compton Castle* was due to be replaced by a new motorship. Finally, down in Pembrokeshire, one of Britain's smallest and least-known paddle steamers, the diminutive *Alumchine*, was due to be withdrawn and would be looking for a buyer early in 1962.

Alumchine manoeuvring alongside Hobbs Point pier with Neyland in the distance. Drivers must have required strong nerves to take their cars down the steep slope before making a right-angled turn to board the ferry over her forward sponson. This lovely tinted view clearly shows the ship's engine room casing, side houses and the large, curved companionway giving access to the small saloon beneath the raised quarter deck. Note that her solid bulwarks have now been replaced by removable railings. Poole Maritime Trust

Alumchine in service on the Neyland to Hobbs Point ferry during the late 1930s or early 1940s. At that time she still had solid bulwarks around her foredeck and large, rather ugly side houses aft of her paddle boxes which housed toilets, a lamp room and a small office. These were later removed. PSPS Collection

In June 1961 John Greed, the Secretary of the Bristol Channel Branch, had received a letter from Pembrokeshire County Council's Neyland to Hobbs Point Ferry Manager, giving advanced notice of her withdrawal and asking if the PSPS might be interested in purchasing her.

Alumchine had been built of steel in 1923 by Abdela & Mitchell Ltd of Queensferry at a cost of £4,396 and, at 76 gross tons (39 net) and measuring only 80 x 17.6 x 5.1 ft (24.3x5.3x1.5m), was undoubtedly Britain's smallest surviving commercial paddle steamer. Originally named *Menna*, she had been designed for Caernarfon Corporation's ferry service across the Menai Strait between Caernarfon and Tal-y-Foel on Anglesey. As built she was a reasonably attractive, if workaday, little ship with an open foredeck where wheeled vehicles and livestock could be carried, two enormous side houses aft of the paddle boxes, a raised quarterdeck with an open deck above and a very basic saloon below. She was powered by a 115 I.H.P.compound diagonal engine with a stroke of 36" and cylinder diameters of 11" and 22", and steam at 130p.s.i. was provided by a single, two-furnace, marine, return-tube

A PSPS member, possibly Eileen Pritchard, stands beside Alumchine *at low tide.*
PSPS Collection

boiler built by Riley Bros of Stockton on Tees. Her bunkers could hold 8 tons of coal which was burned at a rate of 22cwts every 15 hours. She was capable of a top speed of 9.5 knots.

Menna maintained the ferry service reliably for the next six years but, faced with competition from motor lorries which used the Menai Bridges, the livestock trade dwindled alarmingly and in 1929 the ship was withdrawn and laid up at Caernarfon. She was bought by the James Dredging, Towage & Transport Co., renamed *Alumchine*, and her registration transferred to London on 30th September 1929. No details of her time with James have yet been discovered, but it is presumed that they used her as a workboat and personnel vessel in conjunction with contracts on the Thames or South Coast until 1933 when they sold her to Mr F.R. Lee for use on a ferry service across the River Cleddau between Neyland and Hobbs Point slipway near Pembroke Dock. In 1948 the ferry service passed into the direct control of Pembrokeshire County Council.

Alumchine shared the ferry duties with a smaller screw steamer called *Lady Magdalen* but, because her foredeck was strengthened to carry five or so cars of the period along with 216 passengers, became the mainstay of the service until 1956 when a brand new and larger paddle ferry called *Cleddau Queen* was introduced. With the arrival of her larger running mate, which was the last steam powered paddle vessel ever built for commercial use in the United Kingdom, *Alumchine* was relegated to the status of spare vessel covering refits and busy

periods, and spent much of her time laid up in a tidal berth at the Council's Neyland Ferry Yard. This remained the case until 1961 when the Council decided to order a further new ferry in the form of the Voith-Schneider propelled *Cleddau King* and it became apparent that *Alumchine* would soon be surplus to requirements. After a few last spells of relief work her passenger certificates expired on 10th July 1962 and she was permanently withdrawn.

The PSPS committee had, meanwhile, been considering whether to attempt to purchase her. Her small size, which would make her relatively cheap to moor and maintain, and the fact that her attractive machinery had been maintained in excellent condition by the ferry yard staff, with whom the old ship was a firm favourite, were both persuasive factors, and formal negotiations were opened with Pembrokeshire County Council.

By November 1962 the PSPS had agreed to purchase the ship for £806 and a 10% deposit was paid. It was intended to move her to The Solent where she would be more accessible to members and the public, and berths at Hythe or on the Beaulieu River were explored.

During the winter Tony McGinnity and Syd Roberts of the Preservation Sub-Committee began to visit the ship on a regular basis and one her former engineers, George Beare, agreed to act as shipkeeper and check her on a daily basis. Plans were then announced to bring *Alumchine* round to the South coast early in June 1963, steaming "day and night, probably for five days, and stopping only to refuel". A radio and various items of safety equipment were offered by sponsors and various T.V. and newspaper companies offered to cover the voyage. On 12th January 1963 a letter was sent to all members appealing for donations to pay for refit costs, coal, voyage expenses and other contingencies and, remarkably, it was calculated that a sum of £5 per member would ensure "freedom from any financial worry"! Volunteers were asked to muster at Neyland for the week beginning 26th May to complete fitting out and to take part in steering and steaming trials. In a *Paddle Wheels* article which reflected the now-unacceptable attitudes of the times, it was suggested that even "Lady members" might contribute, possibly by providing "packets of sandwiches… to hungry paint-chippers", "running up curtains" or "advising on the equipment necessary for this particular task… spiked shoes and a sewing machine clutched firmly in hand!" Excitement was high as PSPS members began to picture the Society's paddle yacht *Alumchine* steaming proudly around the Solent on summer weekends and providing a cosy venue for winter meetings.

Reality, however, quickly began to bite. Despite the facts that

George Beare continued to visit daily, pump the bilges and keep an eye on the ship, that the County Council had offered the use of their grid iron at the Ferry Yard to enable the ship's bottom to be scraped and anti-fouled, a supply of useful engine room spares had been obtained at nominal cost and several additional sponsors had been identified, Messrs McGinnity and Roberts soon discovered that their long and difficult rail journey from Southampton to Neyland combined with a lack of PSPS members living close to the ship made it impossible to carry out all but the most essential jobs on board.

Some paint-chipping and red-leading was done, but the list of outstanding tasks began to grow: "There are a host of woodwork repairs which require attention… the ships lacks a mast… a large quantity of heavy timber (originally installed to strengthen the fore deck for car carrying) needs to be removed to lighten the ship… the aft saloon is bare and will need painting and soft furnishings… there is no toilet fitted and fresh water is only available from the boiler." Insurance cover and a boiler survey had to be arranged and slowly the project began to look a little more expensive and challenging than originally thought.

Until now, the Society's subscription income had easily covered the limited expenses of printing *Paddle Wheels*, postage, etc. but the Central Committee quickly realised that becoming ship owners would mean "treading a path that could easily become thorny". In order to avoid any future claims or losses in connection with *Alumchine* falling upon the Society or its members, it was resolved to form a private limited company to own and operate the ship. Called Paddle Steam Navigation Ltd (PSN) it was incorporated on 27th March 1963 with a nominal capital of £100. All of the initial directors were members of the PSPS Central Committee and the Articles of Association were carefully phrased to ensure that the Society would always hold a controlling interest. Loans from the PSPS Preservation Fund would enable PSN to purchase and move the ship and, in the event that she ever generated a profit from future operation, it was anticipated that some of this would be used to pay off the original loans and recharge central funds.

By August more "reasonably favourable" surveyors' reports had been received and it was hoped to complete the purchase by October. It was acknowledged that the original plan to move *Alumchine* to the South Coast under her own steam was too risky and unrealistic to be attempted and instead it was decided that she would have to be battened down and towed round by a tug. Unfortunately, the cheapest quote which could be obtained was for £600, which placed the overall cost beyond the Society's means. When they learned of the problem

Pembrokeshire County Council generously reduced their asking price to £500 but, despite a second appeal being issued to members, the overall cost of the venture was still too high and in November 1963 the Central Committee reluctantly recommended that it be abandoned. A stormy A.G.M. held in Salisbury on 17th November 1963 confirmed the decision. The PSPS withdrew its offer of purchase, lost its deposit and, after being sold to a Mr Gull for £420, *Alumchine* was later scrapped during 1965.

The failure of the *Alumchine* project was a severe blow to the morale of the Society and inevitably raised differences between members, some of whom even suggested that the word "preservation" should be removed from the Society's name as

One of a series of photos taken by Syd Roberts during the maintenance visits he and Tony McGinnity paid to the ship during the spring of 1963. A ladder has been produced to allow access to the ship.

PSPS Collection

it was now abundantly clear that it would never own or run an excursion steamer. Others, however, drew attention to more positive aspects: A Preservation Fund had been kick-started, membership expanded, and it had been acknowledged that both of these would have to be significantly increased before another attempt at ship-ownership could be made. Some hard lessons had been learned about the true costs and difficulties of resurrecting an elderly paddle steamer but the newly-created Paddle Steam Navigation Ltd remained in existence to own and operate any future acquisition.

With hindsight it is easy to see that the project came just a little too early for a fledgling and cash-poor society with a very limited membership, and that *Alumchine*, for all her charm as a workaday ferry steamer, may not have been the most suitable vessel to buy. Although she would undoubtedly have generated an influx of new members, she had neither the beauty of the passenger river paddlers, nor the size, speed and lines of the classic seagoing excursion ship and might have struggled to operate as anything other than a members' yacht and headquarters ship. More importantly, the cost of her maintenance might well have ruled out other exciting developments which were to come.

Reliant, the last steam paddle tug in Great Britian, working in Seaham Harbour on 2nd. August 1967. Built in 1907 as Old Trafford *for the Manchester Ship Canal Co. Ltd. she was sold in October 1950 to the Ridley Steam Tug Company of Newcastle and re-named. In September 1956 she was acquired by the Seaham Harbour dock Company, and spent the rest of her career handling colliers within the tight confines of that port. Following the withdrawal of her running mate, the paddle tug* Eppleton Hall *in November 1967, she became a spare vessel and only worked occasionally. In 1969 she was acquired by the National Maritime Museum and preserved, substantially intact, within the Neptune Hall at Greenwich. Tragically and controversially, the museum later changed its priorities and broke the vessel up, retaining only her side lever engine and a paddle wheel for display.*

Bernard Dixon / PSPS Collection

28

CHAPTER FOUR

THE EVENTFUL 1960s

With contributions from Victor Gray, Peter Lamb and Chris Phillips

THE plans for the purchase of *Alumchine* meant that 1963 had opened with a general sense of optimism, which was soon to be tempered by events. Prophetically perhaps, two L&HC Branch meetings heard from speakers who, while wishing the PSPS every success, had some sober messages to share. Frank Marshall, Secretary of the New Medway Steam Packet Co., spoke about operating *Medway Queen* and revealed that, while her operation over the last 39 years had given his company much satisfaction, she "had ceased to provide them with any jam on their butter since 1959". At the next meeting Mr W.J. Philpott, a former manager of Eagle Steamers, gave a highly entertaining lecture on the economics of operating large Thames passenger ships and warned : "If you want to gamble go in for premium bonds, don't go into the steamship business."

Strength was added to these ominous warnings when, in January 1963 Cosens & Co announced that their veteran *Consul* had been withdrawn and that there would be no steamer service from Weymouth for the first time since 1848. She had made a loss for the past three seasons and, with expensive repairs and a load line survey looming, her retention could simply not be justified.

The bombshell came at a somewhat ironic moment, for during the winter of 1962-63 Weymouth had played host to the widest variety of paddle steamers for many years. *Embassy* and *Consul* were in their usual winter berths when, in October and November respectively, the railway paddler *Sandown* and P.& A. Campbell's *Bristol Queen* arrived for overhaul by Cosens. For a few days, therefore, four paddlers belonging to three different companies lay together in Weymouth Harbour, surely the last time such an event would happen in Britain.

The news of *Consul's* demise came as a shock to many local people and on 30th March the PSPS called a public meeting at Weymouth Guildhall to discuss whether anything could be done to ensure a continuation of sailings from the resort. Among those attending was Commander Edmund Rhodes who surprised and delighted the meeting by announcing that he would bring his *Princess Elizabeth* to Weymouth for the 1963 season. The ship's 1962 Bournemouth season had not been a financial success, so the move to Weymouth suited

A unique gathering of paddle steamers in Weymouth Harbour on 14th November 1962. Consul, *her career with Cosens over, lies in her traditional berth at Trinity Quay. At Custom House Quay* Bristol Queen *is about to cast off and make her way through the Town Bridge to begin her refit at Cosens' engineering works in the Backwater. Astern of her* Sandown, *her own refit complete, prepares to run trials in the Bay before returning to Portsmouth.*

Maureen Attwooll

For the 1963 season only South Coast & Continental Steamers Ltd chose to paint Consul *in a distinctive livery of green hull, red boot topping and primrose yellow funnel which is clearly visible in this splendid view of her approaching Newhaven on 18th August 1963. Close examination of the photograph raises two intriguing questions: Why are the handful of passengers gathered right in the stern?; and why is the steamer displaying two black balls indicating that she is 'not under command'? One can only assume that she has recently experienced one of the many mechanical crises which dogged her Sussex season and is retreating to Newhaven to undertake repairs.* PSPS Collection

Commander Rhodes very well indeed. The meeting, which concluded with a talk and film show about Cosens' steamers, provided some positive publicity for PSPS and also resulted in the formation of a Weymouth Branch of the Society under the chairmanship of Mr Lionel Poole. In January an Isle of Wight Branch had also been formed, to be followed in April by a Sussex Branch, but all of these proved to be short-lived and were soon reabsorbed into their "parent" branches.

Everyone had assumed that *Consul* would soon depart for the breaker's yard but, to general astonishment, it was announced that she had instead been purchased by South Coast & Continental Steamers Ltd and would be returning to

PSPS members on Consul's *bridge during the spring of 1963. Tom Cadman and Iris, Mrs Pritchard's friend and apprentice, are on the bridge wing while Richard Roberts peers through the wheelhouse window. Syd Roberts is up the funnel attending to the ship's whistle.* Peter Lamb

service. This was the third of the four "private" attempts at preservation which took place during the 1960s. Behind the new company was Tony McGinnity, one of the founder members of the PSPS whom we encountered earlier in this narrative. He had come into a modest legacy and, with the financial support of Wessex Branch Secretary Eileen Pritchard and other backers, decided to try to turn his preservation ideals into reality.

As winter turned into spring, *Consul* became a hive of activity. While a former chief engineer worked to reassemble her engine which had been disconnected in readiness for the tow to the breaker's yard, PSPS members were welcomed on board to help with preparation for the season ahead. Brushes were wielded with varying degrees of skill as the ship was re-painted in a bright new livery of primrose yellow funnel and green hull, and her accommodation was spruced up. Members could be seen cleaning, varnishing and even climbing a wobbly ladder to polish up the whistle on the funnel. Health and safety was never mentioned and the sense of jollity was somehow captured by the bright yellow and highly untraditional curtains which Mrs Pritchard produced for the Captain's deck cabin!

Behind the scenes, however, worries were already beginning to accumulate. With Commander Rhodes' announcement that *Princess Elizabeth* would be operating from Weymouth, *Consul* was deprived of her traditional cruising grounds, and would have to find another suitable base. It was eventually announced that the ship would operate on the Sussex coast and attempt to succeed where *Sussex Queen* had failed only a few years earlier. *Consul* duly departed for slipping at Poole, where her owners received a series of sharp lessons in the expensive reality of ship-owning. Symbolically perhaps, she arrived with her yellow funnel blackened and blistered because some cheap paint from the local Woolworth's store had been applied instead of the

Bristol Queen *sweeps into Mumbles Pier.*   PSPS Collection

correct, heat-resistant type! Then things got significantly worse. The Board of Trade applied their "change of ownership" policy and insisted that a range of expensive safety, subdivision and fire-fighting regulations be applied, demanded new stability data, insisted that her ballast be removed and weighed, and finally reduced her passenger certificate from 450 to 230, making her future earning potential extremely marginal.

Down but not yet out, Tony McGinnity pressed on with his plans and dispatched the ship to her summer base at Newhaven. A fuel pump problem en route caused her to miss her inaugural trips, and a series of subsequent mechanical problems meant that she missed a high proportion of her public sailings from Brighton. The dire financial situation was eased slightly by a successful September charter to PSPS member Don Rose who, trading as New Belle steamers, brought her to the Thames for a week of sailings from Tower Pier and Southend. A true enthusiast, Don Rose had previously chartered *Medway Queen* for a special day trip to London and was later to make his own attempt to re-open paddle steamer services on the Thames. Following her few days in the limelight *Consul* limped home to Weymouth for the winter while her owners considered their options.

PSPS members made the most of *Consul's* Sussex and Thames adventures and savoured the pleasure of sailing on *Princess Elizabeth* from Weymouth. Her many-coloured sailing bills were a breath of fresh air after Cosens' familiar but rather dull format and, in addition to all the usual local trips, it was once again possible to take regular long day sailings to Yarmouth on the Isle of Wight. On the Bristol Channel a large group of members joined *Bristol Queen* in May for a splendid, three-day excursion to Penzance and the Isles of Scilly, the conception and promotion of which had been heavily backed by PSPS; and later in the summer on nominated excursions to Lundy Island and elsewhere. Another group was on board *Medway Queen* to witness the last Thames & Medway Sailing Barge Race and in July the Admiralty invited another party into Portsmouth dockyard to visit the diesel-electric paddle tug *Forceful*.

Yet again, however, the pleasures of the sailing season were tempered by the withdrawal of more familiar paddle steamers. First to go were the four Woolwich Free Ferries, *Squires, Gordon, Will Crookes* and *John Benn*. Although only dating from the 1920s and 30s these ships were of an extraordinarily antiquated appearance, with twin, widely-spaced bell-topped funnels, coke-fired boilers and independent paddle wheels. Although dismissed by some as mere, humble ferry-boats, their endless crossings of busy Thames tideway required unique ship-handling skills and were fascinating to observe. Replaced by modern Voith-Schneider-propelled ferries, the four paddlers had been sold to Belgian shipbreakers and were due to depart during August. Accordingly, having previously made a detailed photographic and audio record of the ships, members of the L&HC Branch paid an official farewell visit on 29th July. Down in Devon, the River Dart paddler *Totnes Castle* was withdrawn at the end of the season and converted into an accommodation ship, leaving her sister ship *Kingswear Castle* as the only steamer in the fleet.

Even more melancholy was the weekend of 7th-8th September when the much-loved *Medway Queen* made her final sailings. Her withdrawal had been announced well in advance, so regular passengers and admirers turned out in force to give her a resounding send off and on the final day there were poignant scenes at Southend and Herne Bay piers as civic dignitaries and local residents wished her farewell. *Paddle Wheels* described the day as "one of unrelieved sadness and gloom both weather-wise and in every other respect" and noted how, after "finished with engines" was rung down for the last time at Strood Pier and "three cheers" had been raised for Capt. Horsham and his ship, the last passengers had "wended their way home in the darkness, tired, hungry, cold and dispirited, many facing all-night train journeys."

Due in large part to her distinguished role in Operation Dynamo, the Dunkirk evacuation, during which she made repeated Channel crossings, brought home some 7000 men and earned herself the nickname "The Heroine of Dunkirk", *Medway Queen's* demise did not go un-noticed. The Dunkirk Veterans' Association became involved, the national press took a considerable interest, and pressure began to build for her preservation. The PSPS called a public meeting at The Baltic Exchange, London, on 18th October at which The Medway Queen Trust was set up with the aim of raising sufficient money

to purchase and preserve the ship. The new trust, although separate from PSPS, had many joint members, including Dr Robinson, Don Rose and PSPS Chairman Nick Knight.

A fund-raising appeal was launched, and PSPS offered to make a substantial donation from its own Preservation Fund, but despite a long subscription list the target looked unlikely to be met. Then the National Trust began to take an interest and suggested that, for a couple of years at least, they might steam her around the coast to host receptions in aid of their new "Project Neptune" coastal preservation appeal. Unfortunately, however, a survey indicated that her hull needed much expensive work before a seagoing role could be considered, so different options had to be considered.

The Medway Queen Trust and the National Trust then worked together to find an alternative solution and succeeded in persuading Chares Forte & Co to purchase the ship for use as a restaurant and Dunkirk Memorial, moored on the Thames Embankment. The scheme received much positive press coverage but Fortes were unable to obtain the necessary berth and licences, so were forced to sell the ship once again, this time to a Belgian ship breaker. Hearing of the campaign to save the ship, the breakers agreed to delay her departure until a buyer could be found. In August 1965, in a scheme supported by the Dunkirk Veterans' Association, PSPS and Medway Queen Trust, she was purchased by a group of Isle of Wight business men who planned to use her as a club and centrepiece to a yacht marine development on the River Medina, halfway between Cowes and Newport. She arrived under tow on 28th September 1965, was manoeuvred into her berth and refitted

Ryde approaching Clarence Pier, Southsea.

PSPS Collection

32

for her new role. A PSPS loan assisted in the process and the ship opened to the public on 14th May 1966, with PSPS members enjoying corporate membership and at least one Society AGM being held on board.

The efforts to save *Medway Queen* combined with failure of the PSPS's own *Alumchine* project sparked a major internal debate about the future direction of the Society and the meaning of "preservation" which came to a head at the 1963 AGM. Some members believed that static preservation was the only affordable way forward, while others countered that dull museum pieces were of limited interest and that every effort should be made to purchase and operate a suitable vessel. Another group argued that the best way to retain existing steamers in operation was to support their operators by supporting and promoting their services, arranging large group bookings, stimulating interest by chartering the ships to undertake unusual or innovative sailings, or even "adopting" and subsidising a particular vessel.

These diverse views were carefully noted and under the strong leadership of Chairman Nick Knight the Society drove ahead. A Cruising Sub-Committee was formed to plan and promote future charters and links with operators, while the existing Preservation Sub-Committee continued to investigate suitable candidates for preservation. *Compton Castle, Totnes Castle* and the paddle tug *Houghton* were all considered and rejected as unsuitable, but it was agreed to keep the still-operational *Kingswear Castle* under close review.

The principle of encouraging operators to innovate was put into spectacular action on 5th July 1964 when Cosens' *Embassy* was chartered to make the first paddle steamer sailing around the Isle of Wight since 1958. Vigorous and effective advertising

Medway Queen departing from Herne Bay pier during her last day in service, 8th September 1963.   A.E. Bennett/R. Clammer Collection

Bristol Queen at Hugh Town, St.Mary's, Isle of Scilly. Keith Abraham

The Woolwich Free Ferry Squires *pictured on 7th January 1961*   A.E. Bennett/R. Clammer Collection

With her windows boarded up for the tow from the Thames, Medway Queen *is eased into her new berth in the Mill Pond at Binfield on the River Medina by the motor barge* Seaclose *at high water on 28th September 1963. The photograph was taken by Wessex Branch Secretary Eileen Pritchard who was on board the motor launch used by Southern Television to cover the paddler's arrival.* PSPS Collection

by Messrs Gray and Dougan had the desired effect and on the afternoon of the sailing a blackboard at the entrance to Bournemouth pier bore the rare message "Isle of Wight Steamer Fully Booked."

Departing at 2.15pm *Embassy* steamed clockwise round the Island in beautiful weather, called at Shanklin for time ashore, and arrived back at Bournemouth pier at about 9.20pm, before offering a one way sailing to her overnight berth at Poole. The event was an unqualified success, made a healthy profit for the Society and, very importantly, persuaded Cosens to offer two repeat sailings on their own account later in the season.

Frequent nominated excursions on the Bristol Channel continued, including *Bristol Queen's* three-day trip to the Scilly Isles, her annual marathon to Milford Haven, and trips to Mumbles, Ilfracombe and elsewhere.

At Weymouth 1964 turned out to be a unique and exciting season. Having realised the severe difficulties of operating the 1896-vintage *Consul* away from her home port and without engineers who really understood her, Tony McGinnity announced that he would be basing the ship at Weymouth once again and reviving her traditional service to land at Lulworth

COME ABOARD ! !

YOUR FIRST OPPORTUNITY FOR SIX YEARS TO SAIL

ROUND THE ISLE OF WIGHT

(Time ashore at Shanklin)

By Paddle Steamer "EMBASSY"

SUNDAY, 5th JULY, 1964

DEPART BOURNEMOUTH PIER — 2.15 p.m.

DUE BACK ABOUT 9.20 p.m.

FARE - 23/6

N.B.— Tickets May be purchased at a
SPECIAL REDUCED FARE OF 18/- Prior to the day of sailing
Children under 15 half fare
(Fares refunded in the event of cancellation)

THIS IS A MAGNIFICENT 85-MILE CRUISE OF PICTURESQUE SCENERY
PASSING THROUGH THE SMOOTH WATERS OF THE SOLENT AND SPITHEAD,
ROUND THE FORELAND SOUTHWARDS TO SHANKLIN WHERE TIME WILL
BE ALLOWED ASHORE. "EMBASSY" WILL RETURN WESTWARDS PAST
ST. CATHERINE'S POINT AND THE NEEDLES

TEAS and LIGHT REFRESHMENTS AVAILABLE ON BOARD
LICENSED BAR OPEN THROUGHOUT THE SAILING

TICKETS AVAILABLE FROM :

G. V. W. Gray, 22 Gerald Road, Bournemouth
D. L. Dougan, The Mill House, Donyatt, Illminster, Somerset
The Customers' Bureau, Beales, Old Christchurch Road, Bournemouth
or from The Steamer Office, Bottom of West Cliff, Bournemouth

*Promoted by the Paddle Steamer Preservation Society, with the co-operation of
Cosens & Co. Ltd., under whose Conditions of Carriage as exhibited at
their Offices, Agencies and on board their ships passengers are
carried. Sailing subject to weather and circumstances.*

Sherrens - Weymouth

Dressed overall, Embassy *awaits her passengers at Bournemouth Pier, 5th July 1964.* R. Clammer Collection, photographer unknown.

A Sailing Bill (inset) for Embassy's *Round the Isle of Wight charter.* PSPS Collection

7.30am on 5th June 1965 and the early morning sun is desperately trying to break through the thick fog lying over Weymouth Harbour. Embassy, with Princess Elizabeth lying ahead of her, is loading passengers for her PSPS charter sailing round the Isle of Wight which went ahead despite the challenging visibility. R. Clammer

electric paddle ferries, *Queen Margaret, Robert the Bruce, Mary Queen of Scots* and *Sir William Wallace* which had previously maintained the crossing between North and South Queensferry. The first three were swiftly broken up, but the *Wallace* found further employment in Holland and survived until 1970. A more serious blow to enthusiasts was the withdrawal of *Jeanie Deans*, one of the all-time favourite Clyde steamers. She made her last passenger sailing on 28th September and retreated to Greenock to await her fate.

Encouraged by the success of the1964 *Embassy* charter, the Cruising Sub-Committee decided to offer three major trips in 1965. The first was another Round the Isle of Wight sailing by *Embassy* but this time beginning at Weymouth, the first such trip since 1914. Fresh from her refit, the ship looked superb but the day dawned foggy and departure had to be delayed. Off Swanage she encountered another fog bank and had to be guided into the pier by the ringing of a bell, before departing again for Bournemouth. It was on this leg of the journey that the charter almost ended in disaster. *Embassy* strayed slightly off course as she left Swanage Bay and the cliffs at Ballard Point suddenly loomed into view. Fortunately the cliffs are very steep-to at that point so, with her helm hard over and the engine full astern, the ship was able to claw off the rocks and make her way to Bournemouth. Among the passengers seen embarking at Bournemouth was John Betjeman in his distinctive pork pie hat. Although the ship was now running very late, the rest of trip was without incident but things could have turned out very differently indeed!

Cove. This, of course, brought her into direct competition with the resident *Princess Elizabeth*, resulting in much ill-feeling. The sight of two competing paddlers operating from Weymouth Pleasure Pier was a delight to the enthusiast but really did not make economic sense. Although by mid August *Consul* was making a small profit, it became clear that this would be insufficient to pay off her creditors from the previous season and her owners went into voluntary liquidation. Thus, on a sunny summer's day on 28th August 1964, *Consul* made the last ever steamer landing at Lulworth Cove and was withdrawn.

The failure of this private preservation attempt must have been a bitter blow to Tony McGinnity, Eileen Pritchard and their backers. Aware of the precarious nature of steamer ownership, Tony had sensibly diversified some time before by setting up a ship-broking and marine surveying firm, so was able to handle the sale of the ship himself. Resisting an early offer from a breaker's yard he managed to sell *Consul* for conversion into an accommodation ship for a firm offering sailing holidays on the River Dart, and she departed from Weymouth for her final voyage in steam on 4th February 1965. Her operational days were over, but her short-term future had been secured.

In Scotland the completion of the Forth Road Bridge on 4th September 1964 meant the end of the four diesel-

PSPS members and other passengers relax in the evening sun on Princess Elizabeth's *foredeck as she approaches Weymouth Bay on the return leg of her charter sailing to Torquay on 27th June 1965.*

R. Clammer

The second charter was on 27th June and took *Princess Elizabeth* from Weymouth to Torquay and back, an unusual and very attractive itinerary which had not been attempted for 16 years. Unfortunately the week leading up to the charter was one of unremitting cold and windy weather which discouraged casual bookings so, although the day itself dawned calm and sunny, there were disappointingly few passengers on board. Those who did sail enjoyed a perfect day's cruising. The sun beat down, the sea sparkled, passengers relaxed in deck chairs and the ship herself seemed to be in her element, running smoothly and ahead of schedule in both directions. Sadly though, the poor support meant that her owners were not tempted to repeat the trip later in the season.

The third and final charter, organised by Pat Murrell of the Bristol Channel Branch, was on Sunday 8th August 1965 when *Bristol Queen* sailed

Since its completion in 1882, Craigendoran Pier had been the north bank railhead for and headquarters of the Clyde steamers belonging to the North British and London & North Eastern Railways. In this fine photograph, taken on a bright but blustery 30th June 1964, the incomparable Jeanie Deans *lays alongside while one of the Maid Class motor vessels – most probably* Maid of Argyll – *is just visible on the other side of the pier.* PSPS Collection

from Ilfracombe to Padstow, with through bookings available from Swansea and Mumbles. The charter was a huge success, carrying a full load of 1004 passengers in perfect weather, and making a profit of over £200 (compared with £18 profit for the Embassy and a loss of £192 for *Princess Elizabeth*), and persuaded P&A Campbell to plan two similar sailings in 1966.

In addition to the formal charters there was the usual crop of nominated excursions, a specially-arranged cruise through the Solent from Portsmouth on board Ryde on 30th May and a group visit to the Admiralty paddle tug *Grinder* on 2nd October. On this occasion the party were taken out by launch to join the tug as she finished a towing job ad were given a trip round the harbour before mooring back alongside her sister ship *Forceful*.

1965 closed with discouraging news that the Dart paddler *Kingswear Castle* and the Portsmouth-based *Sandown* had been withdrawn from service but, more optimistically, that a fourth private preservation project was under way. *Jeanie Deans* had been purchased by the Coastal Steam Packet Company financed by Mr Don Rose and a consortium of other PSPS and World Ship Society members. The ship left the Clyde in November 1965 and steamed round to the River Medway, encountering severe gales in the Irish Sea en route. Once safely moored at Chatham she was renamed *Queen of the South* and Don Rose made a direct appeal to members of PSPS and other ship societies to save the company money by becoming directly involved with the fitting out, volunteering to help with advertising and clerical duties, or using contacts to procure equipment and supplies at favourable rates. During the months ahead work parties were convened and contributed a good deal, but a lack of training and professional direction meant

that they were not as effective as perhaps they could have been.

The Coastal Steam Packet Company initially had no clear idea where the ship would operate from, but as the spring of 1966 progressed it was announced that she would operate from Tower Pier, London. Timetables and attractive advertising bills were designed by a well-respected enthusiast and the ship made her first sailing on 28th May. Things, however, did not go according to plan. Possibly because too much had been spent on internal refit and not enough on mechanical issues, the ship suffered a whole series of breakdowns and other misfortunes and her stop-start season came to an abrupt end on 6th August. During the winter while the ship was laid up on the Medway, Don Rose managed to raise some additional financial backing, allowing creditors to be kept at bay and the ship to return to service for the 1967 season which, sadly, proved even more disastrous than the previous one. After running on only a handful of days the splendid ship was withdrawn and sold to Belgian ship breakers, bringing to an end the fourth and last of the gallant "private" preservation attempts of the 1960s.

1966 was not a happy year for paddle steamer enthusiasts. The National Seamen's Strike stopped some operators completely while general uncertainty kept many passengers away from those who were unaffected; the weather was dreadful; and the much –publicised loss of life in the wreck of the *Anzio I* on Donna Nook during April together with the sinking of the small pleasure boats *Darlwyne* off Cornwall and *Prince of Wales* at Penmaenpool, put off many members of the public from taking sea trips at all. The opportunity for interesting charters was somewhat limited by circumstances. As the only remaining Portsmouth paddler, *Ryde* could not be spared for charter work. Enquiries about taking *Princess*

Elizabeth were rebuffed but the reason soon became clear when, instead of emerging for the season, she remained in Weymouth Backwater and was advertised for sale. However, on 24th July *Embassy* was chartered once again, this time to run from Poole and Bournemouth to Ventnor where passengers would be allowed 2¼ hours ashore while the ship made a coastal cruise from Ventnor pier, which had not received a call from a Cosens steamer since 1954. Unfortunately this imaginative itinerary was ruined by the weather. Strong winds and rough seas made the Ventnor call untenable, so the ship was forced to return to the shelter of the Solent and offer time ashore at Yarmouth instead.

As the season progressed the news simply got worse. The opening of the new Tay Bridge on 18th August rendered the 1921-built Tay paddle ferry *B.L. Nairn* redundant along with her two screw-driven companions, so she was withdrawn and later broken up. On the Bristol Channel a combination of poor weather, mechanical problems and other factors combined to make 1966 financially disastrous for P&A Campbell Ltd. Having introduced the motor ship *Westward Ho (ex. Vecta)* into the fleet they rapidly concluded that two ships were quite sufficient for their dwindling clientele and withdrew *Cardiff Queen* after her last trip to Lundy Island on 21st September. PSPS, having taken her on her first ever visit to Padstow just ten days earlier, tried unsuccessfully to persuade her owners to move her to Bournemouth for the 1967 season and, after a failed attempt to establish her as a nightclub on the River Usk at Newport, she was broken up in 1968.

At Bournemouth *Embassy* performed well until 28th July when she broke a paddle float while homeward bound from the Island, and severe damage was caused to the port wheel and paddle box. After a week under repair she returned to service only to be greeted by a succession of gales and cancellations but soldiered on until 22nd September when she made her last trips to Totland Bay and then sailed for winter lay-up at Weymouth. Although the local papers carried assurances that she would be back next season Cosens' Board already knew that the extremely expensive work required on her hull and boiler before she could obtain an new passenger certificate

The Admiralty diesel-electric paddle tug Grinder *assisting the RFA* Wave Prince *in Portsmouth Harbour on 2nd October 1965. The photograph is taken from the launch which ferried the PSPS party out to join the tug.* Richard Clammer

PSPS volunteers sanding and varnishing deck seats on board Queen of the South (ex. Jeanie Deans) *during the spring of 1966.* John Richardson

A volunteer sign writer preparing Queen of the South's *fan boards for the season ahead.* John Richardson

The Tay paddle ferry B.L.Nairn *awaiting disposal at Dundee on 5th June 1967. The masts of* HMS Unicorn *and the spire of St Paul's Church are visible in the background.* Les Ring/PSPS Collection

Embassy alongside Swanage Pier at the beginning of her last season, 1966, displaying her mainmast which was fitted during the previous winter to meet new lighting regulations. Capt Iliffe is on the bridge while Mate Eric Plater and Bosun Sandy Rashleigh stand at the head of the gangway to welcome passengers on board.

Chris Phillips (Swanage)

Bristol Queen *at Padstow, August 1965.*   Les Ring/PSPS Collection

Cardiff Queen *makes a splendid sight as she goes hard astern from Ilfracombe Pier en route to Lundy Island, 1964.*   PSPS Collection

simply could not be justified. Cosens regretfully announced that "the day of the paddler was over", *Embassy* was advertised for sale and departed to a Belgian scrap yard in May 1967.

Finally, following various engine problems which caused her to run at reduced speed, the Clyde diesel electric paddler *Talisman* made her last sailing from Gourock to the Holy Loch on 17th November, and was scrapped during the following year. Intriguingly, *Talisman, Princess Elizabeth* and *Cardiff Queen*, were all advertised for sale by Tony McGinnity, PSPS member and former owner of *Consul*, through his ship broking, surveying and delivery firm. Tony has already handled the sale of *Jeanie Deans* and *Consul*, and would go on to sell *Caledonia* and *Bristol Queen*. Some enthusiasts struggled to understand how he could be an enthusiast and also sell much-loved vessels for scrap, but the truth is that he always regarded the breaker's yard as the last resort, and was successful in finding static roles for several significant paddlers.

This grim list of withdrawals was certainly a source of widespread depression and could have led to a disintegration of the Society, which seemed to be failing in its aim to keep existing steamers in operation. Society Chairman Nick Knight however, rose to the occasion and issued members with a direct challenge. Referring to *Queen of the South's* dreadful season he opined: "Much talk took place, but working parties provided by the society never got properly organised or turned up in sufficient strength and regularity. It is my considered opinion that a contributory cause to the failure of this brave venture was the reliance placed upon volunteer labour, contrary to professional advice. Once again this episode showed the dearth of skill and enthusiasm from the society for work in a ship."

He went on to express the view that *Kingswear Castle*, which had been advertised for sale at Dartmouth, was the right size for the Society and represented the last practical opportunity to achieve its stated objective of preserving a paddle steamer. He believed however, that due to the lack of practical support demonstrated by the *Alumchine* and *Queen of the South* episodes, it was unreasonable to suppose that the Society could achieve this alone, and that it needed "to find someone who can take the vessel on a bare boat charter and put her to work to earn her keep in some way, either statically or part-operationally."

Members were asked to express their views and commit to offers of help and, with the endorsement of the AGM held on board *Medway Queen*, Nick Knight and the Central Committee opened negotiations simultaneously with both the River Dart Steamboat Company and potential charterers in the form of Messrs Ridett, owners of the *Medway Queen* on the Isle of Wight. Once a formal charter agreement had been signed *Kingswear Castle* was purchased for £600 on 20th June 1967 and arrived under tow at her new mooring in the River Medina on 28th August.

1967 can therefore be seen as a pivotal year in the history of the PSPS. Despite the loss of so many operational paddlers, the society had at last acquired its own ship and apparently found

Kingswear Castle on her mooring in the River Medina, Isle of Wight, on 25th January 1969 shortly before 'Operation Shipshape' was launched.
PSPS Collection

a practical way to see her future safeguarded.

With options increasingly limited, the Society arranged only one charter in 1967, that of *Bristol Queen* for a grand long day cruise from Cardiff to Tenby on 10th September. In the event the trip never took place as, after experiencing increasingly frequent mechanical problems during the season, the ship suffered serious paddle wheel damage on 26th August 1967 and was immediately withdrawn, never to sail again. The Society supported proposals to turn her into a floating museum in Bristol city centre, but the plan was ahead of its time and she departed for breaking up in March 1968.

1968 opened with only eight British paddlers still in operation: *Caledonia, Waverley* and *Maid of the Loch* in Scotland, the three Humber ferries and *Ryde* together with the diesel car ferry *Farringford* on the Solent. Others were in static use or for sale and PSPS did what it could to encourage their retention. Of particular concern was the former *Consul* which as *Duke of Devonshire* was struggling to make a profit as a sailing school headquarters at Dartmouth. As Britain's last surviving Victorian paddler she was of great historical significance and, when her owners suggested that she would have to be sold, PSPS offered to meet her mooring costs for a few months while options were explored. The National Maritime Museum expressed an interest in preserving her 1896 John Penn engine, but this came to naught and she was towed away for breaking up in Southampton during October. *Princess Elizabeth* ended up in the same breakers yard where her engines were removed before she was sold on for use as a marina HQ on Hayling Island.

On 15th September, a day of torrential rain and strong winds, the Wessex Branch operated a very enjoyable charter from Southampton on board the steam powered former Gosport

ferry *Venus*. Although it made a small loss the event was judged sufficiently encouraging to be repeated the following year when, on 21st September, she made a cruise down the western Solent on her last ever voyage in steam before being converted to diesel power. *Venus* was to feature in several other Wessex Branch charters.

Meanwhile, there was increasing concern about *Kingswear Castle* on the Medina. The Ridetts had not carried out the maintenance or restoration work required by the charter agreement and, preoccupied with their marina development and the *Medway Queen* did not have any clear plans for the smaller paddler. They claimed to be keen to retain her on the Medina but seemed unable to give the Society any firm assurances. With leaking decks and an uncapped funnel, the steamer's condition was visibly deteriorating so PSPS Central Committee began to discuss terminating the charter agreement and moving the ship elsewhere, with Poole Harbour and the Medway both considered. Nick Knight suggested that he might be able to use her commercially in conjunction with his steam yacht *Cresset* at Rochester.

While possibilities were being considered the Society launched "Operation Shipshape" in March 1969. A letter to all members explained that the aim was for work parties to meet on board *Kingswear Castle* each weekend to carry out essential maintenance and attempt to halt her deterioration. Stocks of tools and paint would be available on board, and the return ferry fares of members travelling from the mainland would be met. It was hoped that ship would be in a more presentable condition by 20th July 1969 when it was planned to hold an open day on board to celebrate the Society's 10th Anniversary. Peter Lamb, who was a key member of the Society at that time, has vivid memories of that period:

"The arrival of the "KC" on the river Medina brought its own

Cardiff Queen *at speed between Cardiff and Penarth, c.1966. The area where she is pictured is now enclosed by the Cardiff Bay Barrage.*
Les Ring/PSPS Collection

Talisman *laid up in Albert Harbour, Greenock, on 4th June 1967, shortly before she was broken up.*   Les Ring/PSPS Collection

Bristol Queen *under tow from Cardiff to the breakers yard in Belgium on 21 March 1968, with the tug* Fairplay XI *ahead and a local tug astern. The ship's premature demise was a tragedy as her relative youth combined with a powerful, seaworthy design should have made her an ideal candidate for operational preservation.*
Les Ring/PSPS Collection

*After having her engine and boiler removed at Ferry Services &
Supplies breakers' yard at Woolston, Southampton,* Princess Elizabeth
*was granted an eleventh-hour reprieve when she was purchased by Mr
Harold Butler for use as the centre piece of a marina development in
Langstone Harbour. Mr Butler's plans did not come to fruition but the
ship survived to serve as a restaurant on the Thames and in Paris and
currently as a conference centre in Dunkirk.*
R. Clammer Collection/Photographer Unknown

set of challenges. She was very remote for those travelling from
the mainland by Red Funnel to Cowes followed by an
infrequent bus to Binfield Corner and a twenty minute walk.
The ship was moored in the river and access was by a collection
of WWII vintage pontoons strung together. A number of these
pontoons quickly started to take on water. Other than at high
water they tended to lie at crazy angles on the mud, making
transit virtually impossible. However, this did not deter many
enthusiastic members. Chris Phillips, then National Secretary,
launched 'Operation Shipshape' and his clarion call was
answered with a team of regulars. The work achieved was very
superficial as we had no tools other than those that could be
carried, no power and zero facilities.

On one occasion I convinced my mother she would enjoy a
day out on the IOW and we should call upon the *KC* to show
her what was being achieved. My very supportive wife-to-be
also planned to come along. Upon arrival it became quickly
obvious neither of the ladies would be able to access the ship
via the pontoon bridge that had, by this time, acquired a snake-
like shape and was an utter disaster. Fellow member, Andrew
Patrick, kindly offered to row the ladies across to the KC if I
could scramble across the pontoon in order to assist them

aboard on arrival. This I duly did and made things ready
aboard for their arrival. Andrew produced a fibre glass dingy
and a set of oars and the ladies embarked and set sail.

After a couple of minutes Andrew calmly called across to me
'we are sinking', to the alarm of the ladies whose feet were now
nearly immersed in seawater and handbags floating. He
managed to pull alongside and alight his passengers who,
remarkably, found the incident quite amusing. However, the
problem was there were now four of us aboard, the tide was
ebbing and only two of the party had any chance of clambering
ashore as the pontoon bridge was now lying drunkenly on the
mud. Andrew and I managed to roll the dingy and empty the
water only to find the bung had popped out. We made some
repairs and prepared the dingy for the return journey of a few
minutes. Andrew rowed towards the shore. By this time the
tide had dropped and the slanting wall of the river bank was
longer and covered in seaweed and slime and not accessible. I
saw a rope hanging down the wall attached to a bollard and I
said I would take a jump and climb the wall with the aid of the
rope. I duly jumped and caught the rope, only to find it was not
attached to the riverside bollard and I duly slithered back down
the wall landing in the stinking mud of the river Medina.

To cut a long story short, IOW member Richard White had
arrived by this time and was quick to assist. The passengers
were safely brought ashore. I was completely covered in very
aromatic mud. A quick search around the MQ site produced a
dirty and much used set of overalls for me to change into.
Unfortunately they had no buttons down the front that was
completely open. I gathered my clothes into a large bag and had
to hold them in front of me all the way back to Southampton.
As I smelt so foul I was not allowed into the ferry saloon! Upon
arrival at Southampton we landed in the middle of the town
carnival and I had to negotiate large crowds in my parlous state
before managing to get into the car and make for home.

Owing to the decks leaking badly, the KC was continually
filling with rainwater. We had no pump but I acquired a WW
II stirrup pump with which my wife and I (by this time the
work-parties had dwindled to two!) took stints at pumping the
ship out. A hose ran up through the accommodation and was
dangled over the side with the water draining away into the
river Medina. Having left Nora below, I went back on deck to
chip some rusty areas. Without realising it I had tripped over
the hose and it whipped back on to the deck and all the waste
water was spewing over our bags and lunch. When this was
discovered, divorce nearly resulted but I was forgiven as she
supports me still to this day."

Chris Phillips also recalls the ritual of launching a leaky
rowing boat in order to row out to the ship in mid river. All
equipment had to be carried in this manner and as no
lifejackets were ever available, the whole procedure was
extremely risky. On one occasion he and Peter Lamb lost track
of time and, having struggled ashore through the mud and
missed their bus, had to run along the riverside path in a vain
attempt to catch their ferry at East Cowes!

Despite the trials and tribulations of the attempted maintenance work, *Kingswear Castle's* engine was still in good order and during 1969 she made two brief forays into the Solent under her own steam. She ran trials off Cowes on 4-5th May and on 8th June crossed the Solent and steamed up the Beaulieu River to Buckler's Hard while being filmed for an episode of the BBC "Bird's Eye View" series. The poetic sound track was provided, most appropriately, by PSPS Patron John Betjeman. By an odd coincidence this was also the day that a CCA charter took *Ryde* to the Western Solent, so the two steamers came within sight of one another.

The 10th Anniversary year was marked by a number of PSPS events. There was a tea-party on board *Medway Queen* at which Eileen Pritchard – PSPS Member No 1. – was presented with a bouquet on behalf of the Central Committee and the Society flag flew proudly above *Kingswear* on her mooring in the river. On 1 June the Society chartered Campbell's motor ship *Westward Ho* for a day trip to Tenby but, probably because she was not a paddle steamer, the sailing was poorly supported by members and made a small loss. Far more successful was the charter of *Ryde* on 7th September from Portsmouth, Southsea and Ryde to Southampton . All 850 tickets were sold in advance and long queues of would-be passengers had to be left behind. National secretary Chris Philips, who was doing a two year management training programme with British rail, had been instrumental in setting up the charter and was able to use his contacts within BR's Signals & Telegraph Department to get a public address system set up on board for the day. This allowed passengers' attention to be drawn to the PSPS and CCA stalls on board and for Bert Moody to give a highly informative commentary. From the perspective of today's health & safety conscious world, it is hard to believe that, as late as 1969, the officers of a major Isle of Wight ferry had no regular means of communicating with their passengers in case of emergency!

The Society's flag flew from the foremast, passengers were welcome to visit the engine room and stoke hold and the day was declared an outstanding success, making a profit of £220 plus £92 from the PSPS stall. Sadly, the charter turned out to be *Ryde's* last ever cruise, for one week later, on 13th September, she made her last crossing between Ryde and Portsmouth and was laid up awaiting sale.

Buoyed up by the success of the *Ryde* charter Chris Philips persuaded the Central Committee that something should be attempted in Scotland and, because no PSPS branch then existed in Scotland, approached the Caledonian Steam Packet Company direct with a view to chartering *Maid of the Loch* in the summer of 1970. When this became known he received a very firmly-worded letter from Douglas McGowan pointing out that the *Maid* was not as highly regarded as *Waverley* and *Caledonia*, which were the really important Clyde steamers, and insisting that the society reconsidered its proposal. Chris replied that he was only too happy to think that a group of Scottish members might take on the organisation of a *Waverley* charter and after an exchange of correspondence travelled north to attend the inaugural meeting of the new Scottish Branch on 15th December, which is described in greater detail in Chapters 10 and 11.

The Scottish branch never got the chance to charter *Caledonia* as she was withdrawn after making a final sailing on the Gourock to Tarbert mail service on 8th October 1969. The year ended with the slightly brighter news that two Tyne paddle tugs had been saved from the breakers. *Reliant* had been purchased by the National Maritime Museum for display at Greenwich while the *Eppleton Hall* had been saved from the scrap yard by Scott Newhall on behalf of the San Francisco Maritime Museum. After a complete refit she departed from Dover on 27th September and by the end of the year had reached Georgetown, Guyana, via Lisbon, Madeira, Las Palmas and the Cape Verde Islands, en route for the Panama Canal and California. A truly inspirational end to the decade.

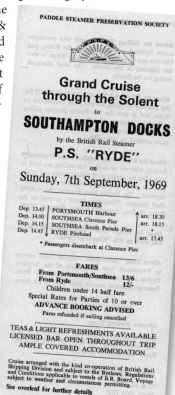

Sailing bill for the PSPS charter of Ryde *on 7th September 1969.*
PSPS Collection

Ryde *hurries away from Ryde pier, 7th August 1966.*

R Clammer

Lincoln Castle, *dressed overall, alongside the river quay at Goole during a charter sailing on 18th July 1976.*   Les Ring / PSPS Collection

CHAPTER FIVE

A CHANGE OF PACE – THE 1970S AND BEYOND

With contributions from Carol Clammer, Nigel Coombes, Jeremy Gold, Peter Lamb, Pat Murrell,
Chris Phillips, Helen Strachan and Terry Sylvester

THE dawning of the new decade heralded an important change in pace and emphasis for the society which was greater and more radical than anyone could have imagined at the time.

On the River Medina, despite the best efforts of the Operation Shipshape volunteers, *Kingswear Castle* continued to deteriorate. The Ridetts were focused on their marina development and seemed unwilling or unable to spend the necessary funds on *KC* whose decks were now leaking badly and required various urgent repairs. Then, in the spring of 1970 she was moved from her mid river mooring to a mud berth beside the riverside path where she quickly fell prey to vandalism. Her etched glass windows were smashed and your editor and his wife-to-be recall spending hours recovering broken shards and storing them for future reproduction. Meetings followed at which the Ridetts made proposals to

extend the charter party, to move her into the non-tidal yacht basin as soon as it was completed, or to buy the ship outright. However, no firm assurances could be obtained as to the date or scope of restoration work so, with great reluctance, the Central Committee agreed in July to terminate the charter and move the ship to the River Medway. The rest of her remarkable story is told in Chapters 7-10.

Whilst the newly-formed Scottish branch quickly arranged a stimulating programme of winter meetings and summer charters, which continue to this day, sadly, this was balanced by the near-demise of the Bristol Channel Branch. The loss of *Bristol Queen* and *Cardiff Queen* had seriously demoralised local members, many of whom were reluctant to sail on the replacement motor vessels and for whom *Kingswear Castle* was too small and too distant to be of much interest. Attendance at meetings dwindled and but for the sterling efforts of Pat

PSPS chartered Lincoln Castle *on a number of occasions during the 1970s. In this view she is seen approaching New Holland Pier on 22nd August 1976 to collect her passengers for an unusual cruise up the River Humber and into the River Trent.*   PSPS Collection

Waverley *arriving at Fleetwood on 8th May 1977, from a fully-booked afternoon cruise. Her earlier arrival from Liverpool had been delayed by lively sea conditions and she ran later and later as the day went on, but that did not dissuade huge crowds from gathering to watch the arrival and departure of the famous steamer on her first venture away from the Clyde.* Richard Clammer

Queen of the Broads, *a charming wooden steamship dating from 1889, was chartered by the London Branch for cruises on the Norfolk Broads from Great Yarmouth.* A.E. Bennett/R. Clammer Collection

On the bridge of Lincoln Castle *during the first PSPS charter sailing of the ship on 15th August 1971. L to R: Capt. 'Stan' Wright, Senior Deck Rating Ken Edwards, Senior Deck Rating Bill Garton, Mate George Richardson and Chris Phillips who was then the Society's National Secretary and had organised the cruise.*

Chris Phillips (IOW) Collection

Murrell who continued to organise fund- and morale-raising charters, the branch might have died completely. As it was it remained in semi-hibernation until 1980 when *Waverley's* appearance on the Bristol Channel led to a major revival.

Apart from *Waverley* and *Maid of the Loch* in Scotland, the three Humber ferries, *Wingfield Castle, Tattershall Castle* and *Lincoln Castle* were now the only operational paddle steamers left in Great Britain. Of distinctive design, they were coal fired and carried passengers and cars on a year-round service between New Holland and Hull and now began to attract the attention they deserved. The Central Committee decided that a charter should be attempted and Chris Phillips, who was then working for BR's Shipping Division at Newhaven, persuaded his General Manager's secretary to write to the Humber Ferry Manager on official paper to request his co-operation. Chris subsequently got his knuckles rapped for employing the secretary on PSPS business, but the charter was agreed for 15th August 1971! The trip attracted widespread interest and advanced tickets sold so fast that enquiries were made as to the availability of a second steamer to take the overflow. Unfortunately this proved impossible, so many would-be passengers were left behind when *Lincoln Castle* sailed with her full capacity of 500 on her cruise "towards Spurn Head". The cruise received a great deal of publicity from local newspapers, radio and TV stations and was judged an unqualified success.

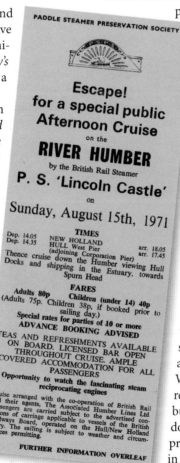

A sailing bill for the 1971 charter cruise. PSPS Collection

When work started on the long-awaited Humber Bridge, which was initially due for completion in 1976 (later delayed until 1981), it became obvious that the ageing ferries were now on borrowed time. *Tattershall Castle* was withdrawn in April 1972 and later sold to become first an art gallery and conference centre and later a pub on the Thames Embankment where, minus her paddle wheels, she remains to this day. Fears that BR might choose to close the route before the bridge was finished led to a vigorous local "Save our Ferry" campaign, while those concerned that at least one paddler should be preserved for posterity formed the Humber Paddle Steamer Group (HPSG), which immediately set about publicising the historical and amenity value of the steamers.

Campaigners' concerns proved well-founded when, in September 1973 *Wingfield Castle* was withdrawn and replaced by the diesel-electric paddle ferry *Farringford* which had been transferred from Lymington. The HPSG, led by the indomitable Esther and Barry Beadle of Hull, redoubled its efforts to persuade Humberside residents and Councils of the importance of retaining *Lincoln Castle* in the long term, issued newsletters, held fund-raising events and operated a series of popular charter cruises. There was a considerable overlap between HPSG and PSPS membership and the two groups worked harmoniously together until 1977 when the HPSG was wound up. Anxious that the good-will and contacts generated by this energetic group should not be lost, PSPS then encouraged the formation of a new group called the "Save P.S. Lincoln Castle Campaign" (SPSLCC). Although the two groups remained independent they were closely affiliated and shared a common policy towards the future of the ship.

PSPS chartered *Lincoln Castle* every year from 1971 to 1978, taking her downstream towards Spurn Head, up the River Trent, and up the Ouse to the port of Goole where she was sometimes able to land passengers for time ashore. With other groups such as the CCA, Wirral Railway Circle and HPSG also making regular bookings, the old ship was kept extremely busy between her ferry runs and this would doubtless have continued had not a major boiler problem been discovered during her annual refit in March 1978. She was withdrawn immediately.

The Humber paddlers were perhaps not the most obvious candidates for preservation, yet all three went on to enjoy long lives in static roles. *Tattershall Castle* has now been in London for over 23 years. *Wingfield Castle* led a nomadic life for several years as various plans for her use failed to materialise, but was eventually sold to Hartlepool Borough Council and moved back to her birthplace, restored and given a central place in the Town's Maritime Heritage Centre. After PSPS/SPSLCC efforts to persuade Humberside County Council or the National Railway Museum to preserve her had failed, *Lincoln Castle* was sold to Mr Francis Daly who berthed her on the foreshore at Hessle in the shadow of the new Humber Bridge where she enjoyed several successful years as a bar and restaurant before moving to Grimsby in 1987. Chapter 15 describes subsequent developments and, despite PSPS's best endeavours, the ultimate scrapping of the ship and her engines in 2010.

While these developments were taking place on the Humber, something even more momentous was brewing on the Clyde. In 1970 PSPS had formed a "Waverley Study Group" of six members, including Terry Sylvester, Douglas McGowan and Iain MacLeod, which spent a year looking into ways in which *Waverley* could best be operated and promoted as a major tourist attraction for the Clyde area. Following the receipt of the report by Caledonian MacBrayne's General Manager John Whittle in 1971 a series of meetings was held, some of the recommendations acted upon, and a warm relationship developed. How this resulted in *Waverley* being gifted to the Society in 1974 is now the stuff of PSPS legend and is described in greater depth in Chapter 10. One can only imagine the shock of the Central Committee at being confronted with such an unexpected offer and the soul-searching which went on before agreeing to accept it. What Douglas McGowan modestly fails to mention is that, in order for the transfer of the ship to the newly-created Waverley Steam Navigation Co. Ltd., he, Terry Sylvester and Peter Reid had to take a considerable personal risk by indemnifying the vendors against any financial loss suffered as a result of any breach of the agreement.

The gamble paid off and over the next 46 years, through triumphs and crises, *Waverley* gradually established herself as the national icon she is today. In May 1977 she ventured away from the Clyde for the first time in her life to run a series of trips from Liverpool, Fleetwood and Llandudno, and the following year ventured round Lands End for a month's cruising on the South coast, Thames and Medway. In 1979 she spent even longer down south and included a five day visit to the Bristol Channel, an event which resulted in the revitalisation of the local branch of the Society which held its first formal meeting under a new committee at Clevedon on the day of *Waverley's* first 1980 arrival. The economic effects of these trips away from Scotland was dramatic for in 1979 she carried 230,000 passengers, nearly double the 1975 figure. This pattern of spending the summer season on the Clyde and the spring and autumn away from home was varied and extended over the years to include Ireland, the Western Isles and the East coast, so in 1981 *Waverley* became the first coastal paddle steamer to circumnavigate Britain, offering trips from various ports as she went. Her annual wanderings are described in more depth in Chapter 13.

While this intensive use of the ship made economic sense and boosted both passenger numbers and public profile, it also highlighted the need for constant repair, refurbishment and improvement. Her boiler was re-tubed in 1976 and completely replaced in 1981, decks were re-laid, windows replaced, accommodation upgraded, safety equipment kept fully compliant, and more. All this, of course, along with *Kingswear Castle's* needs, meant that the requirement for PSPS to raise funds became more pressing than ever. There was no National Lottery in those days, so all income had to be generated by sheer hard work, and charter sailings provided a lucrative, if somewhat risky, way forward. Chris Philips continued to co-ordinate the charters through the Central Committee, but later in the 1970s, as *Waverley* ventured further afield, responsibility was passed to the Branches who rose to the challenge splendidly and have continued to do so ever since.

Over the years different branches have tended to favour particular patterns of charter. As will be seen in Chapter 11, the Scottish Branch has attracted large crowds by taking *Waverley* on unusual itineraries to and from seldom-visited piers in addition to co-operating with other shipping societies to charter smaller local passenger boats for Christmas and other members' cruises.

The London & Home Counties Branch began a pattern of annual charters almost as soon as Waverley began to visit London in the 1970s and has always focused on selling tickets to parties and individuals living in central London and to organisers of coach parties from further afield. In the early eighties Branch fundraising was focussed on raising money for the ongoing restoration of *Kingswear Castle*, which at the time had no earning capacity of her own, so it was always made clear that money raised from *Waverley* charters could be applied to *Kingswear Castle*. Subsequently publicity material for the sailings has always declared them to be in aid of funds to support both of the Society's steamers. In the circumstances it was also thought right that the charter fee paid to Waverley Excursions Ltd should be at a market rate, although PSPS was not required to lodge the deposit normally required of charterers, on the basis that the Society was unlikely to disappear. In practice the sailings were a good earner for the company, with assured operating revenue and, even in the leaner years, very high catering revenue. Earnings from the charters fluctuated over the years. The best result, a surplus of over £4,500, was achieved in 2008, although the following year, despite the "crunch", was nearly as good. There were also a few financial low-points, and it was soon learned that it was very difficult to substitute *Balmoral* for *Waverley* in that particular market. The ultimate disaster occurred prior to the 2005 sailing, when Tower Bridge malfunctioned and could not be lifted for the incoming *Waverley* to take up the sailing. Nor would the bascule locks go back in, leaving the bridge closed to road vehicles and south-east London traffic in gridlock. The sailing took place eventually, from Greenwich Pier, but smoothing ruffled feathers took the next two years!

Over the years the L&HC Branch has also operated a number of imaginative charters on smaller vessels. These have included

Having left Weymouth at 08.45 and Swanage at 10.40, P. & A. Campbell's Balmoral *has just arrived at Bournemouth Pier to collect a large queue of expectant passengers for her PSPS charter cruise to Yarmouth and round the Isle of Wight on 1st May 1971. The fare for the 12¾ day from Weymouth was £1.70 and the Bristol Channel Branch had laid on a connecting coach from Bristol at the inclusive cost of £2.20.* PSPS Collection

the sailings on the Rivers Stour and Orwell on board *Torbay Prince*, Norfolk Broads cruises from Great Yarmouth on board the wonderful old steamer *Queen of the Broads* and trips on Thames sailing barges.

On the Bristol Channel Campbell's motor ships *Westward Ho* and *Balmoral* were chartered on a number of occasions for some memorable long day trips. One in particular springs to mind: on 5th July 1970 the Branch chartered *Balmoral* from Bristol to Lundy Island, but at very short notice her departure point was moved to Avonmouth, as Brunel's famous *Great Britain* was scheduled to come up the Avon that morning on her triumphant return to Bristol from the Falkland Islands. All the *Balmoral's* passengers were treated to a privileged view of the historic scene as they were transported from Hotwells to Avonmouth on board a fleet of double-decker buses.

After 1979 when *Waverley* began her annual visits to the

Bristol Channel and from 1986 when *Balmoral* became established as the local ship, branch members put much effort into boosting income by organising or encouraging large group bookings in co-operation with Terry Sylvester and Sue Coops at WEL's Barry office.

On the South Coast the Wessex Branch ran a series of very interesting and largely successful charters. In 1970 and 1971 during her P&A Campbell days *Balmoral* ran two successful trips round the Isle of Wight from Weymouth, Bournemouth and Swanage. When she returned under the WSN flag the branch took her on a number of occasions including, on 22nd May 1993, the first steamer call at Totland Bay Pier since the paddle steamer *Embassy* had made her final sailing in September 1966, and a rare visit to the Wareham Channel in the upper reaches of Poole Harbour. The motor vessel *Bournemouth Queen* was also chartered in 1972 and 1974 for

The motor vessel at Bournemouth Queen *Poole Quay before her PSPS charter sailing in August 1974. Three years later, while sailing under the name* Queen of Scots, *she took over* Waverley's Clyde *timetable for six weeks after the paddler had grounded on the Gantocks.* R. Clammer

After her withdrawal from the ferry service Lincoln Castle *enjoyed several successful years as a pub and restaurant on the foreshore at Hessle, and was a regular venue for PSPS Northern Branch meetings. She is pictured on 18th April 1982.* R. Clammer

sailings from Poole and Bournemouth to the Isle of Wight.

The branch also specialised in the charter of smaller, local passenger vessels for unusual trips in the Solent area. These included the *Island Queen* and *Boscombe Queen* for trips to view the NATO fleet assembled for the 1977 Jubilee Fleet Review at Spithead, and the Blue Funnel vessels *Venus, Princessa* and *Solent Scene* for cruises to view the Cowes Week firework displays, and to visit the Beaulieu River and the River Medina. One of these, which took place on board *Venus* 22nd June 1974, somehow encapsulates the fun and occasional unpredictability of chartering in a slightly more informal era. The trip's organiser **Peter Lamb** takes up the story:

"On one of the many Blue Funnel charter cruises the chosen vessel was the *Venus* (always a favourite but, in my view, the least successful conversion) by then with diesel propulsion. The cruise, from Southampton, crossed the Solent and sailed along the river Medina allowing passengers the opportunity to enjoy viewing the *Medway Queen* in the mill-pond at Binfield. Alas, on a falling tide the *Venus* grounded. The skipper instructed

passengers to congregate on the bow deck in the hope of lifting the stern. After much mud churning, without success, the tactic was reversed all the passengers surged towards the stern of the craft. By this time quite an audience had gathered on the nearby bank to witness the theatrical performance and a private launch came alongside. After all efforts had failed, a lorry driver on the shore said if a line could be put ashore he would attach it to his back axle and try to pull the bow around with the engines going full astern and the helm over, it might shake the *Venus* from her embarrassing situation. The line was passed ashore and attached to the lorry. As the lorry took the strain it could not get sufficient traction and the 'lookers on' were asked to climb aboard as ballast to try and weigh the back down. Quite remarkably the tactic was successful and the *Venus* shook herself free. One of the passengers, Bert Moody, said he had never been on a ship requiring the services of a four wheeled tug before. Thankfully, a long wait for the tide to flood again was avoided!"

The static preservation of *Lincoln Castle* and the occasional appearances of *Waverley* on the East Coast, prompted the formation of a PSPS North of England Branch by Helen Strachan during 1981. At the inaugural meeting on board *Lincoln Castle*, a committee was elected consisting of Frank Gradwell (Chair), Helen Strachan (Secretary), Charles Taylor (Treasurer), Don Bays, George Coles and Iain Paxton. Although *Lincoln Castle* was always a favourite venue, both at Hessle and later at Grimsby, the large geographical area covered by the new branch meant meetings were also held in a wide variety of other locations. A decade or so along the way and with *Waverley* and *Balmoral* offering sailings on both the east and west coasts, new members from North Wales area had joined and it was decided to change the branch name to the North of England & North Wales Branch, after which winter meetings tended to alternate between York and Liverpool. Other branch activities have included a charter of the Humber Keel *Comrade*, nominated trips on *Waverley* and *Balmoral*, together with visits to museums, steam railways and other sites of interest.

When PSPS was founded in 1959 it was simply a society of like-minded people interested in a specific topic and, like many thousands of such societies, it established rules for its own organisation and governance. However, things began to change when the Society's activities graduated to the acquisition of ships. **Jeremy Gold**, PSPS Chairman from 1988-91, explains what followed:

"As an unincorporated association PSPS could not itself legally own ships. Therefore separate limited companies were set up. These were conventional companies limited by shares: Paddle Steam Navigation Limited (PSN) later renamed Paddle Steamer Kingswear Castle Trust Limited (PSKCT); and Waverley Steam Navigation Limited (WSN). A small number of shares in each were issued to leading Society members who were to become directors, and it was a stipulation that all directors had to be PSPS members. This requirement was the only direct link between the society and the companies.

Soon after the ships entered public service, separate operating companies were established in order to protect the assets against the possibility of the operations failing financially. These were Waverley Excursions Limited (WEL) and Kingswear Castle Excursions Limited (later Paddle Steamer Kingswear Castle Trust (Trading) Limited – now dissolved since KC's transfer to the Dart). Again, directors of these companies had to be PSPS members.

Waverley was the first of the ships to be restored to service, and from the start in 1975 – under the leadership of Terry Sylvester as chairman and commercial director – it was billed as a non-profit making organisation. There were three reasons for this: to emphasise to passengers and potential passengers that all monies they paid for and during a sailing would go into *Waverley's* continued operation and preservation and not into private dividends; to encourage the public and organisations to donate; and to encourage suppliers (and most particularly pier and port owners) to moderate or even waive their charges.

When *Kingswear Castle* entered full service in 1985 the same policy was adopted.

After some years it was realised that more could be achieved if PSPS and the two owning companies could be registered for charitable status. The leading advocates were Terry Sylvester – who saw that the non-profit point would be stronger if the organisation could be seen to have the official imprimatur of the Charity Commission – and PSPS national treasurer Martin Longhurst who saw the charity tax advantages of legacies as a means of encouraging bequests to the society. It would be essential for the three organisations to move together, as a charity PSPS could only give money to the two ships if they in turn were owned by charities.

The task of converting an unincorporated society and two companies into linked charities would not be easy, and if full legal fees had to be paid it would be very expensive. Fortunately, an enthusiastic supporter of the idea was Margaret Russell, a long-standing member of the society, whose interest had arisen because her late husband had been ship's cook on *Medway Queen* during the Dunkirk evacuation in 1940. When she joined PSPS Margaret had almost single-handedly rescued the London & Home Counties Branch by volunteering as secretary in 1976 at a time when its fortunes were at a low ebb. Now, having found a successor for that role, she volunteered to lead the work on charitable status. Margaret, although not herself a qualified lawyer, was a very experienced clerk in a London solicitors' office. She took on what turned out to be an immense task, working in her own time, and persuaded her solicitor principal to oversee her work without charge.

Complications arose because the normal organisational form for a charity was to set up as a company limited by guarantee (i.e. without shareholders). This was no problem for PSPS itself, but the two ship owning companies were already established as limited by shares and there were good reasons for keeping them this way. A further complication was that WSN was registered under the different legal regime applicable in Scotland and where charities were then registered by the Inland Revenue rather than the Charity Commission for England and Wales. Thus it was necessary to persuade the Charity Commission that PSN could become a charity in England whilst limited by shares, and likewise the Scottish Inland Revenue in respect of WSN, to embrace the different laws of the two countries and to satisfy both authorities about an effective linkage between PSPS and the ship companies. It was also necessary to satisfy all concerned that the separate trading companies could continue as before.

The upshot was that PSPS was converted from an unincorporated association into a charitable company limited by guarantee in 1987, but it took until 1988 for the work to be completed for PSN and WSN. The extra time was needed for the WSN aspects to be cleared by their Scottish lawyer, and to confirm that a requirement to allow PSPS to hold shares in the two companies would be acceptable.

The value of Margaret Russell's work became apparent when

PSPS members began to remember the society in their wills, and both ships were able to proclaim their official status as charities. Even better – and of course quite unforeseen when the decision to become charitable was taken – was the introduction of Gift Aid in 1990 giving tax benefits for donations by taxpayers and the founding of the National Lottery and Heritage Lottery Fund in 1994. Neither of these valuable sources of funds would have been available to PSPS and the ships without charitable status.

Compared with being an unincorporated association, charitable status imposes administrative burdens in meeting the requirements of the Charity Commission. However the funding available to PSPS as a charity has without doubt proved to be worth the extra work. Without it, to name just two major projects, it is difficult to believe that the Waverley rebuild between 2000 and 2003 could have gone ahead, and Kingswear Castle's new boiler in 2001 would at best have been delayed and at worst might have been unachievable."

To reflect these changes the PSPS Central Committee was renamed the Council of Management and its members became the Society's Charity Trustees and Company Directors, governed by charity and company law and Charity Commission guidance. Thus by the late 1980s the structure, aims and governance of the PSPS as a charitable organisation were firmly established and, along with its educational and archival activities, fundraising, volunteering and programme of winter meetings, charters, etc. continue to this day. The years since have, of course, been filled with numerous milestones, memorable moments and sometimes quirky occasions, only a tiny proportion of which it is possible to describe here.

In October 1980 the Society's 21st Birthday was celebrated at a splendid formal dinner at the Savoy Hotel in London. The guest speaker was Sir Patrick Baily, KBE, CB, DSC, Director and Chairman of the ships committee of The Maritime Trust. Douglas McGowan acted as Master of Ceremonies. Four years later the 25th Anniversary was marked by an equally enjoyable but slightly less formal meal held at St Katherine's Dock. In the same year the PSPS was represented at a very auspicious occasion, recalled by Nigel Coombes: "The highlight of my 8 years as PSPS Chairman was to represent the membership at

Menu card and order of proceedings for the Society's 21st Birthday dinner at the Savoy Hotel.

PSPS Collection

the Thanksgiving Service of our then Patron Sir John Betjeman in 1984 in Westminster Abbey. Prince Charles read a lesson and one of our current Patrons, Prunella Scales, recited one of Sir John's poems." There was extensive coverage in the Court and Social page of the *Daily Telegraph* of Saturday 30th June, and "Mr N. D. H. Q. Coombes, National Chairman Paddle Steamer Preservation Society "is listed amongst the hundreds of guests attending.

The church of St Helena, on Lundy, cannot compare with Westminster Abbey, but it has featured over the years as an iconic place for both *Waverley* and *Balmoral* passengers and especially PSPS members. For some it is the first sight of the imposing church building on the island top after a long day's sail, for others the rigour of the climb up the steep path, with periodic pauses to admire magnificent views, is rewarded by a delightfully peaceful retreat to rest in, probably followed by a quick pint at the pub before the descent! However, for many it is the memorable annual Evensong church services which stay in the memory. The cry of "first boat ashore for vicars, bell ringers, readers and choir only" has now, with the pier at Lundy, been replaced by a similar call for the first land-rover trip up the hill. The first such service was held on Sunday 17th June 1984 and have continued, "weather and circumstances permitting", ever since. **Nigel Coombes** vividly recalls:

"Our members were never short of exciting cruises. Either *Waverley* or *Balmoral*, weather permitting, would attend a church service at St Helena Lundy Island, often with a peal of bells provided with ringers from both sides of the channel. Terry Sylvester was the supreme organiser and always found a choir (including Prunella Scales), an organist (Jonathon Cohen or John Brown) and lesson readers (Timothy West or the ship's Chief Officer)." On 9th June, 1996 *Waverley* landed 322 passengers at Lundy Island for the annual evensong service at the church which was full for the 50th Anniversary of *Waverley*. In *Paddle Wheels* he described how "it is a privilege to worship in this wild and beautiful place and once again to hear how its peal of bells fills the air with its breezy harmony. The organ, as eccentric as ever, was finely controlled by John Brown... I read the first lesson and the second was read by Tom Clammer with impressive poise and sincerity... Whatever a person's view on life these strictly casual occasions served to underpin the verities of truth and beauty, in a spirit of friendship and enjoyment... that's what being a member of P.S.P.S means to me."

Dinners became established as a popular part of several Branches' winter programmes. The Bristol Channel Branch's events were, for many years, ably organised by the late Howard Jones, and guests were able to welcome a range of visiting speakers including captains of our steamers, local pilots and padres. A Christmas event, often including an excursion, talks and an optional overnight stay, has become an established feature of the Wessex Branch and equally lively events have taken part both in London and North of the Border. On 18th November 1994 at the Scottish Branch's Silver Anniversary Dinner at the Glasgow Art Club, Douglas McGowan presented John Whittle (former General Manager of Caledonian MacBrayne) with the framed pound note that he had donated to allow the Society to purchase *Waverley* on 8th August 1974.

1996 saw the 50th Anniversary year of the launch of *Waverley* and on the Bristol Channel both *Balmoral* and *Waverley* took significant roles in the formal opening of the Second Severn Crossing (now re-named The Prince of Wales Bridge) and also

An historic occasion. Waverley *and* Balmoral *at anchor together in Lundy Roads on 18th June 1986. The motor ship had returned to service under the WEL flag during April, the paddler had just arrived to open her Bristol Channel season and the Lundy supply ship* Oldenburg *was present as well. While some 700 passengers were enjoying time ashore, the crews of the three ships went visiting, and* Waverley *was awarded the trophy for the best turned-out ship.* Stuart Cameron

in the historic first Bristol Festival of the Sea. *Waverley* was moored in the city centre while *Balmoral* continued in service, bringing people to the Festival by sea. On Wednesday 26th June 1996, at the other end of the country, Auberon Waugh and the poetry judges for the *Mail on Sunday's* Grand Poetry Prize used *Kingswear Castle* as a base for the judging. **John Megoran** recalled in *Paddle Wheels* that " it was a perfect day in calm water, plenty of sun and a blue sky and they were all much taken by the delights of paddle steamer cruising. So much so, in fact, that Auberon declared in his column in the *Daily Telegraph* in the following week that sailing aboard *KC* was so pleasurable that it was 'mean' of him to let too many people in on the secret!" Other literary events followed in subsequent years.

The following year saw many celebrations. May 24th 1997 was the 44th birthday of *Maid of the Loch*. Over 2,000 people attended the celebrations and were greeted with the paddler dressed overall, the local Sea Cadets piping guests aboard and the *Maid's* very own lone piper playing on the bow. Star celebrities Prunella Scales and Timothy West as were aboard as well as Jimmie MacGregor.

This was followed by the Golden Jubilee of the first ever *Waverley* sailing on 16th June 1947, marked by the publication of the book *Waverley – the Golden Jubilee* compiled by Joe McKendrick and Leslie Brown. A public Jubilee sailing on 15th July 1997 was joined by 700 passengers and, on the following day, a birthday cake was cut on board by former bosun Roddy McIsaac during the "official" birthday cruise to Loch Goil with specially invited guests on board. This was not the last celebration. There was a very special call at Douglas Pier, part of HM Naval Base Clyde, on Wednesday 18th for the PSPS Scottish Branch's Midsummer's Eve Cruise. Guest of Honour for the evening was Commodore Eric Thompson from Faslane, who cut a cake and fulfilled a childhood ambition by standing on the bridge of a paddle steamer! *Kingswear Castle* was not left out – she had her own celebration too. It was 30 years since she was purchased and arrived on the Isle of Wight in August 1967.

On 27th September 1997 a framed picture of *Jeanie Deans* was presented by PSPS Society Chairman Nick James in the presence of Captains Peter Tamblin and John Megoran on board *Waverley*, to Mr P Abbot – PSPS member number

A few days later, on Sunday 22nd June, Waverley *was back at Lundy with 800 passengers, a good number of whom attended the annual church service at the Church of St. Helena. This group, pictured on the porch steps after Evensong incudes (l to r) John Haysom, Nigel Coombes, John Brown, Ann and Terry Sylvester (robed), organist Jonathan Cohen, and the Rector of Barry.* Nigel Coombes Collection

Bristol Channel champion raffle ticket seller Betty Saunders celebrating her 80th Birthday on board Waverley, *20th June 1999. Chief Steward Craig Peacock, Steward John Davis and Terry Sylvester are behind Betty who was joined by large numbers of friends and fellow members for the happy occasion.* R. Clammer

10,000. *Paddle Wheels* also noted that during the season's Solent cruises under the command of Captain Peter Tamblin, *Waverley* unusually flew the Guild of Master Mariners' flag at the bow, the pennant of the Weymouth Yacht Club above the bridge, and the blue ensign at the stern.

Princess Anne embarked on *MV Balmoral* in 2004 at Avonmouth for a special Missions to Seafarers Charter. **Nigel Coombes** recalls that "Commander Tom Foden, a constant help and advisor for Waverley Company, had co-ordinated the event and Cap. Kit Lee had presided on board. It was noted that

One of the Diamond Jubilee Cakes which was cut on board Waverley *during the 2007 season.* R. Clammer

A special logo adorns the cover of an invitation to attend a reception on one of the regional sailings to celebrate Waverley's *Diamond Jubilee. On this occasion, 31st May 2007, the ship took invited guests and members of the public on an afternoon cruise round the Holm Islands from Clevedon Pier.* R. Clammer Collection

the Princess shook hands and spoke to everyone on board, which caused immense pride among visitors, guests and Society members."

In October 2006 there had been a successful weekend of commemorative sailings to mark the 60th Anniversary of *Waverley's* launch followed, a year later during 2007, by special events in all sailing areas for the 60th Anniversary of *Waverley's* first sailing. Particularly memorable was the occasion during her Western Isles season, when over 100 passengers were landed and made their way to a special service at Iona Abbey. **Iain MacLeod** made mention in issue 189 of *Paddle Wheels* of the tremendous work put in to arranging the service by Society member Deryck Doherty, who also played the organ. Ian reflected that "it was right to have that special opportunity in Iona Abbey of thinking about the long line of enthusiasts and professionals who have between them brought *Waverley* to her Diamond Jubilee." The steamer flew a special Diamond Jubilee flag in each cruising area throughout the sailing season, which was then auctioned during the last trip to raise funds.

A special logo was designed to celebrate the 50th Anniversary of PSPS in 2009 in what may well go down as "the year of cakes!" The celebrations began in the spring with 60 guests at the Bristol Channel Branch Dinner on 25th April in Cardiff, attended by National Chairman, Myra Allan and our Founder Alan Robinson, whose speech was "one of encouragement and reflected that preservationists were focussed and rather obstinate – but in the nicest sort of way!" During the event the 60th 'birthday' of *Balmoral* was also celebrated.

The BBC's *Countryfile* programme makers were aboard *Kingswear Castle* later that spring on Tuesday 19th May to mark the 50 years and the programme went out in May of that year. Her own special Anniversary sailing was on 13thJune to Darnet Ness and up to New Hythe with a block booking by the Wessex Branch, organised by Peter Lamb. The Wessex Branch's own celebration was a special charter of *Waverley* from Poole.

On the Bristol Channel there was a special service on Lundy Island on 7th June, and *Balmoral's* 21st Anniversary with WSN was marked on September 10th by a cake cut by former Captain Ted Davies, watched by his son and fellow Captain, Luke. A cake of a different sort was cut on 19th June for Bristol Channel Branch stalwart and volunteer raffle ticket seller *par excellence*, Betty Saunders, who celebrated her 90th birthday aboard *Waverley*.

An official Diamond Jubilee sailing of *Waverley* was held on 4th October by the London & Home Counties Branch of PSPS, during which there was a small reception for invited guests, including the Southend Pier Management, when a cake was cut by Martin Longhurst, Society Treasurer and WEL Director, and shared with all the passengers.

The year culminated in two cakes being cut at the Society AGM on 7th November, both beautifully decorated; the first by Professor Alan Robinson to celebrate the Society's Diamond Jubilee and the second by Captain John Megoran to celebrate

Kingswear Castle's 25th year of operation on the River Medway.

More recently, following *Kingswear Castle's* return to the beautiful waters of the River Dart, yet more cakes have been cut! During 2014 she was awarded the Engineering Excellence Award by the Institution of Mechanical Engineers and so, on 20th May, Trustees, PSPS Members including Lawrie Beale, Chris Smith and Guy Hundy from the original volunteer restoration team, family and friends and representatives from PSPS and the Institution met for an award presentation, buffet and cruise. A year later, on 13th May 2015, the 30th Anniversary of *KC's* return to full passenger service on the

Medway was marked by another event which attracted considerable attention from the local press.

Never a society to miss a celebration opportunity, Timothy West and Prunella Scales were guests of honour at a Ruby Anniversary Luncheon in London in February 2016 to mark 40 years since *Waverley's* return to service under the WSN flag.

The remainder of this book describes a number of key aspects and events in the society's 60-year history in the words of the people most closely involved.

Among the many guest who met on board Kingswear Castle *for the Institution of Mechanical Engineers' Engineering Excellence Award on 20th May 2014 were four PSPS Chairmen. From left to right are: Jeremy Gold(1988-91), Douglas McGowan (1980-82 & 2012-13), Iain Dewar ((2013-17) and Nick James (1991-2004).* R. Clammer

To mark the 30th Anniversary of Kingswear Castle's *return to full passenger service on the Medway, a celebration event was held on board at Dartmouth on 13th May 2015. Here Carol Clammer, Phoebe Redfern, Tom Shell, KC's skipper Richie Swinglehurst and Trustees Richard Clammer and Roddy McKee gather to cut the cake which was subsequently distributed among the passengers*

Waverley's distinctive livery is reflected in the calm waters of the Solent as she steams away from Yarmouth pier on 19th September 2015. Roy Tait

Clad in waders, one of the Eltridge brothers gets his model of the Thames steamer Royal Sovereign underway at the Blackheath Rally on 5th September 1964.   PSPS Collection

CHAPTER SIX

PADDLERS ON PONDS
Roddy McKee

FROM its inception the London & Home Counties Branch membership embraced a significant number of modellers and others interested in ship models. It was therefore decided to form a PSPS Modelling Group, the inaugural meeting of which took place on 19th August 1961 after a visit to the Model Engineering Exhibition. Rules and aims were decided, future programmes discussed and H. Collard Stone was appointed Group Leader. Members' interests included small waterline models, larger working pond models, restoration of "rescued" display and shipyard models and, in a few cases, live steam propulsion. Although London-based the group was open to all members nationally and some travelled considerable distances to attend meetings and display their models.

Interest grew rapidly and, as the group began to receive more and more requests for information, plans and advice Patrick Taylor and Guy Hundy were appointed as Assistant Group Leaders to share the workload. Work also began on attempting to create a register of paddle steamer models in museums, company premises, piers, stations or private hands. Members were asked to locate and attempt to save any which were at risk of destruction, and a library of modelling literature was established.

In the summer of 1963 the London Branch and the Modelling Group arranged a highly-successful exhibition in Margate which featured H. Collard Stone's fleet of 20 waterline models, a fine pond model of the *Royal Eagle*, various items of steamer memorabilia and numerous photographs. The exhibition built valuable links between the PSPS and the management of General Steam Navigation and the New Medway companies, and brought the history of the Thames steamers to the attention of the public. An expanded version was mounted at Folkestone in the summer of 1964.

Early in 1964 the Modelling Group was incorporated into the London & Home Counties Branch and renamed the Models Group. The late Arthur Rickner was appointed Models Secretary within the Branch Committee, a post he was to occupy for the rest of the group's existence. Arthur would arrange an annual model ships rally at the Prince of Wales Pond at Blackheath in south-east London on a convenient Saturday afternoon, usually in early summer, with the participation of Society colleagues and members of other organisations, including the Society of Model Shipwrights and the Thames

Arthur Rickner, stalwart organiser of the Blackheath Model Rallies from 1964 until 1990, enjoying a day trip on board Medway Queen.
Tony Horne

Ship-lovers and Ship Models Society. The inaugural rally took place on 5th September 1964, attracted seven models and generated much interest.

The experiment was repeated on 29th May 1965 and was a huge success. No less than 18 superb models were on display during the morning while sailing demonstrations on the pond occupied the afternoon, despite the miniature high seas kicked up by an unseasonably biting easterly gale. Models included the Watkins' tug *Iona*, the pleasure steamers *Medway Queen, Bristol Queen, Royal Sovereign, Victoria, Bournemouth Queen, Westward Ho, Golden Eagle, Glen Gower* and *Royal Eagle*, plus various stern wheelers and a supporting cast of screw vessels.

The Blackheath Rally quickly established itself as a popular part of the annual PSPS calendar and the Modelling Section/London Branch repeatedly gave its support to other exhibitions and events at Greenwich, Ipswich, Norwich and elsewhere. The 1966 rally was themed "London welcomes *Queen of the South*," and was intended to generate as much

Tony Horne with his Bournemouth Queen *and Dave Abraham with* Cornish Queen, *built to his own design, at a Blackheath Rally.* Tony Horne

publicity as possible for the Coastal Steam Packet Company's exciting attempt to re-introduce paddle steamer trips on the Thames using the former Clyde favourite *Jeanie Deans*.

Arthur's 25th Blackheath Rally was on 17th June 1989 and to mark the 30th Anniversary of the PSPS the Branch decided to draw the event more into its wider publicity initiatives. A PSPS display and sales stand was pitched beside the pond; for the first time a commentary was provided for the information of interested spectators, and it was possible to arrange for a march-past by the Whitstable Sea Cadet Corps Band, familiar

to many for its enthusiastic musical welcomes for *Waverley's* visits to Whitstable. By fortunate co-incidence the Sea Cadets were visiting Greenwich that very day. Among the models on the water were Peter Stocker's *Royal Eagle* and David Abrahams' freelance *Cornish Queen*, both model paddle steamers that had been at the first rally back in 1964.

Sadly making the models rally more prominent did not assure its future. Blackheath, and the pond, had been in the care successively of the London County Council and the Greater London Council and those authorities had kept the

Four paddlers on Westcliffe boating pond for the opening event of the first Ramsgate Paddle Steamer Week on 20th September 1987. Peter Stocker's Royal Eagle *is closest to the camera, Jack May's* Waverley *and David Abraham's* Cornish Queen *are alongside, and Mr Wilkinson's tug* Chieftain *is about to berth.*   Roddy McKee

Ken Adams chatting to a customer at the PSPS stand at the Rushmoor Steam & Vintage Rally, Aldershot, in July 1987.   Roddy McKee

Magnificent examples of models made by current members: On the left is Chris Woods' Embassy *and on the right Tony Horne's* Ryde *and* Bournemouth Queen.

Chris Woods & Tony Horne

pond in good repair, dredged and weed-free. After abolition of the GLC in 1984 the heath came under the control of the local borough council and maintenance standards began to slip. A further rally was held in 1990, although by then there were some problems with weed, and the council wanted to charge for erecting a temporary enclosure to protect the models, which hitherto had been given free. The following year the council sought to formalise the process further by seeking insurance indemnities that the Society was unable to provide. Thus the rallies came to an end, ultimately a casualty of modern litigious culture.

Ship models featured in Society affairs in another way. September 1987 saw the first of a series of annual publicity drives under the banner of "Ramsgate Paddle Steamer Week", organised by the branch under the leadership of the late Ken Adams with support from Thanet District Council. They began the weekend before the start of *Waverley's* September visit although, as it happened and for reasons beyond everyone's control, the 1987 visitor proved to be *Balmoral*. Though styled as a Ramsgate happening, activities spread across Thanet as a whole, with exhibitions in the museums at both Ramsgate and Margate, and at Westgate a show of archival steamer films compiled by John Huntley. The opening event on the Sunday of each paddle steamer week was the Waverley Model Ships Rally at Westcliff Boating Pond in Ramsgate. Here most of the participants from the Blackheath rallies were augmented by display teams from two very accomplished model clubs. The Elmbridge Model Club from Esher in Surrey brought along a range of fine ship models and a number of novelty items to fascinate children of all ages, including a model Loch Ness monster and a severe hazard to model navigation in the shape of a self-propelled iceberg!

On 24th May 1964 a model of Watkins' famous paddle tug Anglia, *often refered to as 'Three Fingered Jack,' takes on an alarming list on Blackheath pond.* PSPS Collection

Fortunately the Westcliff pond was large because the Portsmouth Model Boat Display Team had some very large warship models and gave a show culminating in a re-enactment of the Battle of Jutland with real flashes and bangs.

A visitor to the 1990 Ramsgate models rally from his home in Leicester was PSPS veteran Basil Craggs. Basil's fine model of the steamer *Royal Eagle* had been on loan to Margate Museum for some years on static display, although it was a working model. As a surprise for Basil it was extracted from the museum, checked over by a local modeller and taken to the model ships rally to allow Basil to meet his model again and be handed a controller to drive it round the pond.

There was a fifth, and final, Paddle Steamer Week in 1991; the formula was not one that could be sustained indefinitely. As a promotion it had proved popular, but it did not succeed in boosting *Waverley's* and *Balmoral's* traffic from Ramsgate, which is largely why the Society had devised it. But the intention was that the models ship rally, now to be under the auspices of the Ramsgate Model Boat Club, would carry on.

The demise of the Models Group and the annual rallies did not, of course, mean an end to members' interest in model paddle steamers. Individuals continue to collect and restore vintage models while many others continue to share their technical skills and enthusiasm and produce some superb new models. Classics from the Blackheath days such as Tony Horne's *Bournemouth Queen* have now been joined by Tony's *Ryde*, Chris Woods' *Embassy*, Nick James' *Cardiff Queen* and *Waverley* and several others, while the PSPS Collection itself includes a fine range of display and pond models including *Glen Gower*, *Koningen Wilhelmina* and several live steam examples.

Kingswear Castle in her mud berth at Medway Bridge Marina, early 1974

PSPS Collection

CHAPTER SEVEN

THE RESTORATION OF KINGSWEAR CASTLE, 1973 – 1983
Guy Hundy

Setting the scene

As explained in the previous chapters, the early 1960s was a time when the society was trying hard to formulate its objectives. In 1960 there were about 100 members and around 300 by 1963. It was a time when the few remaining commercial operators were getting out of steam, or indeed getting out of the business altogether. What could PSPS do? The funds required to buy a ship, especially one in need of attention, were way beyond the means of such a small society, quite apart from what should be done with one and how. Only a small proportion of the membership had any nautical or commercial knowledge and experience.

However we were fortunate at that period to have Nick Knight as chairman. He understood what was happening and knew what could be possible. As discussed in Chapter 3, the first attempt at securing a paddler – the *Alumchine* – had failed due to lack of funds and support, but when the *Medway Queen* became available PSPS, with Nick's guidance, worked with other backers to establish the Medway Queen Trust and thus at least halt her journey to the breakers.

Another sorry story had unfolded with the attempt to operate *Queen of the South* on the London River. How many volunteers were going to turn up at 7.00 am or earlier to prepare the ship and know what needed to be done? Even for professional seamen training and experience are necessary but very little had been made available to the PSPS work parties. By contrast, I well remember the sound of activity coming from the paddle boxes of *Medway Queen* at Strood which started after "finished with engines". Her engineers knew what had to be checked to keep those old wheels secure next day.

So it must have been with mixed feelings that in 1966 Nick Knight went to inspect *Kingswear Castle* which was up for sale at Dartmouth. His report was favourable, and it was realised that this was just about the maximum size of vessel for PSPS, given its resources at that time. Nick ran pleas for money in

On the slipway at Medway Bridge Marina.   PSPS Collection

Paddle Wheels but was clear that the purchase could not go ahead unless the vessel could be chartered to another organisation with some ability to care for her. She was purchased for £600 loaned by the PSPS to a limited company set up by the Society when *Alumchine* was being considered. This company was called Paddle Steam Navigation Ltd, now re-named Paddle Steamer Kingswear Castle Trust Ltd. A charter agreement was duly drawn up with the Riddett Brothers, and the ship was towed to their marina on the Isle of Wight where *Medway Queen* was already securely housed.

PSPS members on the Isle of Wight gave all the support they could, but with the fortunes of the marina diminishing both *Medway Queen* and *KC* deteriorated and became vandalised. It was apparent that if we wished to maintain *KC* she would have to be somewhere secure and more accessible. Nick Knight had facilities at the Medway Bridge Marina just downstream from the present M2 and rail crossings near Rochester, and he was generous enough to offer his tidal slipway for *KC's* use. The tow from the Isle of Wight took place in June 1971 with *KC* arriving on the 18th. The cost just about exhausted PSPS funds.

The next year was spent trying to muster some maintenance resource. Nick made it clear that his own business needed his full-time attention and, if PSPS could not start work, they had better put *KC* up for sale. A ballot of members resulted in a majority for selling the ship and in December 1972 an extraordinary general meeting took place at which Nick presented slides showing the deterioration of the ship since leaving the Dart. At this last minute Lawrie Beal came forward to volunteer for the job of Project Leader, and this swung the meeting narrowly in favour of keeping *KC* and giving Lawrie the opportunity to see if he could make a go of it. On 27th January 1973 the first work party led by Lawrie Beal assembled at the ship to start work.

As with all such endeavours people and their abilities, determination and personalities are so important. This can be even more true for volunteer efforts than professional projects. Both Lawrie and Nick were professionals in their own nautical spheres. Lawrie, a member of the Institute of Marine Engineers, worked on ship propulsion design at Stone Manganese Marine in East London. Nick was primarily a business man, a former Merchant Navy Officer running a boat repair and restoration facility on the Medway. Lawrie had the personality that made everyone feel wanted and useful, would spend time demonstrating how to use tools, but somehow not always appreciating the big picture. Nick was much less approachable and whilst he was usually on site on Saturday mornings, volunteers tended to get it short and sharp if they ventured into his premises without good reason. His sense of humour is perhaps summed up by a remark made following the discovery of some severe wastage of hull plating "You know, Lawrie, that she'll never sail again" or words to that effect. Lawrie looked downhearted, missing the give-away twinkle in Nick's eye. Later the wastage was found to be localised by way of the bunkers.

Stopping the Rot

My first visit to *KC* took place shortly after working parties had started. Having moved to Kent to take up my first job after studying at Leeds and following events from afar, I thought I should go and at least see what *KC* was all about. My visits were somewhat infrequent, but nevertheless Lawrie soon wanted me to become one of the work leaders able to deputise in his absence. The rest is history. With a young family and increasing demands at work, my contribution was somewhat limited, but being local helped to keep me in touch. It must be remembered that communication was limited to mail or telephone; no mobile phones or electronic methods. Lawrie would call in the evening during the week and these were never short conversations. Back at the ship on Saturday or Sunday the Marina's payphone was our link with the outside world. The logbook at the ship became the key progress communication tool where attendees signed in and the work leader recorded progress of the various jobs. Fortunately, everyone appreciated the necessity of keeping a record.

Stopping the rot by painting the hull and preventing ingress of water from leaking decks was first priority. Sounds simple, but it was some time before any paint was applied. Preparation is the key to painting and to chip and scrape the hull exposed

Lawrie Beale scraping the deckhead in the forward saloon.
PSPS Collection

The delights of volunteering! Lawrie Beale working underneath the hull in muddy conditions.

June Bushell

to the weather, and sitting on a slipway that flooded twice a day, needed specialist equipment. Shot blasting was the method adopted, and funding for this was sought from PSPS. Clearing the slipway of mud and painting the treated areas was still down to volunteers. It was a case of achieving the best possible as paint application required lying down flat underneath the hull. Getting this completed dominated the first half of 1973.

It's not possible to start listing all the work that was undertaken in a write-up of this kind, but it should be remarked that in order to progress the project, volunteers found themselves working on all sorts of ancillary tasks. A notable example was moving *KC* from the slipway to a mud-berth and back as required. This required much preparation work and could only happen on a spring high tide. Other "ancillary" tasks were designing, making, and fixing timber blocks to the slipway to allow access underneath the hull, arranging gangways, power and water supplies to the ship, moving stores of tools and materials to gain access to steelwork. All this on a mud-berth with no alongside access!

By the end of 1973 it could be said that the rot was at least paused, but the ship started 1974 on a mud-berth, only accessible by duck boards over the mud or boat at high tide. Interior jobs and deck maintenance become priority. The first couple of months were spent on constructing a gangway from timbers supplied by Nick Knight, fixing water and power supply and generally trying to keep the decks watertight.

Rigging the access gangway from the landing stage to the ship, January 1974.

June Bushell

Working on the leaking decks during 1974. Liz Hundy is caulking a deck seam with caulking cotton, while Guy Hundy is wielding the ladle used for pouring hot tar into the seam. The volunteer with his back to the camera is thought to be Andrew Fox. PSPS Collection

Workers' break. Colin Harrison (in shorts), Ian Watson (in white overalls), Martin Oatway and another volunteer enjoy a well deserved rest. Margaret Scroggs

Getting to Grips

A hull has two sides, and now the condition of the plating on the inside needed examination and treating. The flooring had to be cleared and lifted to gain access. Both saloons were pretty much loaded with tools and stores, and a lot of time was spent moving stuff around. Leaking decks still ensured that bilges needed pumping and steelwork had to be dried out before any treatment could begin. Weather permitting, work on the decks continued. At about this time, attention also started to be given to the engine. Ian Watson, a retired steam engineer from Stevenage would pay a visit, sometimes spending several days at the ship, opening up machinery for examination and preparing it properly for layup.

Other long-distance attendees who generously came to spend a week occasionally during the summer of 1974 were Roy Barclay from Portishead who worked on the decks and Harry Brookbanks from Exmouth, who worked on cleaning up and painting inside.

By October, the workforce had dwindled and workdays were cut down to Saturdays only for the winter. Early in the third year (1975), Colin Harrison paid his first visit. He was rapidly drawn in and became one of the key personalities. He was first to admit not being an engineer or for that matter a paddle steamer 'nutter' but he welcomed the challenge, played a vital role in organising materials and tools, and got stuck in to any job that needed doing.

Working parties picked up again during the summer and 65 people braved the gangway to attend an open day in September.

Operations continued into the winter, but the logbooks tell a story of "holding on" and continuing the dreadful job of cleaning up the bilges in the cold and wet. Here are a couple of log book entries at the start of the fourth year, 1976:

31st January (one attendee)
Too cold to work
28th February (2 attendees)
Taken to Ship
2 – scrapers and handles,

A charming and rather eccentric postcard thought to have been painted and sent by June Bushell. It was addressed to 'Paddle Steamer Waverley, On the Clyde, Greenock? Glasgow?' Remarkably, the Post Office persisted and the card eventually reached the ship at Gourock Pier! Chris Phillips (IOW) Collection

Drilling the slipway for fixing keel block fasteners, May 1977. Lawrie Beale is on the right. Margaret Scroggs

Studding
1 - 3ft ⁵/₁₆ whit, 16" ⁷/₈" whit and 3ft ½" whit
1 – 12" steel rule,
1 – ½" BSF Die
1 – 1½" whit x 8" bolt
Scrap pieces of ¹/₈" and ¼" steel plate
4 – ³/₈" whit deck drawbolts (Job T3)
Job T3 Emergency Drawbolts – completed and hung on port bunker
Bilges – Plates removed for access to stokehold bilges. 2 – 3"water bailed out. Bilges cleaned as far as possible. Port bunker floor plates taken to aft saloon after removing loose scale.
Boiler – some scaling work underneath boiler

During the latter part of 1976 the slipway became vacant, and thoughts turned to getting *KC* out of the water again. The hull was now in need of another paint and, with much better access than on the mud-berth, replacement of some steelwork would also be possible. An additional benefit would be expectation of more visitors and volunteers. The efforts of some begging letters and other contacts were beginning to pay off with firms such as Wolf Electric Tools, BSS, ESAB, and local technical colleges offering various types of help. It was not always easy to explain that access was a 15ft gangway across the mud.

Could the ship be raised higher out of the water than last time? Welding repairs underneath the hull would not be possible otherwise. Close examination of tide levels determined the clearance that could be obtained if the ship was to be floated into position on a spring tide. Lawrie began to prepare drawings showing the arrangement of suitable wooden blocks that would be needed to provide support underneath each frame. Finding suitable material, getting each block cut to the right size, fixing two eyebolts to each, and final delivery to the Marina was a project in itself. Marking out and drilling the slipway to receive the fixings was done at suitable low tides. The next window of opportunity for floating the ship on to the new blocks was in May 1977 when the tide was predicted to reach a sufficiently high level.

All this together with the work on the ship was costing money, and there was none. PSPS mounted an appeal in "Paddle Wheels" which helped.

With *Waverley's* purchase in 1974 and her subsequent needs dominating PSPS resources, much discussion took place in work breaks at *KC*. Why, when more and more funds were going to *Waverley*, couldn't there be a little more for *KC*? It could help *KC* so much. The simple truth of the matter was that *Waverley* just had to be put into operation and earn money so PSPS had to prioritise. Yes, PSPS membership had increased rapidly, but most of the newcomers joined through *Waverley* and she was their prime interest.

Colin had a very simple approach. Okay, there's no money for materials, we cannot work on the ship, how can we earn some cash ourselves? Result: *KC* Jumble Sales in the local village hall, as much local press coverage as possible, begging letters to companies and local authorities.

Tudor Francis at work on the sponson. Note the stack of new sponson brackets supplied by Babcocks.   Margaret Scroggs

Marine Cadets load the refurbished paddle shaft/hub assembly onto their workboat for transfer to the ship, 20th October 1981.   Peter Tullett

Nick Knight received a cheque for £500 from the Mayor of Rochester-upon-Medway City Council, as a donation towards deck timber, 11th November 1982.   John Megoran

Over the Hump!

Prior to returning to the slip, attention was given to the boiler. All the fittings were removed and checked. A first steaming test was made in January 1977 and the boiler was given a final check over by the insurance inspector. Some thought this was a waste of time, but Lawrie argued that we needed to know if the boiler had to come out, and also it would raise morale.

Back on the slip in May 1977, volunteers got to work on painting the hull again. A bit easier this time, but still a tough and long job. It turned out to be a race to get the painting finished because the slipway was needed for another urgent job. There was just sufficient time to get it done and get the paddle shafts removed for refurbishment before KC was floated off the slipway once again on the spring tide in October 1977. And yes, you've guessed it – the gangway had to be reinstated, the slipway blocks carefully removed, numbered and stored for next use.

During 1977 worker strength started to grow again and in 1978 Chris Jones joined the engineering group and took a leading role in getting the boiler hydraulic and steam tests approved. Meanwhile Lawrie prepared engineering drawings of paddle wheel components, sponson brackets, and other items that needed to be renewed. The spokes and other paddle wheel components would be fabricated at Stone Manganese, whilst others such as brackets would be made by Babcock.

Having seen the role Babcock was playing in the recovery of the Mary Rose, the tea break talk turned to wondering whether Babcock could help KC. "Only one way to find out". Colin took the initiative and contacted Babcock's West Midlands HQ, gained an appointment and soon had Malcolm Cockell 'on board'. Following visits to the ship, both he and Richard Martin helped the project in many ways. Malcolm served a term as Trust Chairman, whilst Dick became a trustee – a position he still holds.

She'll sail again

When KC returned to the slip in January 1979 it was clear that all "out of the water" jobs had to be finished before leaving once more. Major repairs, such as new sponson brackets, and some new bottom plates were top priority, and the new wheels had to be postponed a bit, waiting for components. This was the period when folk started to realise that this ship really was heading towards an operational condition. Those who had been quietly thinking that this would never happen, began to change their minds.

There were changes, too in the nature of the volunteer 'team'. A core of regulars meeting most weekends were heading the project forward and the pace was such that Lawrie's capacity to manage the detail was overtaken by events. Recognising this, a planning group chaired by Nick Knight was formed to meet locally on a regular basis to plan the work, control the finances and form the link with PSPS. Later, this group would merge with the owning company board, to form what is now the Paddle Steamer Kingswear Castle Trust. Lawrie was requested to proceed with the component drawings and manufacture at Stone Manganese, whilst others took over the engineering and logistics at the ship. Lawrie, regrettably, stood down from the planning group, but continued his involvement with the components through to their delivery. Without these, the targets could not have been achieved.

A PSPS legacy gave the green light to engage a contractor for key welding jobs; bottom plating, sponson brackets, and repairs to frames inside the ship. It may have been prematurely done because it committed the spending of money that had yet to come from PSPS. It was a touchy topic. Subsequent events showed that it was one of the factors that enabled the timely MCA and insurance approvals. Waiting around for more years could have seen tighter regulatory requirements incur significant extra costs. Soon, Everards of Greenhithe's welders were turning up to weld in the bottom plates and volunteers were making preparations, fire-watching, and following up with a protective coat of paint. The volunteer strength was increased when a number of dockyard employees joined the team.

Babcock were also helping by sending welders, mainly from local power stations where they had contracts, to repair internal frames and bullheads. One of these, Tudor Francis, continued with us after his retirement from Babcock, and made a good job of replacing the sponson brackets provided by his former employer among many other tasks.

It was all starting to come together – use of slipway, blocks to raise the hull sufficiently to allow the welding and plating, modest funding, sponsors of components, and above all sufficient volunteers able and willing to turn up during the week if necessary. Administration, which included letters to sponsors, press links and arranging visits to the ship, was also a time-consuming task.

Final Push

Leaving the slip in March 1981 to move to a berth with much better access and a suitable power supply enabled the internal welding repairs to continue. So what needed to be done?

First and foremost, the new paddle wheels which were under construction at Stone Manganese under Lawrie's supervision. The job could not be hurried. Work could only proceed out of hours and when labour was not needed on the company's own contracts. The components, spokes, rims and paddle-float mountings were all made from scratch. The spokes required bends in two places and this was done in a specially made jig. The wheels were assembled on to the refurbished hubs, components marked up, disassembled and shipped to the Marina for re-assembly.

First to arrive were the hubs, refurbished and mounted on the shafts. How were they to be positioned from outside the ship with only mud to stand on? Answer: float them round at high tide with help from the Marine cadets; a process which generated some good press coverage too. The assembly of the

Kingswear Castle on steaming trials, November 1983.　　　　　　　　　　　　　　　　PSPS Collection

wheels had to be co-ordinated with the re-building of the paddle boxes where Brian Waters was working hard to get the detail right. Brian is an electrician but also an expert with wood. He went on to build two small paddlers, *Monarch* and *Bluebell*, an amazing achievement.

Inside the ship, the engineering team pressed along with the overhaul of the main engine and auxiliaries. Testing the safety valves meant bringing the boiler up to pressure and it had to be done several times. Finally, everything was in order and the insurance surveyor approval was given. The boiler received its certificate in April 1983. Ongoing were welding repairs to inside frames followed by painting with special bitumen, and fixing deck leaks. A KC worker explained to some visitors that we had "replaced all the leaks in the forward saloon with new ones and sent the old leaks to a museum"!

By 1983 things were moving fast. Five or six people turned up for work on the ship each day and at weekends there were usually ten to fifteen. Colin acted as chief steward providing frequent hot drinks and meals. There were so many loose ends to fix before trials could commence – steering gear, dinghy, decking, handrails, glass port light replacement, putting the wheelhouse back together – to name but a few. Another memorable worker comment was "The wheelhouse is only there to stop people nicking the wheel".

Coal was expensive and necessary. Our friends at the

Dockyard had located some suitable fuel stored in an offshore barge because it was slightly contaminated with diesel. Clearance was received in time to enable completion of some heavy work - bagging and offloading it, driving it round to the marina and carrying it to the bunkers.

Proving trials

Finally, the starting date for trials was fixed, David Neill and an engineer from *Waverley* agreed to take charge. The big day came on Friday November 4th 1983. *KC* steamed away from the mud berth, out into the Medway and after making several manoeuvres to the surveyor's satisfaction was granted insurance permission down as far as Gillingham. The team celebrated with a supper on board *Rochester Queen*. The following Saturday and Sunday was taken up with more steaming up and down as far as Gillingham with our own volunteers gradually taking over control and getting used to the handling of a paddle steamer. Finally it was after midnight on Sunday night when the tide became high enough to float the vessel gently back to the mud berth. Bringing *KC* to an operational and reasonably presentable condition was a major milestone, but much still had to be done before and during the early years of commercial operation, as will be described in the next chapter.

With her mast lowered to clear Rochester Bridge Kingswear Castle *heads upstream on 30th July 2011*   Richard De Jong

KINGSWEAR CASTLE – THE MEDWAY YEARS, 1984-2012
With a contribution from Roddy McKee

DURING the 1984 season *Kingswear Castle* was limited to carrying 12 passengers, but was to be seen on one or two days each week operating charters and public cruises up and down the Medway. A number of local pilots together with John Megoran – a long-standing PSPS member and qualified Boat Master - skippered her on a rota basis, Chris Jones manned the engine room, while PSPS volunteers provided the deck and catering crew. During June the ship made the first of many voyages round to the Thames and in September rendezvoused with the *Waverley*. The ship proved mechanically reliable and it was decided that the only way to ensure a financially viable future was to seek a full passenger certificate in order to carry paying loads of passengers.

Consideration was given to taking *Kingswear Castle* back to the River Dart, but in the end it was decided to retain her on the Medway and operate from Thunderbolt Pier within the Chatham Historic Dockyard. John Megoran was appointed master and manager - a post he was to fill for the next 28 years – and after undergoing more intensive work during the winter, the ship was issued with Class 5 and 6 Certificates and made her first full-scale public sailing on 19th May 1985.

One largely forgotten aspect of the ship's time on the Medway was the existence of a Kingswear Castle Supporters' Group (KCS) which was set up in 1984 with the aim of making a substantial financial contribution to the ship's costs. Members agreed to make minimum regular payments (initially set at £156 p.a.) into the fund which gradually accumulated a useful amount of capital which was then disbursed to Paddle Steam Navigation Ltd (PSN) to undertake specific projects. When PSN became a charity in 1989 it was felt more appropriate for members to contribute directly, so the Supporters' Group was wound up and its funds paid over. Although its membership was always limited, the group raised a very useful amount of money at a critical time in the ship's history and deserves to be remembered with gratitude.

The story of *Kingswear Castle's* subsequent life on the Medway has been fully chronicled elsewhere – including John Megoran's *P.S. Kingswear Castle, A personal Tribute* and Clammer &

Kingswear Castle *raising steam alongside J P Knight's tug pontoon on the morning of 21st April 1984 in preparation for her very first 12-passenger Medway sailing, from Strood Pier, later that morning. The pontoon was detached from the shore, so the ship's boat was used to ferry crew out to the ship and has yet to be hoisted into its davits.*
Roddy McKee

Kingswear Castle *normally used a slipway for her annual winter refit or for major work to her hull or sponsons but on this occasion, in April 1991, is seen in No.3 Dry Dock at Chatham Historic Dockyard.* PSPS Collection

Kingswear Castle *embarking passengers at her home berth alongside Thunderbolt Pier, Chatham, on 2nd July 2011. At the foot of the gangway, with his back to the camera, John Megoran is in conversation with Jeremy Gold, then Chairman of the ship's owning charity. Facing the camera, volunteer Roddy McKee counts passengers on board. On deck, with his back to the camera and wearing a dark blue hat and shirt, is another volunteer crew member, Gerry Abrahams, chatting to PSPS Treasurer Martin Longhurst.* Richard De Jong

Kittridge's *Paddle Steamer Kingswear Castle & The Steamers of the River Dart* – so does not need to be repeated in detail here. Suffice it to say that over the years the ship developed a successful programme of short cruises and charters on the Medway interspersed with visits to the Thames and a fascinating and imaginative selection of full day "enthusiast" cruises. She also appeared in a number of films and television programmes and played host to assorted personalities, politicians and even members of the Royal Family.

During her time on the Medway the ship was also continuously refitted and improved. Chris Smith, who had been one of the original restoration volunteers, served as Chief Engineer from 1985-2006 and brought his considerable skills to bear on the varied work required. Landing platforms were reinstated, shelters constructed aft of each paddle box, re-decking took place and in 1994 a major fund-raising drive paid for improved safety equipment required to meet new, tighter regulations regarding survivability. In the winter of 1993-94 the ship's bottom was completely re-plated, during the following year her funnel was fitted with a hinging mechanism to allow her to pass under Rochester Bridge at all states of the tide, in 2001 she received a brand new boiler and in 2005 the access to the forward saloon was modified to improve comfort in choppy water. These were some of the highlights of a carefully planned and meticulous programme of maintenance and repair.

Kingswear Castle's success on the Medway was due to two chief factors. Firstly and crucially there was the skill and dedication of John Megoran who, as well as taking the ship to sea each day of the season, took on the year-round role of, timetabling, marketing, banking, purchasing, overseeing refits and ensuring compliance with increasingly complex maritime legislation. The second was the fact that the existence of a dedicated team of PSPS volunteers and trustees meant that the ship could operate with a very small paid crew, wage bills could be kept to an absolute minimum and John Megoran could benefit from some very useful unpaid support. One of the longest-serving of those PSPS volunteers was **Roddy McKee** who takes up the story:

Kingswear Castle Volunteers

"*Waverley*, as a sea-going vessel must comply with national and international standards of crewing. The formal qualifications needed by officers and ratings are in modern parlance generally known as STCW certificates, after the international convention on Standards of Training, Certification and Watchkeeping. Certificates of competency or proficiency have become essentials for everyone with watchkeeping or safety responsibilities or both, and certificates of medical fitness and proof of training in personal safety are now needed by all who work aboard. It is therefore difficult to contemplate *Waverley* being run other than on a full-time professional basis.

Kingswear Castle operates in a different regime. She does not go to sea, but rather plies what, in the current terminology, are known as categorised waters, those that passenger certificates once referred to as smooth, or partially smooth, waters. The River Dart is defined as Category C water, as are the tidal Medway and the Swale: "tidal rivers and estuaries and large, deep lakes and lochs where the significant wave height could not be expected to exceed 1.2 metres at any time". *Kingswear Castle's* Class V passenger certificate requires only the master of the vessel to have a national qualification, and her propulsive power is insufficient to oblige her to carry a certificated engineer. All other crew members must receive training in the operation of the steamer, including mooring and unmooring the vessel, launching life-rafts and recovery equipment, donning of lifejackets and evacuation, use of fire-fighting and bilge-pumping equipment and the control of passengers in an emergency. That however is done in-house as part of the safety management system agreed with the Maritime and Coastguard Agency. Training and drills need to be logged and the records retained.

The pattern of operation during the Medway years matched the training requirement very well. Apart from all-day special sailings, most operating days did not involve passenger sailings before noon, but the preparation time essential for a historic craft, with steam to be raised and brass to polish, meant that the crew were on hand much earlier. Frequent drills and refresher training, plus induction for new people, could readily be slotted in the period before the day's passengers began to turn up.

On the Medway *Kingswear Castle* was crewed by a combination of a tiny number of full-time staff, a handful of seasonal staff supplemented in the peak-season by offering vacation jobs to a couple of undergraduates, all topped up with a sprinkling of unpaid volunteers. Not all those categories were mutually exclusive because there were instances of volunteers becoming staff, and staff becoming volunteers. Initially the volunteer element came largely from those who had worked on the steamer's restoration, and indeed some stayed. One in particular, Chris Smith, became a key member of the permanent staff for many years. However as time went on there were some changes. When I first considered volunteering I was a bit backward in coming forward. I was all too well aware that I was not one of the people who had spent years on my back in the mud under the steamer, and did not want to get in the way of those who had, and who at last had a live steamer to run. Gradually it dawned on me, however, that some of them had no great desire to be operators, and a few would be happier restoring something else. If I wanted to help run her, I could feel free.

Some volunteers made their main contribution on shore. Patricia Bushell, now sadly no longer with us, acted as John Megoran's secretary for many years. Stafford Ellerman was responsible for the Trust's accounts, initially on secondment from NatWest, but as a volunteer after he retired from the bank. Others busied themselves mainly afloat, although not usually formally as crew members. Jean Spells organised the production and sale of KC branded clothing while Richard Turner produced videos and DVDs. Both of them, together with Richard's brother Charlie, Heather Rooke and others were also heavily involved in on-board raffles and sales of draw tickets. Alan Peake established a reputation as the on-deck bacon-roll chef on full-day special trips and Pam Thomas was known as a formidable lady stoker when relieving husband Nigel on the shovel.

As the 21st century got into its stride, a change in the law brought new complications for steamer operation. Although the rules have always been slightly different among the four constituent countries of the UK, traditionally all had exempted from licensing sales of alcohol aboard things that moved, trains and boats and planes. The same was true of the Republic of Ireland. Alone in the British Isles the Isle of Man required ships to be licensed; if *Waverley* or *Balmoral* were sailing in Manx waters a licence had to be taken out. That was about to change, firstly in England and Wales, when the provisions of the Licensing Act 2003 came into force. Trains and planes remained exempt, but domestic passenger vessels became subject to the same rules as pubs. The legislation required the premises, in this case the steamer, to be licensed and introduced the concept of personal licences for relevant people. That meant attending a course and sitting a test together with a criminal record check and police enquiries. *Kingswear Castle* duly acquired her licence, and John Megoran a personal licence and yet another title of Designated Premises Supervisor. Clearly some back-up was needed, as personal licences cannot be had instantly. Thus volunteers Gerry Abrahams, Roddy McKee and Alan Peake went off to college to obtain them.

In her last few years on the Medway the voluntary proportion of *Kingswear Castle's* crew increased and, outside the peak summer season, it was quite common to sail with master and engineer and otherwise an all-volunteer crew. In part that was because many long-standing volunteers had matured and retired from full-time work, and were thus more available. That was a state of affairs which saved on operating expenses, but might not have been self-sustaining in the longer term. However it lasted as long as needed and five of the seven crew on the occasion of the final Medway sailing were volunteers: Gerry Abrahams, Tim Corthorn, Jill Harvey, David Lawrence and Roddy McKee."

Return to the Dart

Despite the success of this operating model everyone concerned was aware that the status quo could not last forever, and the Trust's mind turned to ensuring a long-term and sustainable future for the ship. Fortuitously, down in Devon the managers of the Dartmouth Steam Railway & Riverboat Company had convinced themselves that an original, coal-fired Dart paddler would fit ideally into their programme of steam train and boat excursions, and made approaches to the Trust. Although initial proposals proved impractical, discussions continued and at the end of the 2012 season it was announced that *Kingswear Castle* would be returning to the Dart on a 15 year charter.

The crew of Kingswear Castle *after her final Medway cruise on 28th October 2012. Left to Right: Chief Engineer Nigel Thomas, David Lawrence, Jill Harvey, Roddy McKee, Gerry Abrahams, Tim Corthorn and Capt. John Megoran. All but the engineer and Captain were volunteers.*
John Megoran

Needless to say, her departure from the Medway caused great heartache for the loyal band of volunteers who had supported her so well over 29 seasons in operation, but it is a testament to them, her skipper and Trustees that they were willing to accept the loss of their much-loved ship in order to ensure her long-term future.

After a long coastal tow and a stop at Portland to shelter from bad weather, *Kingswear Castle* arrived back on the Dart amid great celebrations on 18th December 2012. John Megoran and Chief Engineer Nigel Thomas spent several months training her new crew to handle a paddle steamer and on 7th February 2013 the ship made a trial trip upstream to visit Totnes for the first time since 1965. After a thorough refit on the Dart Company's slipway, the ship entered public service on Good Friday 29th March 2013.

Since then an immaculate *Kingswear Castle* has operated regular cruises on the very routes for which she was built back in 1924 and has established herself as a much-loved and almost iconic part of the local scene. Her new operators have the workshop facilities, under-cover slipway and steam engineering skills to maintain her to an extremely high standard and her new crew take an enormous pride in her. She is still owned by the Paddle Steamer Kingswear Castle Trust on behalf of the PSPS and it is to be hoped that the harmonious relationship between them and the Dart Company will continue indefinitely. Although volunteer crew members are no longer required, several Trustees and members of the PSPS Wessex and Dart Branch now keep themselves extremely busy arranging special sailings, producing books, articles and DVDs and giving talks all over the South West of England to promote the ship, her operators and the PSPS. Volunteering is alive and well!

After the long tow from the Medway by the tug Christine, Kingswear Castle *arrives at Dartmouth on 18th December 2012, after an absence of 45 years.*
Sandi Armstrong

Back on the river of her birth, Kingswear Castle *is pictured steaming downstream near Fleet Mill amid the stunning scenery of River Dart on 19th June 2013.*
R. Clammer

Waverley on one of her regular cruises into the River Medway during her annual Thames season, viewed from Kingswear Castle's wheelhouse. It became a tradition for the two ships to meet somewhere in the river and then steam together, slowing and overtaking each other, sounding their whistles and providing a visual treat for photographers. On at least one occasion arrangements were made for Kingswear Castle to come alongside the larger paddler and exchange a number of lucky passengers who were able to enjoy the experience of sailing on board both ships in a single day.
John Megoran

CHAPTER NINE

59 YEARS OF THE PSPS: A Paddle Steamer Manager and Captain's View
John Megoran

PADDLE steamers have rather dominated my life. My first recollection is of being aboard Cosens's *Consul* in the summer of 1956 when I was five backing out from the Pleasure Pier at Weymouth. From then on, I was hooked, pestering my parents to take me for trips often. As the years rolled by, I hardly missed a day gawping at them laid up in the Weymouth Backwater on my way to and from school in winter or seeing them getting ready for their daily trips in summer. I wrote to operators around the country asking them to send me their steamer notices. I built a mock-up paddle steamer in our back garden complete with engine room telegraph, charts and an almanac from which I taught myself the rudiments of coastal navigation. I was sort of obsessed by them.

In 1960, aged nine, I encouraged my father to take me on the last trip of the season of *Monarch* from Bournemouth to Poole and it was then that Dad and I first became aware of the PSPS. *Monarch's* master Capt Harry Defrates, who was a friend of the family, introduced us to PSPS Secretary Mrs Eileen Pritchard who informed us that *Consul* had been chartered by the Society the following Saturday to raise funds and that we must buy tickets. You didn't argue with the formidable Mrs Pritchard, so we bought tickets although we didn't need much persuading. Mrs P is one of my great paddle steamer heroes from the 1960s. She was tireless in promoting the cause of paddle steamers, encouraging people to do things for them and was in the forefront of all the 1960s attempts at Paddle Steamer Preservation. Later, as a Director of Paddle Steam Navigation Ltd she was vociferous and steadfast in her support for *Kingswear Castle* even in the teeth of sometimes strong opposition.

I insisted that Dad join the PSPS that night aboard *Consul* so he became member number 62. Two years later I became a member in my own right, not a junior member I should add, as such a category did not then exist, but as a full member.

Eileen Pritchard on board Princess Elizabeth *with Iris, her friend and hairdressing apprentice. Mrs Pritchard was a major figure in the early days of the Society, both at national and Branch level who encouraged younger members to become actively involved and helped to finance the attempts to preserve* Consul.   Peter Lamb

During the 1960s I attended Wessex Branch meetings, occasionally contributed items for Paddle Wheels, bought all the books on paddle steamers I could find and so my obsession developed, fired on by the then ever-constant presence of paddle steamers in Weymouth Harbour.

Looking back, I was so lucky to grow up in Weymouth in the 1960s when the harbour was such a centre of paddle steamer activity with, at one time or another in my youth, *Monarch, Embassy, Consul, Princess Elizabeth, Sandown* and *Bristol Queen* all either being laid up there or visiting for refits by Cosens. As a result, I got to know the steamers intimately as well as some of the crew and those behind them. My grandmother introduced me to Don Brookes, Cosens's General Manager. Capt Defrates was ever kind inviting me up onto the bridge and writing me little notes to update me on developments. Through him I got to know Cdr. Edmund Rhodes who bought the *Princess Elizabeth* in 1960 and Tony McGinnity who with others bought *Consul* in 1962.

Tony is one of my tip-top heroes of paddle steamer preservation. Indeed if you tot up his total involvement with PSPS, trying to buy *Alumchine*, being at the centre of the purchase of *Kingswear Castle*, his work as an agent trying to find work for paddle steamers when withdrawn and his decade as a director of Bristol Channel operator P & A Campbell, then nobody else comes close to his achievements in that arena and in that era.

It was also through Capt Defrates that I was introduced to Capt. Stanley Woods, a close friend of Mrs Pritchard, who was master of *Princess Elizabeth* in 1965. He got me steering, loaned me almanacs and other text books about seamanship and navigation and egged me on in my ambition to go to sea. When Don Rose asked him to bring the *Jeanie Deans* round from the Clyde to the Thames in early November 1965 Capt. Woods invited me along for the ride as his private helmsman although in the end I only got as far as Stranraer where I had to leave the ship to return to school. The following Whitsun holiday I was back aboard and on the wheel for the first three days of sailings on the Thames as *Queen of the South* which did not go well with the ship running ever late and, on the Whit Monday, suffering a serious issue with the port paddle wheel necessitating a tow down to Gravesend. I still recall with some embarrassment my fourteen year-old self tucking into a plate of smoked salmon sandwiches which I thought were for everyone but which Don had brought aboard *Jeanie Deans* for his fellow directors on the trials on the Clyde and receiving a mild but nonetheless benign rebuke from Don for my unwitting error.

None of these 1960s' attempts to run paddle steamers lasted beyond two years except for *Princess Elizabeth* which managed five. The zeitgeist was against them and the ships themselves were elderly and in need of significant investment for structural and other maintenance work. For example, I recall part of *Princess Elizabeth's* deck over the boiler room being taken up for survey in 1967 and exposing heavily corroded steel plating underneath with holes where the steel had just rusted away.

By the mid-1960s I was beginning to form the opinion that paddle steamers were on the way out and that my dream of

John Megoran, aged 14, on the bridge of Princess Elizabeth *at Weymouth.*   John Megoran

becoming a paddle steamer captain was just not going to happen so I count myself as hugely fortunate in that I did become a paddle steamer captain in the end and spent nearly thirty years running *Kingswear Castle* on the Rivers Medway and Thames and this despite not going to sea as planned in 1969 but taking a degree in chemistry instead.

In those days you couldn't be a navigating officer deep sea if you wore glasses and by 1969 I was starting to need them for long distance. I could see OK without them but not with pin-point accuracy in the far distance. I took the eyesight lantern test at the old Board of Trade office in Southampton. I struggled to make out the tiny coloured dots reflected from an oil lamp onto a mirror without my glasses. The examiner said that I was border-line so he didn't recommend a sea career. That was not a good day for me. Not a good day at all.

However, I spent my subsequent summer holidays from university working on the 150 passenger *Weymouth Belle* which had taken over the paddle steamer sailings from Weymouth around Portland Harbour, to Lulworth Cove and

Jeanie Deans *moored to buoys off the Gun Wharf at Chatham on the River Medway, immediately after her arrival from the Clyde.* John Richardson

Princess Elizabeth *in Weymouth Bay, August 1965.*   A.E. Bennett/R. Clammer collection

to Portland Bill. Those were lovely summers for me operating on the old routes of the *Consul* and *Princess Elizabeth* and this gave me enough time to start to get qualifications to sail as master of domestic passenger vessels for which glasses were permitted. So, it was in 1972 that I gained my first command sailing as relief captain of the *Weymouth Belle*. As the years rolled on the eyesight restriction was removed enabling

This photograph, taken on board Kingswear Castle *at the start of the 1985 season – her first with a full passenger certificate – depicts a number of key players in the ship's restoration and subsequent commercial operation on the Medway. From left to right these include Jeremy Gold, Alan Peake, engineer Simon Cheeseman, Guy Hundy, Nigel Coombes, Colin Wright, Chris Jones, Roger Toft, Joe Abrahams, Pat Bushell, Chris Smith, Mike Rogers, Brian Waters with his accordion, John Megoran, Lawrie Beal and Malcolm Cockell. John had recently been appointed permanent master and general manager. He made a great success of the business and remained with the ship throughout her Medway years. With the move to Dartmouth he has continued to sail as occasional relief captain and to provide background advice and support for her new operation in her old home waters.*

John Megoran

candidates to go to sea with glasses so by 1997 I had upgraded my certificates to enable me to sail as master of *Waverley* and *Balmoral* both of which were added to my Thames, Medway and Portsmouth Pilotage Certificates.

Handling *Waverley* was interesting and different from *KC*. For a start the captain is in a different position on the ship. *Waverley's* bridge is near the bow. On *KC* the captain is abaft the paddles. *KC* steers well astern up to about force six when she seeks the wind. *Waverley* is a bit hit and miss when travelling astern even in more modest winds and so on. Nonetheless it was fun turning *Waverley* in Portsmouth Harbour (in those days without a tug) and turning her in the Pool of London (with a tug) but most of all it was a pleasure taking her in and out of Bournemouth Pier just like I had seen Capt Iliffe do it on the *Embassy*.

It was to *Kingswear Castle* that I came in 1984 through my final paddle steamer giant, Nick Knight. Although he was PSPS chairman from 1963 to 1967, he was not really a committee man, telling me in later years that in his view the ideal committee consisted of just three with one laid up in hospital and the second out on safari in the Gobi Desert. He had a fiery determination to bend others to his will. He was instrumental in finding a new career for *Medway Queen* on the Isle of Wight and it was Nick who forced through the purchase of *Kingswear Castle* by Paddle Steam Navigation Ltd with a loan of £600 from the PSPS in the teeth of considerable opposition from others who saw her as a liability rather than as an asset.

On board Cosens' Monarch *en route from Swanage to Bournemouth c. 1960. It was on board this steamer that John Megoran first became aware of the PSPS.*   Pat Murrell

Cosens' Monarch *moored at Trinity Quay in Weymouth Harbour probably in the spring of 1960. The ship has returned from dry dock and has been repainted for the season ahead, but has not yet had the canvas fitted to her bridge wings and promenade deck rails.*

R. Clammer Collection.

It was also Nick who persuaded me to throw my lot in with *Kingswear Castle* and take on running the business on the Medway as well as sailing as the steamer's principal captain. I liked Nick a lot. We were kindred spirits. The two of us just clicked.

After sailing as one of the volunteer captains in 1984 I took up my post running the business that autumn to lead the process of returning *Kingswear Castle* to service with full Passenger Certificates in time for the 1985 season. It soon became clear that whilst a lot of good and hard work had gone into the ship in the previous decade it had all been done without the benefit of any major funding and therefore there had been a lot of make do and mend. Indeed. I think that it would be more accurate to say that *Kingswear Castle* was "got into a sufficient state" to return to service rather than "was

restored" because that is just how it was. For example, wood for the new decks was of poor quality, full of knots and shakes and quick to rot. There was insufficient money for proper marine glue for the deck caulking so road tar was used as a cheaper alternative which stuck to passengers' feet and so on.

At the first hull survey the surveyor, Mr Ahmed called me over and said "John, some of these rivets haven't got any heads on them" and he was right. They hadn't. Gulp. Having started his career as a boy on steamers in Bangladesh, Mr Ahmed was a goldmine of useful information and helped me hugely in those early years. I learned a vast amount from him for which I am ever grateful. He was pragmatic and for solving the rivet problem suggested that the shipyard run a circle of weld around each of the affected heads. It was a nice gesture and helped to get *Kingswear Castle* going. If he had taken a different view,

Kingswear Castle *in the Thames Estuary*   PSPS Collection

Kingswear Castle in the Thames Estuary on one of her longer day trips, photographed from Balmoral which was en route from Rye to the Pool of London on 11th July 2007. John Hendy

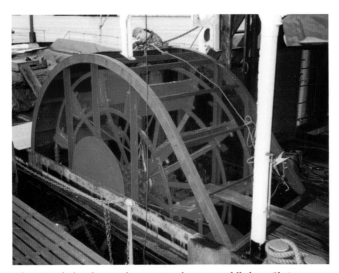

Chris Smith, hard at work renewing the port paddle box. Chris was one of the original restoration volunteers and continued to work on board from 1985 until 2006, starting as a deck hand and purser/steward, but going on to serve as relief Master and permanent Chief Engineer. He had an intimate knowledge of the ship, led her winter maintenance and was responsible for many of the improvements to her structure.   John Megoran

A photograph taken in 1989 just prior to a cruise in memory of Nick Knight. From left to right are Bill Prynne (PSPS Chairman in 1963 and from 1967-76), John Megoran, Mrs Knight, Nick James (PSPS Chairman 1991-2004), Malcolm Cockell, and Pat Bushell wearing her smart KC office uniform. Malcolm Cockell was the Chairman of the PS Kingswear Castle Trust & Trading Company and, as a senior manager at Babcocks who decided to put his company's facilities and expertise at the disposal of the restoration project, was instrumental in enabling the ship to return to passenger service.   John Megoran

then things would have panned out in a different way.

After a dearth of funding for *Kingswear Castle* from the PSPS in the 1970s, in the nearly thirty subsequent years I ran her on the Medway the PSPS were generally supportive when asked for help. Operating the ship also opened the door to proper funding for proper restoration. Excess revenue of income over expenditure provided matching funding for other applications to, amongst others, the Heritage Lottery Fund, the Landmark Trust, the City of Rochester upon Medway and PSPS. And this was needed. A couple of seasons in and I was going round under the bottom on the slipway tapping away with my hammer when I found a couple of places where the hammer went through and made holes. Gasp! And this was on a ship which was supposed to have been restored. That settled it for

Margaret Thatcher, the Prime Minister of the day, accompanied by Sir Stuart Pringle and other aides about to board Kingswear Castle on 1st June 1987 during her election tour of the Medway towns. Chris Smith waits at the gangway to welcome her on board.   John Megoran

me. We had to get on and find the money to do some proper restoration.

On my watch between 1985 and 2012, we re-plated all the ship's bottom from the bow to the stern and from the keel to a foot or so above the waterline each side, put in a new coal-fired boiler, renewed all the decks and caulked them with proper marine glue, replaced both the sponsons in their entirety either side, fitted new paddle boxes, a new fiddley, a new coach roof forward, a whole new bow, a new engine viewing gallery, a new inner funnel, new bridge wings, new generators, a bow thrust, a new general service steam pump and much else.

It was also clear to me from the outset that if the business was to be sustainable beyond the two year failures I had witnessed in the 1960s, then we couldn't rely just on PSPS members and other enthusiasts as passengers. Only a handful of PSPS members ever travelled regularly on *Kingswear Castle* in the Medway years and we needed 15,000 plus visitors or more a year to make the operation viable so what we offered had to appeal to a wider audience. In this we found a real gem in operating our afternoon cruises from the newly opened Historic Dockyard Chatham, from Strood and from Rochester. These appealed to a broader range of market segments and consistently turned in profits. In running a business it may seem obvious but it is crucial to remember that what matters is to produce a surplus of income over expenditure and not be seduced into thinking that a large turnover is of itself necessarily a good thing. I am pleased to be able to report that *Kingswear Castle* never required any operating subsidy on my watch.

People tend to think of me as *Kingswear Castle's* captain over all those years but in truth this was only a tiny fraction of what I did. Top of my list was ever trying to ensure that the business

John Megoran in his familiar place at Kingswear Castle's *ornate wheel during a cruise on the upper reaches of the Medway on 2nd July 2011.*

Richard De Jong

remained solvent particularly given that Chatham was never a honey pot tourist destination. A great deal of work in the winters involved drumming up business. In the end we produced around 100,000 colour leaflets annually which were professionally distributed throughout Essex, SE London, Kent, Surry and East Sussex. We took stands at travel trade fairs in London and the South East which were particularly useful for tapping into sizeable coach party and retired markets. We piggybacked on other organisations' marketing, not least through the City of Rochester Upon Medway, and with Bob Ratcliffe and others we set up the Medway Towns Tourist Consortium to help promote the area. We were in the forefront of setting up online ticket sales.

We were also pleased that *Kingswear Castle* won a number of honours over the years including the prestigious Scania Transport Trust Award as well as a Tourism SE gong for our website which I also managed. We took part in quite a bit of filming both for television and the big screen including one where *Kingswear Castle* was dolled up as the Cross-Channel Packet *Le Bonheur* flying the French ensign. She was spotted in this guise by a Maritime and Coastguard Agency surveyor who rang our office to ask why we had re-registered the ship in France without telling his department. We also carried quite a few famous passengers including the likes of Pierce Brosnan and Eric Idle, Prime Minister Margaret Thatcher, who had a go at steering, and Prince Edward.

In 2011 we were approached by the Dart Railway, which also runs the passenger boats at Dartmouth, about taking *Kinsgwear Castle* on long-term charter. This seemed an offer too good to refuse and made a good fit with the fact that I was then sixty-one and clearly could not go on running *Kingswear Castle* forever. I was therefore delighted to see *Kingswear Castle* returned to run on the river for which she was built in time for the 2013 season. Since then I have retained my involvement in the background providing advice, help and other assistance as required. I was also pleased to lead on the project to buy the engine from *Kingswear Castle's* sister, *Compton Castle* for the Paddle Steamer Kingswear Castle Trust in 2016.

Over all her Medway years *Kingswear Castle* benefitted from the help of a great number of people some of whom were PSPS members and some of whom weren't. Chief amongst these was my right-hand man for over twenty years Chris Smith. I had huge confidence and trust in Chris. He was a real asset. There is a lot of Chris in *KC*.

To all who have helped I say a big thank you. Without their superb efforts we would not have been able to achieve all that we did. Of course, others might have done it differently. Others might have done it better. Others might have done it worse. Who knows? But I stand on my record and will rest easy as all my leaves fall to the ground in the knowledge that the PSPS has been a central part of my life for 59 years and that I have done a little bit to keep at least one paddle steamer sailing in the UK. And what a pleasure it has been doing it.

Waverley hurries away from Largs in the evening sunlight on 9th August 1972. R. Clammer

CHAPTER TEN

DEVELOPMENTS IN SCOTLAND AND PURCHASE OF PS WAVERLEY

Douglas McGowan MBE

IN 1960 aged 12, I was given a Junior Membership of the Clyde River Steamer Club (CRSC) by a family member, costing half a crown! (12.5p) As long as I can remember, I was always fascinated by the Clyde steamers, especially the paddle steamers which as a young boy, I found quite captivating with their thrashing paddles, hypnotic triple expansion engines and the associated intoxicating aroma of hot oil and steam.

My Father had a passing interest in the steamers but he wasn't a first class "nutter" like his eldest son. My Uncle was a sales rep for Hotpoint and frequently travelled to Arran, Bute and Cumbrae. He would bring me back one or two postcards of the steamers and occasionally a little plaster-cast model (costing 7/6d) of one of the fleet which were sold on board, to feed my passion. Family holidays were often spent at Whiting Bay on the Island of Arran which boasted the longest pier on the Clyde. For me, it was the thrill of getting there and coming home just as much as the holiday itself, especially if it happened to be on one of the paddlers such as *Caledonia*, one of my favourites, along with the *Jeanie Deans*. Funnily enough, although I always enjoyed sailing on the *Waverley*, she was never one of my favourites.

The CRSC was primarily a Club focusing on the history of the Clyde steamers and its Constitution did not pretend to become involved in matters of preservation. I became aware of the PSPS in the early 1960s and decided to join in 1966. I soon became aware that the Society had active branches in London, Wessex and the Bristol Channel but I was very surprised to discover there was no Scottish Branch. I considered this somewhat incongruous given the Clyde's famous maritime heritage. It was Henry Bell's *PS Comet*, after all, which became the first commercially successful steamboat service in Europe. By the end of 1967, the Clyde had lost the diesel electric paddler *Talisman* and at the beginning of the 1969 season, rumours were circulating that the charismatic Denny built paddler of 1934, *Caledonia*, was soon to be withdrawn. I had visited Arnott Young's shipbreaking yard at Dalmuir and witnessed the destruction of *Talisman* in 1968 and was determined that the *Caledonia* would not meet the same fate. In early 1969 I met up with a young David Neill, at that time 2nd Mate on MacBrayne's *Lochnevis*. David was an avid *Caledonia* fan, having served on her as Assistant Purser in his student days and was keen to at least attempt to preserve her. Little did I

The magnificent Caledonia *leaving Dunoon during the summer of 1967. Built to cope with the winter crossing to Arran, the ship's heavy construction and distinctive appearance earned her many admirers.*

Douglas McGowan

Waverley at Ardrishaig on 26th September 1970 during the PSPS's first ever charter of the ship.   Les Ring / PSPS Collection

know then that only five years later, we would be operating the *Waverley* with David as Master!

Chris Phillips, at that time Secretary of the Society, was equally enthusiastic to establish a Scottish Branch and offered me much encouragement, even travelling to Glasgow to meet me. The inaugural meeting was held on 13th December 1969 in the Christian Institute, Glasgow, a very large rather austere Victorian building, long since gone. About 25 members and friends attended (more than I anticipated!) and I announced that the Branch would do what it could to keep *Caledonia* sailing, although it had already been announced by the Caledonian Steam Packet Co (CSP)that she was for sale. Our focus would also be on *Waverley* and *Maid of the Loch*. The first Committee was Iain Hunter (Chairman), Bruce Gilmour (Vice Chairman), Douglas McGowan (Secretary), Leslie Puckett (Treasurer), with Committee members Alistair Goodman, Lawrence Macduff, Peter Reid and David Neill. The branch didn't waste much time: the first full-day PSPS charter of *Waverley* was September 1970 to Tarbert and Ardrishaig - an outstanding success. Gordon Wilson takes up the full story of the branch later in the next chapter.

But other matters at the end of 1969 were far more pressing: just two weeks after the Branch was formed, although not actually under the auspices of the PSPS, Iain Hunter, David Neill and I got together to work out whether or not it would be feasible to purchase and operate the *Caledonia* ourselves. Our plan was to operate on non-competing routes on the Clyde and

cruises from Oban. (Sound familiar?)Looking back at it now, we were either incredibly brave, naive or stupid, or a combination of all those things! I was aged 21 on a salary of £750 per annum as a sales rep for Terrys of York and I was aspiring to be a shipping magnate! David had worked as Assistant Purser on the *Caledonia* and had access to fuel consumption, crew and annual refit costs etc. So we did our sums and at my suggestion, we went to see the Shipping Correspondent of the Glasgow Herald just before Christmas 1969. He listened intently to our plans. Imagine the surprise of my girl friend of only two weeks (now my wife) waking up the following morning to read on the front page of the Herald about her dashing young man, not just a chocolate salesman of ill repute, but shipping magnate in the making! Impressive, or what!

The coverage in the Herald attracted a fair amount of interest and not just from my girl friend. A PSPS member, Ian Burrows, was Engineering Superintendent with Glasgow ship owner Harrisons (Clyde), who were also the major shareholder and owner of Western Ferries, expressed support and enthusiasm for our plan and offered the expertise of his company. A top level meeting quickly followed with the man himself, Ian Harrison, in their boardroom. Now the adrenalin really started to flow. Harrisons arranged a survey of the vessel in the water in the presence of a BoT surveyor and reported on her condition: "Hull very good except for corrosion on floors under boilers. Machinery good except for main engine valve gear

Caledonia speeds away from Gourock at the end of a busy day, heading for her Craigendoran base.　　Keith Abraham

Waverley sits above her own reflection at Keppel pier on 16th September 1972, the year of her 25th Anniversary.　　Les Ring / PSPS Collection

bushes and main air pump shuttle valve chest".

A major campaign followed and I wrote to MPs and prominent Glasgow businessmen including Sir Hugh Fraser, Sir Hector MacLennan and Sir William Lithgow. I received sympathetic responses from everyone but no large cheques! There is no doubt that Harrisons would have managed the ship on our behalf but then the bombshell letter arrived from Maurice Little, Managing Director of the Scottish Transport Group, parent company of the CSP Co. The letter made it clear that they would not sell the *Caledonia* to Harrisons/Western Ferries as they were concerned we would be in competition. Sadly, it was the end of a dream. Little did I know what was just around the corner!

Down but not out, a few months later I then wrote to Arnott Young Shipbreakers where the *Caledonia* had ended up, pleading with them not to break her up as she was a very historic vessel with distinguished War service. A couple of meetings with their Board followed and they agreed not to break her up for a minimum of 12 months. During this time, in November 1971, Bass Charrington purchased the vessel, had her refitted as a pub and restaurant and berthed at Cleopatra's Needle on the Thames. She was a popular venue for several years until tragically destroyed by a major fire in 1980.

1969 was an auspicious year in more ways than one. I was also introduced to Terry Sylvester on my 21st birthday. It became obvious very quickly that we were kindred spirits with the same ideals and objectives. With the demise of the *Caledonia*, by 1970 the *Waverley* had become not only the last of the Clyde paddle steamers but the last sea-going paddle steamer in Europe. We needed to shout about that! Within the slowly flourishing Scottish Branch of the PSPS, we set up the *Waverley* Study Group led by Terry and myself. Its purpose was to look at ways of broadening the appeal of Waverley, to offer some ideas on marketing and publicity to the CSP Co management and ultimately to improve her commercial viability.

Much to my pleasant surprise, Terry and I started to have regular meetings with the CSP General Manager John Whittle at their Gourock HQ. Here we were, a couple of "steamer dreamers" in the sacred inner sanctum at Gourock with the boss! We had several ideas to discuss but the principal one was for the *Waverley* to have a separate identity from all the other units in the fleet, to make her "stand out from the crowd" as something really special. For instance, we suggested that the funnels were painted red with a black top separated by a white band, the colours of the old LNER. We also suggested painting the paddle boxes black instead of white to make her really stand out from the other ships in their fleet which were predominantly car ferries serving the Clyde and Western Isles. The latter idea was implemented for the 1972 season but we had to wait another 3 years to change the funnels (under OUR ownership!) The Society continued to show their support for *Waverley* by regularly chartering the ship to unusual destinations such as Ormidale, Loch Riddon (landing by

Waverley at Rothesay on 30th May 1967. Les Ring / PSPS Collection

tender) and Inveraray, as well as chartering *Maid of the Loch*. So, in effect, we were becoming loyal customers of the CSP Co as well as their (unpaid!) consultants! My wife Jean and I around this time became very good friends with the *Waverley's* officers and crew and we were treated on board as VIPs. Whether it was because they acknowledged that someone cared passionately about their ship or simply because we were "regulars" I am really not sure, but we were very well respected.

Terry and I were conscious of the fact that in 1972 the steamer was going to be 25 years old, so at one of our meetings with John Whittle, we suggested that perhaps a special sailing could celebrate this milestone with resulting positive publicity. John immediately agreed to this and so on 19th May 1972, *Waverley* sailed on a special afternoon cruise to the Kyles of Bute with invited guests from the PSPS, CSP and the Press. But the CSP went even further... their own splendid bakery at

Gourock produced a magnificent Anniversary cake in the shape of *Waverley's* paddlebox and it was cut at a special ceremony on board by the Captain. The 25 candles were blown out by Terry Sylvester's eldest daughter Sharon. The Society was presented with a very fine collection of ex-railway company silverware and the Society returned the gesture by presenting the steamer with a commemorative brass plaque which was duly unveiled by my fiancée Jean. All of this resulted in considerable TV and Press coverage. However, I have two major regrets about this day: at the end of the 1975 season, the Scottish Branch held an auction of numerous artefacts and steamer memorabilia to raise much needed funds for the Waverley. Most of the unique silverware was included in the auction which raised a very respectable sum but it was a poor decision and the silverware would today have been a worthy asset to the PSPS archive. The other regret concerns the 25th Anniversary brass plaque which was displayed under the 1899 War service plaque for her predecessor on the promenade deck. Following the rebuild in 2001 it never reappeared, which I felt was wrong as it was an important part of the ship's history.

The events leading up to the Society being gifted the world's last sea-going paddle steamer have been very well documented over the years. Suffice to say that during her final 1973 season under Caledonian MacBrayne,

On board Waverley, *9th August 1972.*   R. Clammer

Waverley suffered from boiler tube problems resulting in several days off service and rumours were rife amongst the enthusiast community. So it was probably no great surprise when I received a call from John Whittle asking me to attend a meeting in his Gourock office. As there was no sign of any work going on and the ship was silent, I feared the worst and naturally assumed that John would gently break the news that the old lady was being withdrawn and sold to the highest bidder. 22nd November 1973 was the fateful day. I was nervous and apprehensive. Terry and I had spoken on the phone the previous evening and we had been speculating on the various outcomes: "Maybe they'll just give us the ship", joked Terry and

we both laughed, not thinking for one minute it would actually happen. Maybe Terry had a premonition! There were just the two of us at the meeting, John and myself. John explained that the steamer required considerable expenditure, particularly on the boiler and passenger numbers cruising on the Clyde were in decline. Due to harsh economics, they had no alternative but to withdraw her from service. And then came the bombshell. Following a meeting with their parent company, the Scottish Transport Group, and in recognition of all the advice and support offered by Terry and me representing the PSPS, it had been decided to offer the ship to our Society "as the most appropriate organisation to look after her". "The bad news" said John, "is that you will have to give us £1 to make the deal legal!"

Some time later, John described my reaction as a mixture of exultation and trepidation. To that, I would add incredulity and consternation. It was certainly a surreal moment, one which I will never forget. But I suddenly felt very alone - there was no other witness sitting beside me to soak up this special moment and I felt a little sad that Terry, my "partner in crime" wasn't able to share the special experience. My immediate thought was, "hold on a minute, this is a publicly owned asset, are they able to do this?" and "where's the catch?"

I left the Calmac office dumbfounded and excited and first broke the news to my wife on arriving back home who probably thought I had been on the jungle juice. And then I broke the news to Terry, who like me was incredulous but calm and thoughtful. John had reminded me that to take ownership of the vessel we would need to set up a limited company as the PSPS Constitution did not allow us to own a ship. We would also need to appoint a Ship's Husband. I wondered what on earth a Ship's Husband's duties were? John enlightened me: if the ship were to go on fire or sink at her berth, the Ship's Husband was the person whom the authorities immediately contacted. I also looked up the Dictionary definition: "A person who is responsible for providing maintenance and supplies for a ship in port and acts as a general agent". (Little did I know I would become a Ship's Husband some 8 months later... scary!)

The first move was to convene an urgent Committee meeting of the Scottish Branch the following evening and later the Branch duly acknowledged the offer from Calmac. However, any formal acceptance would have to be considered by the Society's Central Committee in London. A few days later I was on a plane from Glasgow and duly sat in front of the Committee recommending we accept their offer. But it wasn't that easy. There were several "doubting Thomases" on that Committee and who could blame them? Why would Calmac make such an incredible gesture? What were the legal implications? What do they expect us to do with it? What if we fail? In the meantime, who is going to pay for insurance, port dues and a watchman? Those were just a few of the questions fired at me. Fresh in the minds of Committee members was the *Queen of the South, ex Jeanie Deans* which had been acquired by a PSPS member from the CSP Co in 1965 and had two unsuccessful seasons on the Thames. Also, a few years earlier, the Society had acquired the small ex River Dart paddler *Kingswear Castle* and had been struggling for several years to generate sufficient interest and funds to return her to operational condition. *Waverley* was almost three times her size and had a Class V passenger certificate for 1,350! It ended up quite a hard sell but the vote was narrowly in favour of accepting the steamer. Our Society's Founder and President, Professor Alan Robinson, was very supportive and clearly put his faith in Terry and me.

We honestly had no idea at that time what to do with the ship. It was a huge responsibility and our next move was being watched closely by enthusiasts, the general public and the media. Once our feet touched the ground, we began to think about the possibility of having her berthed in Glasgow as a floating museum or pub/restaurant or floating clubhouse for our members, all of which was going to be expensive. Gradually, our thoughts turned to the possibility of actually operating her. Would it be possible? Did we have sufficient expertise to launch such a dream? Did we have the funds? Those and many other questions were going through my mind as 1973 drew to a close and 1974 dawned. *Waverley* had a rather utilitarian reputation, being built immediately after the War when quality materials were in short supply so before we could move any further, we considered it important to professionally establish the condition of the hull and boiler. And so in

Douglas McGowan accepts the ship's papers and bill of sale from John Whittle of Calmac, while Terry Sylvester looks on.
Douglas McGowan Collection

February 1974, with the permission of Calmac and generously paid for by Terry, she was towed from the James Watt Dock Greenock to Lamont's slipway at Port Glasgow, proudly flying the PSPS flag! The underwater survey concluded that the hull was good for a minimum of 10 years without any major re-plating and the boiler with careful maintenance would benefit from re-tubing, something which was not undertaken until the winter of 1975/76.

The fun and games then started but it was not until 8th August 1974 that the steamer was formally handed over at a ceremony in the Gourock office, attended by John Whittle and Sir Patrick Thomas, Chairman of the Scottish Transport Group, Terry and myself representing Waverley Steam Navigation Co, a company which had been bought "off the shelf" by our Accountant Peter Reid, to enable the PSPS to take ownership of the vessel. A pristine Royal Bank of Scotland £1 note was presented to me by Sir Patrick adding that they wanted the transaction to be an absolute gift "just in case we didn't have a spare £1 to stump up!" What a magnificent gesture! My only regret was that I didn't hang on to the £1 as it would have been a worthy addition to the PSPS archive. (or I could have sold it on ebay for a small fortune!) A few days previously, I had issued Press Releases to all major newspapers, TV and Radio and there was a considerable Press turnout on the day. Following the signing of the "Bill of

A Paddler for a Pound!' A well-known but essential photograph taken on 8th August 1974 showing the famous £1 note which purchased Waverley *passing between Douglas McGowan and Sir Patrick Thomas. Second from left is John Whittle of Calmac, and on the right is Terry Sylvester.* Douglas McGowan Collection

The sale of Waverley *to the PSPS and her triumphant return to passenger service in May 1975 generated great media interest. On this occasion Douglas McGowan is being interviewed for a TV documentary at James Watt Dock with the steamer receiving her new livery in the background.*

Douglas McGowan Collection

Sale" and transfer of the ship's papers, there were photocalls on the pier and also at the James Watt Dock, with Waverley in the background. The following day, "Paddler for a Pound" and "Never could £1 have bought so much" were some of the headlines widely announced to the great British public along with further TV interviews. Fame... without the fortune! I did ask John Whittle fairly recently whose decision it was to gift the ship to the PSPS. He replied that it was the STG Chairman, Pat Thomas who believed it was the right thing to do as we had demonstrated such support but would also result in good publicity for Calmac.

Although Calmac probably considered it unlikely that a small bunch of enthusiasts would attempt to operate the ship, nevertheless, a non competition clause was written in to the Bill of Sale... just in case!

The months which followed were frenetic to say the least. Terry and I attended many meetings with tourist groups, local authorities and potential funders to encourage financial support. It became clear that there was a groundswell of support out there from people who genuinely wanted to see the Waverley sail again. In the autumn of 1974, I approached over 50 companies, seeking their support on either a cost basis or donating services or materials free of charge. The response was overwhelming with almost every company responding positively: Esso, Weirs Pumps, White Horse Distillers,

Armitage Shanks, a Glasgow flag manufacturer, a paint manufacturer and even a major chocolate company who (unknowingly) donated the free time of one of their salesmen!

Following the transfer of ownership, we immediately became responsible for the security of the ship as well as dock dues and insurance. Following my approach to the Clyde Port Authority, they agreed to waive charges for a period. The Branch commenced work parties at weekends from August 1974, basically cleaning the ship, getting rid of rust and painting. It amazed me how quickly a ship deteriorates when not in service. For a time, I was in charge of work parties - incredible really as I don't know one end of a screwdriver from another. Usually we had up to 30 volunteers, including enthusiastic children and not a hard hat in sight. Nobody died... as far as I know.

On 25th October 1974, we launched a major Public Appeal in the Scottish and National Press. Leslie Puckett, our elderly Branch Treasurer was expecting a quiet retirement when he volunteered for the role at the inauguration of the branch. Little did he know that 5 years later literally hundreds and hundreds of donations would be tumbling through his letterbox! And he dealt with them all very professionally and revelled in his involvement. The Appeal raised about £100,000, an amazing amount of money back in 1974, boosted by a £25,000 donation from the Scottish Tourist Board. This was enough to have Waverley dry-docked in February 1975 in the Garvel Dry Dock

Waverley approaching Ardrishaig on her first ever sailing in operational preservation, 24th May 1975.　©CRSC Dr. Joe McKendrick Collection

During her first week back in service, Waverley sweeps down the Clyde on Sunday 25th May 1975 looking resplendent in her new WSN livery. Paddle float damage on the previous day had meant that the ship was badly delayed and did not limp back to Glasgow until 3.35am. Nonetheless, she left on time at 10.00am for a successful 11-hour day which took her to Dunoon, Millport, Largs, Rothesay, Loch Riddon and back.

Iain Quinn Collection

in Greenock. Ian Burrows offered his professional help with engineering matters and was duly appointed to the Board. I eventually tracked down Bill Summers who had been *Waverley's* Chief Engineer from 1947 until 1969 and he didn't need much persuading to come out of retirement and help us, offering invaluable advice to our brand new team of engineers. The funnel colours were changed to red, white and black and 8,500 feet of decking was either repaired or replaced. The boiler was given a comprehensive clean and a hydraulic pressure test. I had regular progress meetings with the Dock Manager, a delightful chap called John Hamilton and I amazed myself at the things I learned about overhauling a paddle steamer! He was a good teacher, one of the "old school".

We needed to develop a commercial timetable that didn't compete directly with Calmac's *Queen Mary II* and this was developed by both Terry and George Train who was also appointed to our Board. We needed to find a sales and marketing office and this was duly established at Anderson Quay, alongside our Glasgow berth. In the early months of 1975, I was arranging various Press Conferences which usually resulted in TV and radio interviews. The Press were hungry for updates and I felt it was important to keep them "on side". Next on the list was to advertise for Officers and Crew and a General Manager. David Neill was appointed Captain. I was involved in some of the interviews and appointments. I was also involved in appointing the Purser and Assistant Pursers, sourcing flags, stocking and manning of the Souvenir Shop and local PR.

Just to add to the excitement, our first daughter, Lynn, was born in February 1975. In fact, I was on board *Waverley* during the docking process as my wife went into labour! A gangway was quickly manoeuvred into position to enable me to rather urgently take Jean to the maternity hospital!

Our "maiden voyage" was Thursday 22nd May 1975, a day I will never forget. We decided to make the first sailing by invitation only so we invited some 350 guests including PSPS Officers and volunteers and everyone who had contributed in some way as we sailed down the river to Dunoon. It was a splendid day and Sir William Gray, Lord Provost of Glasgow, who had demonstrated such magnificent support in the early days, joined us for that rather special occasion.

Looking back now, yes, it was scary at the time but we were young (I was 25 when I handed over the £1) and when you are young, you probably don't think about the consequences of what you are doing, you simply get on with it. Which is maybe just as well. 42 years on, a very formal and mysterious envelope arrived on my doorstep one morning. A speeding fine, I thought. But no, I was very surprised and indeed honoured to be awarded the MBE "For services to *PS Waverley* and to charity". As I said at the time, it was a huge honour, not just for me but for the small but dedicated band who succeeded in bringing the good ship *Waverley* back to life to give pleasure to millions. It was also a great honour for our Society.

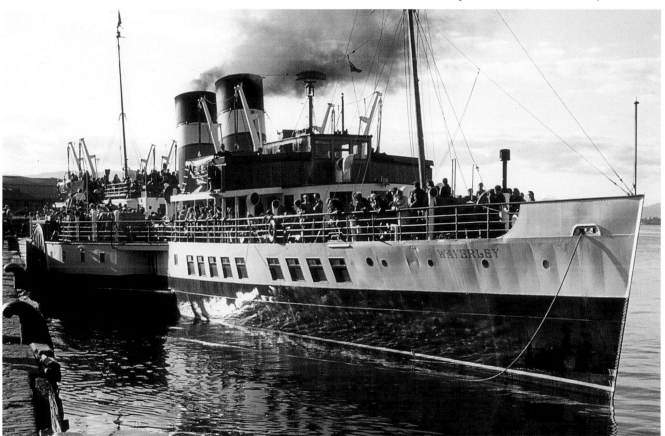

A well-laden Waverley *departing from Greenock on a tranquil evening during the summer of 1975, her first season in preservation.*   Gordon Wilson

Clyde Marine Services' Greenock-based passenger vessel Cruiser was used by the Scottish Branch for its Festive cruises for 13 years. The 119 GT, 24m vessel was built in 1974 as the Southsea Queen for the Gosport Ferry Company. Proving too small for the service she was sold in 1978 to White Horse Ferries and spent the next 17 years on their Hythe-Southampton service as Hythe Hotspur. In 1995 she moved to Poole Harbour on charter to Blue Funnel who subsequently purchased her and renamed her Poole Scene. Since 1999 she has operated charter cruises on the Clyde.

Murray Paterson

CHAPTER ELEVEN

THE SCOTTISH BRANCH

Gordon Wilson

OR the first few years of its existence, there were exciting times for the Scottish Branch, with members engaged in attempts to save *Caledonia* and *Waverley*. However, these years also saw the development of a list of activities, many of which were to become regular features of the calendar.

Branch meetings, which were inaugurated on 13th December 1969, have continued to take place in Glasgow each winter, aimed at spreading the word about paddle steamers, and encouraging those present to develop a deeper interest. Of course, it is not possible to fill the syllabus purely with paddle steamer related topics, so related shipping topics are often included. However, despite the huge increase in Branch membership from the time of the first meeting, meetings still appear to interest only a small minority of members, currently in the order of 5%. However there have been occasions when larger attendances have been attracted, particularly when serving masters and officers have been encouraged to leave

their comfort zones and tell of their seagoing highlights. Members will still recall interesting presentations given by David Neill, Ian McMillan, Jim McFadzean, Gordon Reid, Graeme Gellatly, Steve Colledge, Kit Lee, Ian Clark, John Megoran and David Howie. Branch meetings have taken place at various Glasgow venues including the Christian Institute, Transport Museum and College of Building, before settling down in the Renfield St Stephens Church Centre from 1979 to date. For a few years, the Committee also ran 'Roadshow' presentations in locations such as Greenock, Helensburgh, Largs, Ayr and Edinburgh, but these attracted patchy attendances and did not appear to generate new members, so they were discontinued after a few years.

The first Branch exhibition stall was set up in Glasgow's McLellan Galleries in February 1971, and 47 years later the Branch is still running its stall at what is now Model Rail Scotland at Glasgow's SEC each year. The stall generates funds

Queen of Scots lays alongside Waverley at Millport on 1st September 1977, the day when the paddler returned to service following the completion of hull repairs in Govan dry-dock following her grounding on the Gantock rocks off Dunoon on Friday July 15th – a memorable day! Thanks to the kindness of Sir William McAlpine, the motor vessel had been made available to maintain the paddler's sailings during the peak summer season, and carried over 14,000 passengers.

Murray Paterson

through selling shipping related merchandise and second-hand books, and also hands out copies of *Waverley's* Scottish sailing programme for the coming season. This still remains an important means of contacting members of the public who may never have thought of sailing on *Waverley*. Over the years, stalls have also been set up at transport exhibitions in Paisley, Saltcoats, Greenock, Bridgeton, Cathcart and Johnston, and at Ship Ahoy Exhibitions in Glasgow, Hamilton and Irvine, but the most memorable was a two-day open-air event in Irvine when the stand staff arrived for the second day to find that the stall and the tent housing it had blown away overnight. Needless to say, outdoor exhibitions have been treated with caution ever since, although for a few years we did participate in the short-lived Clyde River Festival and set up a stand in a gazebo adjacent to the Science Centre.

Charters are another regular feature of the annual Branch programmes, and it is interesting to note that the first of these was on 5th April 1970, when *Waverley* had carried a large group of Scottish National Party members to a conference in Rothesay. During the free time the paddler had there, the

During its fifty year history, the Scottish Branch has produced a number of authoritative publications. The first, entitled "The Royal Route Retraced" appeared in 1970 to be sold on board Waverley *during her Glasgow to Ardrishaig charter on 26th September. A second, pictured here, was published in 1971 to coincide with the charter of* Maid of the Loch *on Loch Lomond with an overland connection to Trossachs for a sail on board* Sir Walter Scott. *Written by Lawrence Macduff, Douglas McGowan and Jeanie Martin (later to become Mrs McGowan) with a cover illustration by John Innes it sold for 12p in the new and unfamiliar decimalised coinage which had been introduced that year.*

R. Clammer Collection

Branch chartered her for the princely sum of £50 for a cruise Round Bute, and a large profit of £7.37 was generated. On 26th September of the same year, there was a full day charter to Tarbert and Ardrishaig and this was quickly followed by a charter of *Waverley* round Arran in September 1971, then to Ormidale in 1972 with *Rover* acting as tender. Generally profitable charters of *Waverley* continued until 1980, latterly with considerable support from large parties arriving by trains organised by the Scottish Railway Preservation Society, but thereafter it was decided that a day charter of the paddler was too much of a financial risk, although they did take place to mark special anniversaries in 2012 and 2014. It was *Waverley's*

Maid of the Loch had been chartered several times by the Society before she was finally withdrawn from service at the end of August 1981.

PSPS Collection

Hardy members brave blizzard conditions to board Countess of Kempock *at Gourock for the first ever Scottish Branch Festive Cruise on 30th December 1978. Weather conditions were so severe that the cruise was almost cancelled, but in the event the ship made it to her intended destination of Carrick Castle in Loch Goil, where the owners of the local hotel and shop were bemused but delighted by the sight of eighty enthusiasts streaming ashore in search of warmth and sustenance.*   Murray Paterson

Passengers on the 1978 charter received a slice of Christmas cake and a dram of whisky, and were entertained by William Tennant's Old Time Steamer Band. Many commented that it was the first time that William Tennant had been seen wearing his "willies" during a performance, or the violinist playing with his woolly gloves on!
                                                    Murray Paterson

40th Birthday in 1987 which was the catalyst for trying an evening charter of the ship and, although this was a great success, there was a gap until 1993 before a further evening charter was organised to celebrate the reopening of Greenock Custom House Quay. So successful was this that evening charters have taken place each year since, with the exception of 2000 when *Waverley* was in Great Yarmouth for her rebuild. In 2001 *Waverley* was uniquely offering Christmas Party Cruises from Glasgow, so the opportunity was taken of running a daytime Lunch Cruise aboard her on 16th December.

Over the years, charters were not limited to *Waverley*, and in 1971 the Branch organised an ambitious charter of *Maid of the Loch,* including coach connections between Inversnaid and Stronachlachar to allow the option of a return trip to Trossachs aboard *Sir Walter Scott.* Unfortunately, this made a loss of over £300, a very significant sum at that time. In 1973 a group of PSPS members chartered the puffer *Auld Reekie* for a weekend outing, an event which was repeated in 1974, and over the years the Branch has chartered such diverse vessels as the *Ferry Queen* on the Forth and Clyde Canal, the waterbus *Sir William Wallace* to Paisley, the steam yacht *Carola* on the Clyde, the *Forth Belle* on the Forth, *St Magdalene* on the Union Canal, the steam yacht *Gondola* on Coniston Water, and *Lomond Duchess* and *Silver Marlin* on Loch Lomond. The Branch has also organised trips to various destinations such as the Lake District and Loch Katrine.

In December 1978, *Countess of Kempock* was chartered for the first PSPS Festive Cruise, an event which remains profitable and still takes place each year 40 years later. Somehow the idea of a day out with lunch is appealing after the hectic Christmas period, and before the excesses of New Year, to the extent that the number supporting this cruise has increased significantly over the years. The *Kenilworth* was the chosen vessel for the subsequent 21 years, and then as we all became older, we turned to the slightly larger and more comfortable *Cruiser* for 13 years, before settling for the almost

PSPS 2010 Christmas cruise. Pictured on Cruiser's *upper deck are, left to right, Peter Reid, Elizabeth Wilson, Heather Reid, Gordon Wilson, Kathryn Paterson & Joe McKendrick.*
                                                    Murray Paterson

During one of the Branch's regular winter work parties the late Dr. Joe McKendrick is seen caulking Waverley's *foredeck during the winter of 1994.*
Gordon Wilson

luxurious accommodation aboard *Clyde Clipper* for the last four years. In 2001, *Waverley* offered Christmas party cruises, and in that year the opportunity was taken to run the Branch Festive Cruise aboard the paddler. *Kenilworth* was definitely very basic, with limited and spartan internal accommodation, so most participants spent the time outdoors, clad in as much clothing as they could put on. Because there was no space for on-board catering, the cruise usually included a call at Carrick Castle where the Hotel or Eversley House supplied a hot meal. It also allowed a prominent committee member to feed the local geese. When the chosen vessel changed to *Cruiser* and *Clyde Clipper*, there was covered accommodation available for on-board catering, so buffet lunches were served during the cruises. Of course, this also meant that the itinerary could be changed in the event of bad weather.

PSPS work parties first appeared on *Waverley* shortly after her sale to PSPS, and from 1980 they were organised on a more formal basis. Regular jobs included painting the deck shelters, and varnishing the buoyant seats and deck seats, but in 1994 the opportunity was given for PSPS volunteers to assist with the replacement of the wood on the foredeck, leading to experience in caulking and fitting wooden plugs over the fixing bolts. More recently, volunteers have tended to be skilled tradesmen, who work on weekdays when the ship's professional crew are in attendance. Branch work parties also made their mark aboard *Maid of the Loch* in 1986 and again in 1993. In 1986 the work involved fitting Visquene sheeting to stem the flow of rain water through the vessel's deteriorating decks, and

then in 1993 permission was given for Branch volunteers to carry out a much more extensive clean and paint of the *Maid*, which eventually saw her funnel become red and black, and her hull become black to spread the message that she had a future. Branch members have continued to offer their services to keep the *Maid* 'ship shape' ever since.

Of course, Branch members did not need to be afloat to enjoy themselves, and a number of celebration events ashore have been arranged over the years. In the early 1970s, two Branch 'social nights' were held in a Glasgow scout hut, the idea being for the mothers of the scouts to be the dancing partners. This formula was not entirely successful, and it was minuted at the time that the event would not be repeated since it was recognised that steamer enthusiasts do not dance! Much more successful were formal dinners to mark anniversaries of the Branch, and these were held in 1979, 1984, 1989, 2000 and 2009.

Over the years the Branch has raised hundreds of thousands of pounds mainly for *Waverley* through its charter sailings, grand draws, raffles and auctions. For many years it was considered that *Waverley* herself was the best fund raiser, so Branch members concentrated on encouraging the public to come for a sail, through publicity at exhibitions, and through distribution of *Waverley* timetables and hanging cards over a large area of Scotland. For several years, the Branch was instrumental in producing and distributing a 'candy striped' pocket timetable which it was felt presented information on *Waverley's* Clyde cruises in a more convenient way, thereby

In recent years the Branch has chosen the spacious and comfortable Clyde Clipper *for its Festive Cruises. She is seen here at Ormidale, Loch Riddon on 27th December 2017.*
Murray Paterson

encouraging a few more to come aboard. When the decision was made to run Grand Draws, Branch members embraced these fully, whether by selling or buying tickets, and very considerable sums were raised through this. The Branch also raised large sums through the publication of books including "Birth of a Legend" in 1987, "Clyde Steamers Remembered" in 1994, "More Clyde Steamers Remembered" in 2001, and more recently a special edition of Waverley Times, a Clyde Cruising Guide, and booklets commemorating *Waverley* anniversaries and unusual sailings. Apart from draw proceeds which go direct to the ship, the funds raised were generally for particular projects such as a padded bench seat in the forward deck shelter in 1983, a chilled display for the restaurant in 1984, and more recently replacement paddle floats, replacement covers for life jacket lockers, and an upgrade of the galley fire prevention system. Funds have also gone towards a dehumidifier, a scanner for the PSPS Archive, and towards various projects associated with the restoration of *Maid of the Loch*.

Throughout the Branch's 50 years individual members have made considerable contributions through their work on the *Waverley* Boards and on PSPS National Council, giving talks to clubs and societies, and assisting with the purser's office, shop and commentary on board. Some talented Branch musicians have also raised considerable sums entertaining the passengers around *Waverley's* decks, and in more recent times individuals have also been active publicising the ship through postings on the PSPS website, YouTube, Facebook, Twitter and Instagram.

Without doubt, the work of the Branch has made a very significant contribution towards keeping *Waverley* sailing over the years, and the challenge to all members is to maintain the momentum – even for another 50 years!

After Maid of the Loch *passed into the ownership of Dumbarton District council in December 1992, members of the Scottish Branch were able to become centrally involved in her conservation. In this 1993 view a work party, having chipped and red-leaded from one of ship's boats, has begun painting the hull black for the very first time.*
Gordon Wilson

View looking aft from the bridge just after the Phase One drydocking. The funnels and aft deck house are still missing, while the new sponson houses and the empty boiler and engine rooms are clearly visible

Nick James

CHAPTER TWELVE

WAVERLEY REBUILT

Nick James

IN 1988, PSPS achieved its then major aim of obtaining charitable status. It was a huge milestone, its achievement spearheaded by Nigel Coombes as the Society's Chairman, with very substantial support from Margaret Russell, one of our early members. Before this, we might have been seen as a bunch of supremely enthusiastic enthusiasts who had achieved the seemingly impossible by establishing the reliable operational preservation of *Waverley* against all the odds. The right individuals, namely Douglas McGowan, David Neill and Terry Sylvester, had been there at the right time to make it happen, and they had the vision, the tenacity, and the ability to succeed where, with other paddle steamers, others had repeatedly failed. *Kingswear Castle* was also in the process of establishing her reputation under the skilled stewardship of John Megoran. Now, charitable status was in some senses a "coming of age" for the Society, bringing with it a sense of both recognition and responsibility.

It didn't come a moment too soon. It was becoming obvious that both *Kingswear Castle* and *Waverley* would soon require major capital expenditure if they were to continue to operate. *Kingswear Castle* would need very substantial hull replating, and both ships would require what seemed an unattainable sum of money to enable them to comply with new legislation. PSPS had appointed a professional fund-raiser to undertake a feasibility study. He was very concerned about the then loose structural relationship between PSPS and the Waverley companies, and estimated that once this had been resolved so that major donors were more likely to want to support us, the Society could hope to raise up to £250,000 with the help of professional fundraising. The structure of the relationship between the Society and the Waverley companies was strengthened, and many more of the fundraiser's suggested reforms were implemented, largely thanks to Jeremy Gold who had taken over from Nigel Coombes. When Jeremy had to resign as Society Chairman due to pressure of work in his paid employment, I was persuaded to succeed him for a period of 6 months, until a *deus ex machina* in the form of a well-known and well-connected politician would take over to lead the much-needed fund-raising campaign.

The *deus ex machina* did not materialise for the PSPS; he was instead diverted to higher things. As fund-raising was already showing promise, we decided to go it alone and develop our own fund-raising strategy, without professional help. A target of £350,000 was set, to be raised by 1 April (!) 1995. Three months ahead of schedule, we had raised £360,734 purely from efforts by Society members. No big donations from the great and good, no high-profile fund-raising events or dinners, just sheer hard graft.

It had seemed almost an impossible task when we started out. But there were very strong elements in our favour. PSPS had some 3,500 members all supporting a single cause - the preservation of a unique living tradition symbolised in the reality of two historic paddle steamers in operation. The essence was that those ships were operational, "not stuffed, sanitised and mounted in a museum" as the then Environment Secretary John Gummer once memorably put it when he was aboard *Waverley* in London. And there was a massive and unavoidable reality in that if we did not raise the £350,000 there was no question but that our ships would cease to operate. The Society's strength and unity of purpose, combined with the fact that we had a captive audience of many already-motivated potential donors in the form of the ships' thousands upon thousands of passengers, was the key. Individual members did their bit, and the Society's five local Branches were set fund-raising targets which they attacked with relish and exceeded, often by spectacular amounts. We were not far from the days when *Waverley* carried a record 234,000 passengers in one season, so there were plenty of pockets to be opened. If we had the same challenge now, it is a sobering statistic that in 2018 *Waverley* carried 90,000 passengers. Of course a huge number of things have changed; not least hours of work regulations, endless other regulations affecting the operation of ships, the minimum wage, and the price of fuel, and many more. All of these militate against *Waverley* operating in the same way now as she did then, and there is no way the clock can be turned back. In the early nineties, when we had to raise these funds, we were very lucky indeed in that our requirement coincided with a peak in passenger (and therefore supporter) numbers.

The £350,000 had been set, sensibly, as a "worst case" estimate of what would be needed. Fortunately the worst case did not happen. In addition, Society members were now, partly thanks to the Society's Chairman haranguing them in every edition of Paddle Wheels, almost pathologically addicted to fund-raising. We had raised £368,734. The necessary work had cost £242,776. So, for the first time in the Society's history, we had a six-figure sum in hand (£125,958 to be precise) that was

The £8 million rebuild of Waverley *described in this chapter took place in two phases, both at George Prior's Norfolk shipyard. The ship made her last public sailing from Clevedon on 18th October 1999 and after spending several weeks stormbound at Avonmouth arrived at Great Yarmouth via Southampton on 21st December. Work started on 3rd January 2000 and within three weeks the sponsons, paddle wheels, funnels, boiler and fuel tanks had been removed and dismantling of the main engine was well under way. On 11th February she entered dry dock where the hull was extensively rebuilt, refurbished windows were fitted and much work took place on the main and lower decks. She is seen here, still without her sponsons, being floated out of the dry dock on 20th April 2000.*

Nick James

not immediately needed. Of course it was a lot to us, but relatively speaking it was chicken-feed compared to the best part of the £2.5-£3 million needed every year to keep *Waverley*, *Balmoral* and *Kingswear Castle* sailing, the vast majority of which had to come from fares and on-board sales.

That £126,000 soon paled into insignificance, but Lady Luck was again going to play into our hands in a quite extraordinary way. In so far as the £126,000 paling into insignificance is concerned, here are some extracts from the Chairman's Comments in the Autumn 1995 edition of "Paddle Wheels":

"*Kingswear Castle* is in fine fettle. "New" hull, shining and silent engines, cosy saloons. But have you looked closely at the deck lately? By the turn of the century it will have to be renewed. The ship's boiler is fine now, but is over thirty years old, and will need attention or possible replacement within the foreseeable future. The cost of these two projects combined goes well into six figures."

"*Waverley* is in fine fettle too. But she is nearly fifty years old. By the time they reached her age, nearly all her predecessors had been through one - or in some cases two - World Wars. And what happened on their conversion back to civilian use? Most of them were virtually rebuilt. *Waverley's* continental

sisters, which work fresh-water lakes, are also rebuilt, and they emerge "as new" from, for example, the covered shipyard of Lake Lucerne."

"*Waverley*, let us be honest, has never been rebuilt in the same sort of way. What has been achieved with her is nothing short of a miracle, but she is in essence a forty-eight-year-old ship kept operational by supremely skilled and dedicated repair and maintenance. That cannot go on forever without a real rebuild becoming necessary.

"Waverley Excursions' Engineering Superintendant Ian McMillan has now taken the bull by the horns... I will not frighten you with the cost, other than to say it runs well into seven figures."

Just in time, the Heritage Lottery Fund(HLF) had been set up and was the only way this project could have been funded. Their support, if obtained, would need very substantial partnership funding, not least from PSPS.

Thus began the *Waverley* Rebuild. The project developed over many iterations until it finally started in late 1999, was partially completed in August 2000, and fully completed in the winter of 2002-2003 at a total cost of some £8 million. The Society again had a unity of purpose and commitment second to none, and the fund raising continued apace. Through the efforts of PSPS members, the quite astonishing sum of £1.1 million was achieved for *Waverley*, and *Kingswear Castle* got her new deck and new boiler as well. Substantial support for *Waverley's* Rebuild was also secured from the European Regional Development Fund, as well, of course, as the HLF. And, although it's a separate story and was separately financed, MV *Balmoral*, then *Waverley's* fleetmate and support ship, received new engines, decks, and restored passenger accommodation, almost all thanks to the efforts of the same people working with different hats on. PSPS had, in 10 years, raised £1,323,500 on its own account from its own members and from the ships' passengers, without professional help. This was over five times the original perceived "ceiling" of £250,000.

The above is, put as briefly as someone as wordy as me can put it, the nub of what happened between 1990 and 2003. It has been documented elsewhere in other ways, and is the essence of what happened in those years insofar as PSPS is concerned. There were of course all sorts of other things going on, and more personal tales to be told. I hope that some of the latter will not be out of place, as they have not been told elsewhere.

Some time after Ian McMillan (*Waverley's* and *Balmoral's* Engineering Director) had "taken the bull by the horns" as mentioned above, he prepared an initial document for the HLF. It was not confined to engineering matters, but of necessity dealt with all aspects of the proposed rebuild of *Waverley*. It didn't make much mention of the interior outfit of the ship, but did suggest that it should be done in "Art Nouveau" style and made mention of Charles Rennie Mackintosh, the celebrated Glasgow-born architect who had died some 20 years before *Waverley* was built and who, as far as I'm aware, never designed a ship's interior. When we eventually made contact with the HLF, this met with what can only be described as fierce if bemused opposition, and we were told in no uncertain terms that to meet with HLF approval the ship's passenger accommodation would have to be restored to as near its 1947 configuration as was possible.

Ian had uncanny powers of persuasion, and somehow managed to make me agree to be the Waverley director responsible for the ship's internal outfit. I was also to be in charge of the overall application to the HLF. No pressure, then...

Ian, for obvious reasons, was Project Director and responsible for the engineering and technical elements of the HLF application. I wrote the short volume that dealt with the ship's heritage, and Dennis Oxby of Second City Associates was contracted to write the business plan. Those who knew Ian will be aware that, being a perfectionist, he had a tendency to meet deadlines with little room for manoeuvre. He also wrote almost everything by hand, in handwriting that looked artistically beautiful from a distance but on close examination often proved to be almost, if not totally, illegible. He had completed his part of the Rebuild application in his inimitable handwriting and given it to a lady in Lynmouth to word-process. The deadline arrived for him to get it to me. That very

Afloat again, and three of the four new sponson houses, which were prefabricated ashore, have been fitted. Large holes in the upper deck mark the position of the engine and boiler rooms.　　Nick James

The crankshaft main bearing being examined by Project Director Ian MacMillan and Project Manager Gordon Reid.　　Nick James

The main engine partially reassembled.　　Nick James

day, Ian was aboard *Waverley* as Chief Engineer and the lady delivered it to him at Ilfracombe. I was due to pick it up, in both a hard copy and on disc, at Clevedon Pier that same evening.

Ian went through it, making handwritten additions, all the way from Ilfracombe to Clevedon where *Waverley* disembarked all her passengers. He carried on making additions for the best part of another hour, while the ship delayed her departure for her overnight anchorage, the tide fell rapidly, and Ian's crewmates, who were going to end up stopping work an hour later than anticipated, became more and more adventurous in their use of language. Eventually, I was given the document in both hard and electronic form and I headed off back home to Southampton while *Waverley* hurtled into the night to go to anchor.

The following day, I looked at the document, which amounted to about 300 pages and had a lengthy and detailed index, itself occupying about twenty pages. One of the first things I noticed was that the page numbers mentioned in the index bore no relation to the reality of the document as typed. Whether Ian had handwritten the index and made it refer to his handwritten page numbers which remained

Gordon Reid standing beside a refurbished paddle wheel frame, ready to be fitted after dry docking. Nick James

unchanged by the lady in Lynmouth, or whether she had done it from scratch and got it wrong, I shall never know. I do know that it took days to fix! And I wonder if anyone ever used it...

There were numerous other things that needed to be sorted out before the document could be handed over to the HLF, mostly due to the lady in Lynmouth having little engineering knowledge and therefore being even more at a disadvantage when deciphering Ian's script. One of these is worth mentioning.

At a late stage, and after the document had been typed, Ian had instructed the lady to change the acronym "WEL" to "Waverley Excursions Limited". As a result, whenever a certain method of repairing or fabricating steel parts was referred to throughout the document (which was very often), the following sort of thing would appear:

"The port paddle frame is to be crack-tested and repaired where necessary by Waverley Excursions Limited ding."

Yes, the word "welding" had become "Waverley Excursions Limited ding" every time it was used in the whole document.

The lady from Lynmouth had simply got her word-processing software to automatically replace the letters "wel" wherever they appeared with "Waverley Excursions Limited". She probably didn't have the time to do anything else! I forget how many hours it took to sort it out, but I clearly remember deliberately leaving one example of it uncorrected. Nobody ever mentioned it to me; not Ian, not the HLF experts and monitors, no Company directors, nobody. Which part of *Waverley* was repaired using the lost technique of Waverley Excursions Limited ding, I don't know; I have so far not spotted it. Hopefully, it's not below the waterline!

Negotiations with the HLF, once they had received the full application, were not always plain sailing but were always cordial. They initially appointed as Project Monitor the UK's leading Naval Architect with a special interest in historic ships, well-known for his work with the National Maritime Museum. At our first meeting which involved him, he was there together with the HLF Project Officer, an HLF museum expert, Ian and me. The Naval Architect took a very practical and sensible line with which Ian and I fully agreed, saying that while those areas of the ship visible to passengers should be restored with as much historical sensitivity as possible, those areas not seen by the public (for example the boiler-room) should incorporate modern technology which would make the ship cheaper and easier, and even possible, to operate in the modern world. A "frank discussion" ensued with the HLF's museum expert. At one point, the Naval Architect said: "No-one in their right mind would suggest installing a double-ended coal-fired Scotch boiler". (This was the type of boiler fitted to *Waverley* in 1947, fuelled by men with shovels.) Immediately, the museum expert said "I don't see why not" and a fierce argument ensued between the HLF's museum expert and their Naval Architect. Ian and I were reduced to amused spectators. We were less amused when, a few days later, it emerged that the sensible Naval Architect had been removed from the project. Despite that, *Waverley* was fitted with two modern oil-fired boilers.

Other complex matters had less of a humorous side. New regulations for domestic passenger ships were in draft form while we were planning the Rebuild. This meant that we had

Looking aft along the starboard side of the dining saloon, showing the new plating completed in dry dock and the refurbished window frames.   Nick James

The completed dining saloon, restored to 1947 style with period flooring, light fittings and newly-constructed furniture.   Nick James

to plan with the assumption that the regulations would apply when they had not been ratified either by the EU or by the British government. Through the national organisation "Heritage Afloat", and particularly through the efforts of their Chairman, David Morgan, we succeed in getting the EU to exempt all ships built before 1955, or replicas of ships built before 1955, from the impending regulations. This seemed to be a triumph, and would have been but for an established British tradition. The EU effectively exempted historic ships from the new regulations, but left it to the individual member states to legislate for their safe operation. The British

government decided to apply the new proposed EU regulations in full to historic ships, thus in effect overturning the EU exemption within the UK. Britain is famous in the other member states for "gold-plating" EU regulations; this was another example of it and left us in exactly the same position of having to plan for regulations which at the time were uncertain. A huge amount of ingenuity had to go into, for example, fireproofing what look like traditional wooden bulkheads by giving them and the doors contained within them a steel core. Even the use of real wood in any form was contentious. It was solved, again through the good offices of

Phase 2 of the rebuild took place between 14th October 2001 and 9th June 2002 and concentrated on the forward end of the ship. Too wide to fit into the local drydock, Waverley was lifted out of the water on a submersible barge, and provided a startling sight for passing motorists. The bridge, forward deckhouse, Jeanie Deans bar, and crew accommodation were all rebuilt, more work carried out on the engine, new masts fitted and fresh timber laid on the promenade deck.

Richard Clammer collection

Before and after. The Jeanie Dean's *bar stripped for deck renewal and after completion with its carefully chosen 1940s fabric and flooring.*

Nick James

Heritage Afloat and David Morgan. We reached an agreement with the British authorities that, if we installed a fire-extinguishing sprinkler system with double the number of heads that would normally be specified, we could use real wood and real wood veneers in the passenger accommodation.

And so on and on... The open engine-room, fire-exits, ventilation, adequate crew accommodation, passenger numbers and numbers of seats on board (I even resorted to thinking about enquiring if toilet bowls could be counted as seats, but didn't...); these and many, many other issues unthought of by the majority of fare-paying passengers had to be teased out and answers found which did not compromise historical integrity.

Going back for a moment to 1992, there appeared in the Winter issue of *Paddle Wheels* an article under the headline "*Waverley* to cross Atlantic!". The article was an appeal for volunteers aboard both *Balmoral* and *Waverley* for winter work. Its last sentences read: "And if you are still wondering about the headline: no, it's entirely untrue. But at least it got you to read this".

One of those who actually did read this was a certain Gordon Reid, then working for IBM in Renfrewshire. As a result, he decided to volunteer on board *Waverley*. Thanks to Ian McMillan's legendary powers of persuasion, seven years later Gordon became *Waverley's* Project Manager for the Rebuild. And, as the hapless author of that article in Paddle Wheels, if things were getting more than a bit difficult during the Rebuild, or afterwards when Gordon was *Waverley's* Chief Engineer, or even later when he was relief engineer having moved on to the *Hebridean Princess*, Gordon would approach me with a glint in his eye and the words "You b*****d. It's all your fault". Gordon was essential to the success of the project. Knowledgeable, efficient, seemingly unflappable and when flappable keeping it to himself, he was one of the rocks on which the project's success depended. Another, of course, was George Prior's shipyard in Great Yarmouth. The quality of their management

A revitalised Waverley *at speed off Penarth on Sunday 15th October 2000, pictured from* Balmoral *which met her at sea to celebrate the paddler's first return to the Bristol Channel after the Phase 1 rebuild .*

Chris Jones

and workforce was without equal; the results peerless. It was a massive loss when the yard closed not long after the *Waverley* Rebuild was completed.

So it all came together, thanks to the astonishing unity and sense of purpose of PSPS members and the vision, skill, dedication, sheer unrelenting hard graft and goodwill of those professionals who led and undertook the work and the colleagues and volunteers who supported them with utter reliability. It happened too because PSPS and the owning and operating companies shared the same values and the same expectations, and worked together to make things happen. Each valued the contribution of the other, and none more so than Ian McMillan, who was the greatest rock upon which the project depended, and whose untimely and tragic death after he had left *Waverley* subsequent to the Rebuild deprived us of so much. There were, of course, differences of opinion and of style, but everyone was singing from the same hymn sheet. That may have been made easier by the fact that, both for the initial campaign and for the *Waverley* Rebuild, the alternative was oblivion for the ships, the traditions they keep alive and the pleasure they give to thousands upon thousands of people. Or at best the future would have been for them to have become museum pieces, the life gone out of them, gradually deteriorating as money could not be found to maintain them adequately. That was, and to us still is, unthinkable.

When *Waverley* was in the final stages of the first phase of the Rebuild, my commitments to my paid employment meant that I was out of the country. I heard her paddle-beat on trials on my mobile phone in a minibus in Spain. When I got back, she was already on her way round to Glasgow via the Pentland Firth. As soon as I could, I got the sleeper to Fort William and made it to Kyle of Lochalsh in time to see her sweep into the pier at 10.30pm on 17 August 2000 to pick up stores so that she would be ready for her first sailing from Glasgow the following evening. It was my first sight of the completed vision we had started working on five years earlier. I shall never forget the impression she made as she silently approached the pier. It was like seeing a 1947 photograph of the ship come to life. We'd done it! And in the ensuing days, it was wonderful to hear the comments of those few enthusiasts who remembered the ship when she was new. One of them summed it up: "I keep finding things I'd

A job well done. Project Director Ian MacMillan and Project Manager Gordon Reid on board Balmoral *at Penarth pier on 15th October 2000. In the background* Waverley *awaits her first post-rebuild Bristol Channel sailing.*   Nick James

forgotten were there. This isn't a new *Waverley*; it's the old *Waverley* that's found herself again".

But in some ways she was a new *Waverley*. The old *Waverley* had been a little overweight even when new, more so with age, and her performance suffered as a result, not least because her paddle-wheels were often over-immersed. In the Rebuild, every effort was made to reduce weight. Funnels and deckhouses were replaced using aluminium, not steel. The rails around the promenade deck are hollow whereas before they had been solid, and so on and on. The result was beautifully commented on by Ian Muir, former first engineer of *Waverley* in the early preservation years. He saw her come up the Firth of Clyde on her return from Great Yarmouth. "I was delighted to see that she was so light-footed", he said. As a consequence, her performance, especially in less than ideal sea-conditions, was transformed for the better.

To the extent that *Waverley* is the old *Waverley*, she is the old *Waverley* but with modern safety and other technical features making it possible to continue operating her in the 21st century. Now, nearly 20 years further on, much, much more has changed. There is now nobody left of working age who remembers how ships like *Waverley* were operated when they were commonplace. Even if there were, their experience would be of limited value as the world has moved on to a position where it is simply not possible to operate a ship in the same way any more. The environment has changed, the infrastructure has changed in that there are far fewer places with available piers and jetties to use, the climate has changed, the regulatory framework has changed beyond recognition, holiday habits and social habits have changed. Yet *Waverley* and *Kingswear Castle* in operation have an ongoing attraction and appeal that would become and have become timeless. Partly this is because they are unique, even in the world of heritage transport preservation, in that they are still doing exactly what they were built to do where they were built to do it, and are being worked as hard, if not harder, than when they were new. In 1959, our founder Professor Alan Robinson saw the timeless appeal of these ships. That is why he set their preservation in motion 60 years ago. What has been achieved is little short of miraculous. Hats off to him, and long may the ships continue to delight their passengers!

On a magical early morning sailing from Oban to Fort William on 31st May 2009 Waverley *steams up a tranquil Loch Linnhe,the silence disturbed only by her own paddle beats.*

Richard Clammer

CHAPTER THIRTEEN

WAVERLEY ROUND THE COAST
Iain Quinn

Scotland

THE main calling points on the Clyde were established in 1975. The new Glasgow berth – Anderston Quay – was totally unique, and remains the company headquarters to this day. For 45 years it has been the link to Waverley's outside world, with PSPS leaflets by the thousand sent from here far and wide accompanying sailing tickets.

In 1975/76 *Waverley* travelled all over the Firth, with regular unusual calls at Ayr and Campbeltown, and rarities such as Stranraer, using timetables drawn on the knowledge of George Train, a well -known PSPS member who died in 2006. From 1975-1977 George devised long-forgotten itineraries including Sunday transfers at Largs and Dunoon to *TS Queen Mary* –

Waverley continuing to Ayr and the *Mary* to Glasgow – surely an enthusiast's dream today!

There are high hopes that Helensburgh's future may be more certain in 2019, but a call there during a PSPS charter in September 1977 convinced the local Council to put the pier and approaches on their repair list, allowing it to be a vital artery for Waverley's business from 1978 – 2018. The Clyde piers such as Largs, Rothesay, Brodick, Dunoon and Ayr have all seen changes since the first season, and although Largs was lengthened and given wonderful fendering, the calling place at Dunoon has become a concrete breakwater, barely able to take *Waverley*.

Later, in the 1990s, Captain Steve Michel put in the timetable

Waverley sweeps through the narrows in the Kyles of Bute, en route to Tighnabruaich on 25th August 2012.

Ashley Gill

During one of her annual visits to the Western Isles, Waverley is pictured from the Skye Bridge en route to Broadford from Kyle on 27th April 2011.

Ashley Gill

one-off calls at Otter Ferry, Portencross and Carradale, piers not visited for many years. Portencross had closed in 1914 and Carradale in 1940, and these calls allowed hundreds of passengers to take part in history. Girvan, a convenient port for Ailsa Craig cruises, was re-established as a *Waverley* call in 1975, again with superb results.

Unique one- day- only visits certainly command attention. *Waverley's* annual visits to the Hebrides started in 1981, taking the ship to a very special area, rich in grandeur, and made totally magical by the sound of a paddle steamer. PSPS members have swelled the support for *Waverley* in some of the remotest corners of Britain, and hundreds of school children have boarded at places like Uig and Dunvegan in Skye, and Lochmaddy, Lochboisdale, Stornoway and Tarbert in the Outer Hebrides. Now in their 30s, I wonder if they remember *Waverley*?

The Northwest Of England, Ireland & Wales

The North West of England, Isle of Man, Northern and Southern Ireland and North Wales were all short spell visits which attracted incredible support including that of local PSPS members. Willie Coats single- handedly made arrangements in Ireland, Richard Danielson in the Isle of Man, and a good many in Llandudno got behind the efforts to bring *Waverley* to their ports, and made them work.

While the Isle of Man has good berths, regulations now prohibit departures from Garlieston and Whitehaven to the Island. Llandudno for its size has a pin head berth which is very susceptible to weather, but *Waverley* arriving or leaving Llandudno is particularly impressive and commands total attention. The Northern Irish visits were very well supported but difficult logistically, so following calls there in 1985 and 1986 there was a long gap before she returned in 2001, unfortunately with much poorer support. However the Republic of Ireland saw *Waverley* call at 13 locations, including Dundalk, New Ross, Cork and Kinsale.

Waverley has called at Heysham, Fishguard, Rosslare, St Ives and Penzance during light passages, and for a few years rare pictures were possible as a result of charters from Holyhead and Belfast.

Bristol Channel

Waverley first visited the Bristol Channel in 1979, this being the end of the P&A Campbell era, giving an opening for another area to help keep the ship in business. The Bristol Channel season started as a few days, and in 2018 was the same, but at its peak in 1985 *Waverley* spent six weeks in the area, and performed 21 charters. A number of ports and calling points are no longer visited or are replaced by coaches, and notable losses are Newport and also Sharpness where *Waverley's* arrival was amazing to watch as she steamed up the Severn with the

With the famous Clifton Suspension Bridge in the background, Waverley *makes an impressive arrival at the Tongue Head at the entrance to Bristol's Floating Harbour on 30th May 1998. Having got her ropes ashore, the ship will then be warped around the dock head until her stern is in the lock approach and she is pointing down steam ready for departure on a day trip to Ilfracombe.*

Ashley Gill

Waverley refuelling at Poole Quay on her first ever visit to the port, 1978.

Chris Phillips (Swanage)

fierce tide to arrive at high water, and having passed the pier at 21 knots, she would turn to make her approach at about six knots full ahead, thumping against the tide. On departure she was with the tide again, allowing a fast passage to Clevedon.

Clevedon was closed for years, and thanks to *Waverley* and *Balmoral* it reopened in 1989. PSPS was so active in this major project a few members were elected to the Pier Trust, ensuring their involvement for years ahead. PSPS members were utilised at Minehead on every call to assist with passenger transfers to and from the West Somerset Railway and steamer.

Terry Sylvester was based in Barry, and from here came almost all the *Waverley* timetables until General Manager David Duncanson arrived in the Glasgow office in 1979, thereafter taking over all publicity in Scotland, the Isle of Man and Ireland. At that time publicity leaflets were cut and paste, and notable for their drawings. John Nicolson contributed artwork for the timetables and advertisements, Joe Marshalsay for the timetables, and during the period from 1975 – 1977 June Bushell did all the coloured drawings on the timetables.

Of course operation on the Bristol Channel has always been challenging for the ship, especially when westerly winds create huge swells, and north, north westerly and easterly winds prevent calls at Ilfracombe. Fuelling is far more restricted now compared to the 1970s and 1980s, and charters have all but disappeared largely due to the demise of agent Tom Foden, whose ability to sign up charters was legendary.

Countless PSPS volunteers worked the souvenir shop on board, raising thousands for the ship, and particular mention must be made of Patrick Murrell and Lionel Vaughan, both wonderful, long-standing PSPS men with life-long affection for paddlers on the Channel. Pat organised many PSPS charters in the 1960s.

South Coast

Moving round to Devon and Cornwall, for a few years *Waverley* visited *Kingswear*, now again the home of *Kingswear Castle*, PSPS paddler number 1. Although these visits were great, they would have been so much better with *KC* there. Mevagissey, Torquay, Falmouth and St Mawes also saw *Waverley* calls, and on a single occasion there was a cruise west from Bournemouth, Swanage and Weymouth to Salcombe for a tender call. Very, very special.

On the Dorset coast, *Waverley* reopened Swanage in 1988, thanks to hard work by local PSPS members, some sadly no longer with us, but recognised at the time with memberships of the Pier Trust. For 30 years this calling point has offered unique links to the steam railway. Calls at Bournemouth too were first promoted in 1978 by valued local PSPS members such as Denis Thorogood and John Morse, and from 1979 by Geoff Ryder who by 2019 had become the last link with these

Waverley *arriving at Haldon Pier, Torquay, 25th April 1980.*   Les Ring/PSPS Collection

exceptional days. Wessex was a vibrant Branch, and its members took *Waverley* as their own.

I recall a packed *Waverley* at Swanage Pier, and after I had made the usual announcement about the ship now being at Swanage, and all tickets for inspection, followed by and we sail at 1830 for Bournemouth, a semi-naked man arrived on the pier riding a bike and carrying a traffic cone, bellowing 'Thursday is market day at Swanage, Thursday is market day at Wareham'. When I repeated the call for Swanage, he bellowed 'I am the official announcer here – that man is only practising'. Quick as a flash, I repeated his message about market days to loud laughter on board. He waved, cycled off, and never came back.

Poole was the quality berth needed for promotion, and was replaced by Swanage in 1988. Swanage was never the same as Poole Quay. Bournemouth is now a memory, but my recollection of the pier solid with people is as strong now as it was then.

Yarmouth (Isle of Wight) appeared on the timetable first in 1989, the pier has since been rebuilt twice, and has proved of immense value. The original piermaster, Les, would have moved mountains to allow calls for the *Waverley*, and became a valued friend to the crew. Similarly at Sandown, at the other end of the Island, Denis Bunce was again the power behind the pier, the franchise for which was held by Mark Rayment who

also owned Eastbourne and Llandudno. Denis was vital, and from memory also made arrangements at Southsea Clarence Pier pre Harbour Station days.

Southampton calls were originally arranged through the British Transport Docks Board, now Associated British Ports (ABP), and *Waverley* has visited many berths there. Her original calling point in 1978 was the Royal Pier, home of the Southampton, Isle of Wight and South of England Royal Mail Steam Packet Company Limited.

The Solent was the location of perhaps the most emotional two and a half days of Waverley's long career in preservation, namely the Spithead Review in June 1994. *Waverley* and *Balmoral* had an anchorage, and our passengers enjoyed the commemorations including the service at Southsea Common. In attendance were the QE2, *Canberra* and *Jeremiah O'Brien* amongst a vast number of naval craft. *Jeremiah O'Brien* was a preserved Liberty Ship which had sailed from USA, and on the Sunday we steamed to the NAB Tower with her. Their team saluted us, exchanging whistles galore, and over the PA system I said that I doubted whether we would ever witness this again, so three cheers for *Jeremiah* and her preservation team. They responded saying that *Waverley* was truly magnificent and full speed ahead to your preservation team. What a day of memories, and all because in 1974 the PSPS had agreed to take *Waverley* under their wing.

111

London's skyline has changed a great deal since Waverley's first visit. In this view the ship is arriving at Tower Pier on 5th October 2018.

Ashley Gill

Sussex has no calls by *Waverley* today, but in 1978/1979 she had four calls – Worthing, Hastings, Deal and Eastbourne. In fact Worthing was rebuilt in 2015, but not used since.

East Coast

There were eight calling points on the Kent Coast in 1980, whereas now there is only one – Whitstable. Margate has a coach connection to Whitstable, Folkestone is now unusable, and Dover is very costly. The Medway was the superb setting for the rendezvous with *Kingswear Castle* from 1987 to 2012, an event which saw both ships packed for the view of Britain's last two operational paddle steamers sailing side by side. PSPS members were absolutely vital in promoting *Waverley's* sailings in the Kent and Sussex areas, particularly in the initial stages. Deal and Hastings were only in use for two or three visits in the late 1970s, but Deal was used in 1980 for the 40th Anniversary of Dunkirk when Captain John Cameron DSC, master of the 1899 *Waverley* at Dunkirk, and of our *Waverley* in 1947, was present for the very poignant and emotional event. John died in 1989, so was not present for the 50th Anniversary in 1990 when *Waverley* was chartered by Holts Battlefield Tours and sailed with the entire small ships' flotilla. This was a very memorable and unique occasion, and took place in weather similar to that of 50 years before – windy and bright. These sailings used Dover and Ramsgate as Operation Dynamo had done, and on board there were recordings of Bertram Ramsey, Winston Churchill and Vera Lynn, along with flags from all the major companies that had pleasure steamers involved at Dunkirk.

The Thames

Like the South Coast, the Thames Estuary has seen changes to the number of calling points in the period of 40 years since the first visit. Southend is now basically tidal, Clacton and Great Yarmouth unusable, coaches replacing calls at Southwold and Ipswich, Gravesend has a new pontoon and others no longer used. Also much changed is the PSPS support, with huge thanks due to long serving volunteers such as Jerry Gold and, until recently, Roddy McKee who offered invaluable support for sailings in their area, and others who offered assistance with deliveries and stores. PSPS members were also involved in Walton and Great Yarmouth's piers which were rebuilt for *Waverley*. Thanks also go to the Tower Bridge Master, the Port of London Authority staff at Tower Pier, numerous tug masters, and PSPS members, all of whom have given great assistance to *Waverley* in London for 40 years.

The North Of England

The comments so far have related to the areas which still see calls by *Waverley*, but during the years from 1981 to 1983 she also visited ports in the Humber, North East England, the Forth and North East Scotland, very uncharted waters for her, albeit with LNER links in the Humber with the three paddlers *Tattershall*, *Wingfield* and *Lincoln Castles*, which at that time were all in existence although no longer sailing. The *Lincoln Castle* had been chartered by PSPS in the 1970s, and, like *Waverley*, was built by Inglis. Hull, New Holland and Goole were used by *Waverley*, and in 1983 when she made her last visit to the Humber.

Waverley passing through Tower Bridge on her first ever visit to London, 29th April 1978.   Les Ring/PSPS Collection

Waverley *at Scarborough, 23rd May 1981.*   Les Ring/PSPS Collection

Waverley *passing the site of Hawthorne Leslie's shipyard on the River Tyne, May 1981.*   CRSC/Dr Joe McKendrick Collection

Waverley *at Newcastle, 24th May 1981.* Les Ring/PSPS Collection

Not all piers are easy! Exceptionally steep gangways at River Pier, Alexandra Dock, Hull, on 19th May 1982. Les Ring/PSPS Collection

Further north, Scarborough, Middlesbrough, Hartlepool, and Blyth all had calls, and on the Tyne *Waverley* witnessed the final days of the Swan Hunters Yard with the Aircraft Carriers *Ark Royal, Illustrious* and *Invincible* under construction. *Waverley* welcomed *Invincible* home from the Falklands during her visit to the Solent in 1982. As a result of *Waverley's* visit to the area, Helen Strachan founded the PSPS North of England Branch, and subsequently *Balmoral's* visits helped to support the Branch.

East Scotland

On the Firth of Forth, *Waverley* steamed under the Railway Bridge, a spectacle which is still remembered today. The cruises round Bass Rock and along the Berwick Coast were heavily promoted by the Scottish Branch, but after visits to the Forth and Tay in 1981, 1982 and 1983, the condition of Granton Harbour contributed to the decision not to return, as did the stormy conditions which affected the sailings in 1983. *Balmoral* did make several trips to the area in later years as she could access calling points impossible for *Waverley*. It had been many years since the New Galloway Saloon Steam Packet Company last ran a paddle steamer in this area, and the Tay had seen the *Slieve Bearnagh* and *Marchioness of Bute*. Visits to Burntisland, Granton, Grangemouth, Dundee and Montrose were certainly unique. *Waverley* never made passenger calls north of Montrose, although she did call at Aberdeen for fuel in 1984, 2000 and 2003.

Incidents

Incidents with *Waverley* in 43 years have been very rare, but she has grounded three times. The first grounding was on the Gantocks on 15th July 1977, and this brought *Waverley's* Clyde cruising to a halt for 6 weeks. Bill McAlpine made available for no charge his small classic motor vessel *Queen of Scots* which helped to keep the WSN flag flying. She was not everybody's favourite ship, but did signal *Waverley's* return for as long as she kept sailing, and indeed the paddler reappeared at the

A famous and dramatic photograph of Waverley *pinned by the stern on the Gantocks off Dunoon on the afternoon of 15th July 1977. After the ship struck at 13.45 hours all passengers were landed safely but the falling tide left the ship stranded until just before midnight when she floated off. She subsequently moved to Govan dry dock under her own power, where repairs took six weeks. The ship survived what was undoubtedly the worst day in her career and proved the pessimists wrong by returning to service on 1st September.* Douglas McGowan Collection

beginning of September for a season which was extended to cover the Glasgow Autumn Holiday at the end of that month. Photographs of the Gantocks grounding make an interesting image, and show how this could have ended *Waverley's* career. However WSN fought to bring her back, and their will and determination grew. The PSPS fundraised and donations poured in, and PSPS members also promoted the sailings of *Queen of Scots*, meaning that she was surprisingly busy on some days.

In May 1999 *Waverley* grounded late at night at the Horseshoe Bend on Bristol's River Avon. This was also serious given the way the Avon tide ebbs very quickly, but the high calibre of *Waverley's* captain and engineers ensured she was refloated before any serious damage was done. The third incident was in 2010 when *Waverley* touched the bottom off Clevedon Pier.

These three groundings certainly stand out, but the world gets to hear about incidents involving such a unique and good-looking ship.

Paddle trouble, boiler worries and auxiliary machinery failures have happened occasionally, but are usually dealt with by the on-board engineers. In recent years paddle failures have been less frequent, due mainly to reduced running hours, but at least four spare paddles are carried on board as a precaution. In 2016, 2017 and 2018 it was the air pump and boiler controls which caused intermittent concerns, and thankfully in 2018 the air pump issues were eliminated.

PSPS Support For Waverley

Many PSPS members have contributed a huge variety of skills to assist during operation and over the winter. In the early days Chief Engineer Ian Muir led the volunteers ably and with much humour, and until recent times winter work was mainly done in-house. One major contributor was Tony Horn of Worthing who used his superb joinery and carpentry skills to create new bridge wings, a front for the new aluminium wheelhouse, external doors, paddle box steps, stairs at the purser's office, all 36 large windows round the hull, fan boards and much more. I remember assisting him by taking measurements for the 36 windows, and I was fascinated to see him fitting them. Tony is just one example of how PSPS members can make a real contribution.

The reopening of Clevedon was mentioned earlier, and on the Clyde a fight from 1983 – 1994 resulted in the reopening

Waverley approaching Swanage Pier on 19th September 2017.   Chris Phillips

of Millport Pier on the Isle of Cumbrae, only to see it now closed again. Keppel, just a few minutes from Millport Old Pier, is a small concrete jetty which was not approved for use from 1983 – 1994, but has now been made available for use. The Old Pier must reopen, and local PSPS members fight on as I write.

Blairmore Pier on Loch Long was reopened in 2004 thanks to an approach from Agnes Harvey who had purchased the former waiting room and surrounding land including the pier. Many fundraising events and the tireless efforts of the Blairmore Pier Trust led by chairman Dr Joe McKendrick brought the pier back into use after over 30 years of closure. This kind of achievement does not happen often but thanks to *Waverley* and PSPS this one succeeded. Sadly following Joe's passing in 2012 the Pier Trust folded, but I was proud to have been an honorary member.

Tarbert, Loch Fyne, a major cruise destination for *Waverley*, faced closure in 2008. However a WEL team including the late Ian McMillan, myself and Andy O'Brian went to the village to present the case for saving it, and with support from Tarbert Harbour Commission we won our case. Both at Blairmore and Tarbert, Ian carried out a survey which helped enormously, because often it is only simple repairs which are required.

Another example of the close affinity between PSPS and WSN was the reopening of the Britannia Pier at Great Yarmouth and Walton on the Naze for *Waverley* calls thanks to the efforts of *Waverley's* captain together with the late Ken Adams, an active Paddle & Pleasure Steamer Trust member, all under the direction of Bernard See. Keeping a close relationship between PSPS and *Waverley* was essential, and key to that was Terry Sylvester who made it his job to know as many of the piermasters and harbour officials as possible at all

of *Waverley's* calling points, leading to many operational benefits. The on-board farewell announcements thanking pier staff which were made automatically to much public support also helped to give the vessel priority when last minute alterations owing to bad weather led to alterations to her planned schedule.

PSPS involvement at piers was more a South Coast and Thames benefit for *Waverley*, but to take one example at Swanage, the local Pier Trust, and Peter Lamb in particular, set up in 1988 a publicity kiosk with his daughter who was persuaded to carry a red, white and black cheese board advertising local promotions. On the Thames PSPS members were used at Tower Pier and Southend to lessen the pressure on the purser who was trying to cater for a turnover of 1300 passengers. On the Bristol Channel, Terry's office staff often assisted at Penarth, and at Ilfracombe assistance was given by many long-standing PSPS supporters including Albert Fisher, Keith Draper and Fred Birmingham as well as by the loyal harbour team. PSPS publicity was given prominence at the wee kiosk at Ilfracombe, highlighting the work of the organisation.

It was always difficult to deal with *Waverley's* logistics away from home, especially if she was storm bound and didn't make the timetabled calls. Local PSPS members were vital in these cases especially where coaches were involved.

PSPS chartered *Waverley* mainly on the Clyde, where a pattern of evening cruises developed each year around her birthday on 16th June. Trips to Loch Long and Loch Goil were the norm for many years, but in more recent years there have been more imaginative excursions, some of which have sold out, much to our satisfaction.

Day charters have been much rarer, but a few are worthy of

Towards the end of a long day's sailing, Waverley pulls away from Clevedon Pier en route for Penarth on 8th September 2012.

Ashley Gill

The Second Snark *tendering* Waverley *at anchor off Ormidale, Loch Riddon on 11th July 2012.* Paul Semple

mention. On 24th May 1975, *Waverley's* first public sailing in preservation was a PSPS National Charter organised in Scotland, with the ship uniquely flying the Society flag from her foremast. The excursion left Glasgow at 9am, and returned at 3.55am the following morning due to paddle trouble. Again on this day PSPS proved their worth with George Train, a founding WSN Director, a transport expert and the man behind *Waverley's* Clyde timetable in 1975 – 1977 organising a special BR train from Gourock back to Paisley and Glasgow after 1am for those who did not want to sail home. It was a day of euphoric spirit, but also a learning curve.

In September 1978 *Waverley* and PSPS united again for a special visit to Lamlash Bay for a ferry landing by tender Eilean Mhor at Lamlash Pier. Much later, in 2012, *Waverley*, PSPS and the Coastal Cruising Association united for a re-enactment of a PSPS September 1972 outing to Loch Riddon, where a ferry landing at Ormidale was offered using *MV The Second Snark*, built by Denny of Dumbarton in 1938. As it happened, this lovely wee vessel was near decommissioning and it was superb to offer the same pairing of vessels as 40 years before. The excursion could happen again as *The Snark* is home once more on the Clyde and now part of her own preservation project. Fingers crossed.

2014 was the 40th Anniversary of WSN

taking ownership of *Waverley* from Caledonian MacBrayne in the James Watt Dock in Greenock, so on 8th August 2014 *Waverley* sailed to Ardrossan, her first call there since 1985. Leaving Ardrossan she was full with supporters wishing to mark the occasion, including those who brought the project to life all those years ago.

As I sit writing, the 60th year of PSPS and the 50th year of PSPS in Scotland is upon us, and I am reminded that PSPS is *Waverley*, and *Waverley* is PSPS. As the *Waverley* publicity said 'In association with the Paddle Steamer Preservation Society'. Long may it be so.

Waverley has been centre stage at numerous local and national events during her time in operational preservation. On this occasion, amid great celebrations, she officially reopened the restored Clevedon Pier on 27th May 1989, thereby adding a vital calling point for her and Balmoral's Bristol Channel operations. All passengers on that day were issued with commemorative tickets and certificates. R. Clammer Collection

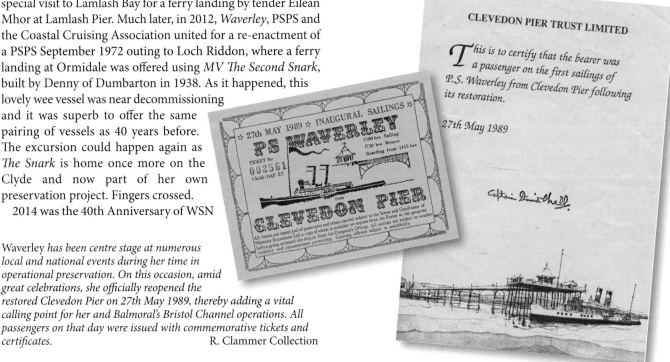

Balmoral arrives at Portishead from her overnight anchorage to collect passengers for an early morning 'Sunrise Cruise' up the Severn Estuary to Lydney where a large crowd joined her for a trip to Ilfracombe, 1st September 2008.

R Clammer

CHAPTER FOURTEEN

PSPS, BALMORAL AND OTHER MOTOR VESSELS

Jeremy Gold

When PSPS was founded in 1959 it was, by definition, concerned with the preservation of paddle steamers and encouraging their owners to retain them in service for as long as possible. However screw vessels had been in operation on British rivers and coastal waters since the mid-nineteenth century, originally steam powered but with motor vessels – usually diesel – on the scene from the early twentieth century.

As well as being interested in the particular features of paddle steamers, many PSPS members derived their main pleasure from the actual sailings regardless of the type of vessel. This distinction showed itself in the formation of the Coastal Cruising Association(CCA) in 1964 by a group of PSPS members who felt that the latter did not really meet their needs. Initially there was some acrimony, but this subsided and the CCA continues to this day as a successful unincorporated society encouraging an interest in cruising coastal and inland waterways. The two societies have many dual members. and many charters of small motor vessels by PSPS branches for (mostly) out of season social and fund-raising cruises – most notably the Scottish Branch Christmas period trips- now run jointly with PSPS's old friends the Coastal Cruising Association.

So far as ship operation is concerned, Waverley Steam Navigation (WSN) chartered *MV Queen of Scots* (on a reduced schedule) to cover for *Waverley* after the Gantocks grounding in 1977, thus enabling the company to maintain a cash flow and retain key staff whilst the paddler was out of service during the peak holiday season. There was also a single evening charter of *MV Clyde* to cover for a (very rare) breakdown of *Kingswear Castle* on the Medway.

This concept of having a second ship to aid business continuity and share overhead costs resulted in a group of *Waverley* supporters purchasing *MV Shanklin* from Sealink's Isle of Wight operation in 1980. Ownership was vested in a separate company (Firth of Clyde Steam Packet Co.) and in 1981, renamed *MV Prince Ivanhoe*, she was operated by WEL primarily on the Bristol Channel where P&A Campbell's service with *MV Balmoral* had ceased at the end of the previous season.

When she re-entered passenger service under the WEL flag in April 1986, Balmoral *appeared with a white hull and buff funnel, reminiscent of the large private yachts of the 1930s. In addition to her core Bristol Channel services, her size and manoeuvrability meant that she could visit many smaller ports around the UK coast which were inaccessible to* Waverley. *She soon earned the title of Britain's most widely-travelled excursion steamer. In this view she is seen arriving at Inverness during 1988.*

Gordon Wilson

After a difficult start, *Prince Ivanhoe's* loadings were coming good but the venture came to a premature end on 3rd August 1981 when she ran over an uncharted obstruction off the Gower coast and had to be beached. As with *Waverley* and *Kingswear Castle*, expenditure on *Prince Ivanhoe* had necessarily been kept under close control. One area affected was the insured value and the damage to the ship proved too costly for her to be refloated and repaired. *Prince Ivanhoe* thus had to be abandoned to the underwriters before her long-term prospects could really be judged. *Prince Ivanhoe's* short life meant that, although she was operated by WEL and benefitted from voluntary support from PSPS members, her role as a motor vessel within the ambit of a society devoted to the preservation of paddle steamers never really became a matter for discussion.

Four Chairmen: Jon Holyoak of the Balmoral Restoration Fund, Terry Sylvester of Waverley Steam Navigation Co. Ltd., Malcolm Cockell of Paddle Steam Navigation (Kingswear Castle) and Nigel Coombes of the PSPS; all pictured on Waverley's bridge wing during a sailing from Sharpness to Ilfracombe on 2nd June 1985. Mike Warrington / Nigel Coombes Collection

Despite the loss of *Prince Ivanhoe* the idea of running a second ship to support *Waverley* remained alive, but it was not until 1985 that anything suitable became available at an acceptable (i.e. low) cost. This was *Balmoral* which, after its withdrawal by Campbells, had ended up as an unsuccessful floating restaurant in Dundee. In like manner to *Shanklin / Prince Ivanhoe*, the ship was purchased with private funds and ownership vested in a separate company, Helseam Ltd., which was later renamed Balmoral Excursions Ltd. Despite being out of service for several years, the ship was able to be sailed under her own power to Glasgow where she was laid up pending plans for her return to service.

Unlike *Shanklin*, which had been in good condition when purchased and needed relatively little work for WSN service, *Balmoral* needed much to be done to bring her up to scratch,

Balmoral *being rebuilt in one of the dry docks at Clydebank Engineering Ltd., Govan, early in 1986. Note the new dining saloon under construction on the former car deck. When PSPS Chairman Nigel Coombes paid a visit to see the work in progress, both the transformation of the vessel and the shipyard's sanitary arrangements left an indelible mark on his memory, for he later wrote: "Any proud Scot will have enjoyed the porcelain majesty of the lavatories of Rothesay Pier, christened, I believe, by the Prince of Wales. But few will have experienced the basic, redbrick design of the Govan fundamentals." Odd what sticks in the mind!*
Gordon Wilson

Between 1992 and 1996 Balmoral *appeared in a number of different paint schemes before finally adopting the classic livery of P & A Campbell's White Funnel Fleet. Here she is seen with a dark green hull and buff funnel during a visit to Blackpool in 1992.*   Gordon Wilson

including construction of a new wheelhouse and a dining saloon on what had originally been her open car deck. This necessitated substantial fund raising but, unlike for *Waverley* or *Kingswear Castle*, PSPS was not able to contribute directly given that *Balmoral* was not a paddle steamer. However many PSPS members were likely to want to support *Balmoral*, for a mixture of reasons: interest in the ship herself; interest in the expanded opportunities she could offer for coastal cruising; the belief that *Waverley* would benefit from having a running mate and (perhaps more subtly) a need to offer a full season of sailings in the Bristol Channel if the costly piers at places such as Penarth and Ilfracombe were to be maintained for use by *Waverley* in the latter's short but at that time lucrative season in that area. Thus it was that leading PSPS members, including Terry Sylvester, Jon Holyoak and Pat Murrell, established a Balmoral Restoration Fund and PSPS provided facilities to circulate their material and published reports about *Balmoral* in Paddle Wheels.

In 1986 *Balmoral* duly re-entered service under the command of Captain Steve Michel, who had been Chief Officer on *Waverley* for several years. A brief introductory period on the Bristol Channel included adventurous sailings on the Gloucester Canal – the largest ship ever to go to Gloucester – followed by visits around Britain(in like manner to *Waverley's* programmes since 1978) before reintroducing high season sailings to the Bristol Channel for the first time since 1981.

Over the years that followed WEL used *Balmoral* to revive the Bristol Channel market, and both *Waverley* and *Balmoral* were served by WEL's ownership of the small launch *Westward Ho* which worked as flit boat at Lynmouth, taking passengers ashore from the ships as they anchored off the picturesque harbour town. *Balmoral* also extended her around-Britain schedules to take advantage of the fact that her lesser beam and (as a screw ship) greater manoeuvrability enabled her to visit many locations which were out of *Waverley's* reach. In doing so she extended the range to include regular visits to the Isle of Man, Northern Ireland and Eire (including some west coast ports) and one-off trips to the Scilly Isles and to Boulogne.

Although not formally part of the PSPS fleet (although in 1992 her ownership was transferred to Waverley Steam Navigation), *Balmoral* benefitted substantially from the support of PSPS members in terms of matters such as publicity distribution and fund- raising raffles aboard ship. She, in turn, benefitted the society by sustaining the membership of the Bristol Channel and the North of England & North Wales Branches. She also fulfilled her function as cash-flow guarantor for WEL on the small number of occasions when *Waverley* fell prey to breakdown, sometimes relinquishing her own schedule in order to take over *Waverley's*. One example of this was when,in autumn 1987, she covered for a broken down *Waverley* down on the South Coast and Thames. Her scheduled service on the Clyde was in turn covered by a charter by WEL of

Balmoral *arrives at Llandudno Pier in the evening sunshine on 7th September 2015.*   R. Clammer

MV Southsea (a near sister of *Shanklin/Prince Ivanhoe*).

The success of both *Waverley* and *Balmoral* in continuing the tradition of large ship coastal cruising was critically dependant on the voluntary and (from 1987) charitable support of PSPS and its members, so it is perhaps no surprise that the status of *Balmoral* – particularly when fund raising was needed – was debated within the society from time to time. Discussion took place at society AGMs and in the columns of Paddle Wheels as to whether PSPS should expand its legal powers to include motor vessels, or contrariwise, was *Balmoral* really an asset to the operation?

On the first question, extension of powers to cover motor vessels was always opposed by the society's Council of Management. The two main reasons were that some members – not necessarily a majority but certainly a significant number – were interested only in paddle steamers and would not wish to see their money given elsewhere, and a fear that opening the door to motor vessels would result in applications for support for many older vessels – doubtless good causes – which PSPS membership and funding could not sustain and which would therefore detract from the ability to support paddlers.

On the second question, the answer seemed to depend on what one meant by "an asset to the operation". In direct financial terms *Balmoral* was certainly not a big money spinner as, although cheaper to operate than *Waverley*, she lacked the popular appeal that the words "paddle steamer" are able to conjure up amongst the public and was therefore more difficult to market. An analysis of her finances in the mid 1990s, with careful allocation of overhead expenditure between the two WSN / WEL ships, suggested that her financial results were at best neutral. However *Balmoral's* presence and her ability to visit places barred to *Waverley* definitely enabled the PSPS message and membership to spread more extensively. This gave the society added strength and therefore benefitted both *Waverley* and *Kingswear Castle*.

If *Balmoral* was, perhaps, a small loss maker, this was probably justified by her role in providing continuity of business when *Waverley* was in trouble, and also by the fact that she provided an excellent training ground for crew who could learn the increasingly unfamiliar skills needed for coastal cruising before moving on to the more difficult *Waverley*. In addition, and perhaps conclusively, it seems inconceivable that the major reconstruction of the berthing facilities which took place at Clevedon, Penarth and Ilfracombe piers in the 1990s would have gone ahead without *Balmoral's* provision of main summer season sailings, and without this work there would by now be no *Waverley* sailings on the Bristol Channel.

In 2002, with the advantage of *Balmoral* now being owned by WSN as a registered charity, Heritage Lottery Fund support was obtained for her to be re-engined. While her original

One of Balmoral's *original Sirron diesel engines being lifted out of the ship in Abel's Albion Dry Dock at Bristol on Monday 7th April 2003.*
Nigel Coombes

engines were of considerable heritage value, spare parts by then had all to be specially manufactured and by modern standards they were noisy and thus obtrusive for passengers. The new engines both reduced costs and – aided by fully sealing the engine room – provided a better sailing experience. This was undoubtedly a bold project, and there was a history of such work in similar size ships going badly wrong, but in *Balmoral's* case all went well.

However throughout the 2000s staff changes, a more difficult operating environment, and latterly a less favourable economic climate all combined to make the WEL operation more difficult. The range of *Balmoral's* sailings was reduced and it became increasingly apparent that whilst the non-financial benefits she could provide remained significant, the cost in terms of operating losses could not be sustained and risked threatening the viability of *Waverley*. As a result, WSN decided to withdraw *Balmoral* from service after the 2012 season. Recognising that by now *Balmoral* had historic value in her own right, and that others might wish to take her on as a separate project, WSN funded her lay-up and allowed volunteers to carry out maintenance work at her berth in Bristol.

Over the next two years a new organisation comprised of a combination of experienced PSPS members and new volunteers established a new operation. *Balmoral* was owned by the registered charity MV Balmoral Fund Ltd. – to whom WSN gifted the ship – and White Funnel Ltd. operated her. She re-entered service in 2015, once again based on the Bristol Channel and with some forays elsewhere – most successfully to North Wales. However despite some innovative ideas and improvements, the difficulties lately experienced under WSN /WEL management were still in place and, struck by bad weather and much bad luck, the operation ceased after the 2017 season. Now in 2019, MV Balmoral Fund Ltd. actively promotes the ship as a static venue in Bristol Floating Harbour whilst researching possible alternative business and funding models to enable her to return to service.

Balmoral *arriving at Clevedon on 27th August 2017, with the coast of South Wales in the background.*
Mike Tedstone

Queen of the South *manoeuvring with some difficulty off Southend Pier on 28th May 1966.*

Bernard Dixon/PSPS Collection

CHAPTER FIFTEEN

PSPS SUPPORT FOR OTHER PADDLE STEAMERS
Myra & John Allen

From time to time, the PSPS has surveyed the membership about the future direction the Society should take. Inevitably one of the questions seeks views on whether the Society should acquire or support more paddle steamers. The usual response is that we should consider doing so, whilst not jeopardising the future of our two, existing, operational paddle steamers, *Kingswear Castle* and *Waverley*.

In practice, this support has taken many different forms over the years. The tricky question is usually one of ownership. There are legal restrictions on the type of organisation that charities can support, and any support must be given with the consent and co-operation of the current owner. Establishing and maintaining a cordial relationship is essential. In reality, the actual purchase of a ship, even today, is within the financial means of many enthusiastic people. Unfortunately, the value of a ship, particularly one in need of restoration, is often little

more than scrap value, and the ongoing liabilities start as soon as ownership transfer takes place. It is often hard to convince owners that they have a liability rather than an asset, and this has been an underlying cause of friction in several cases over the years.

It is also a hard truth that static preservation, over a long period, is hard to make financially successful, and the list of statically preserved paddle steamers and other ships which have eventually succumbed to the breakers is, sadly, ever lengthening. Nevertheless, the Society has always tried to support them when practicable, and has used static preserved paddle steamers such as *Maid of the Loch, Medway Queen, Lincoln Castle, Old Caledonia, Princess Elizabeth*, and *Tattershall Castle* for its Annual General Meeting or for branch meetings.

Of course, those involved in the active preservation of other

Queen of the South *on the buoys off Tower Pier, London, on 9th June 1967.*   Bernard Dixon/PSPS Collection

Old Caledonia, *the former Clyde favourite* Caledonia, *two days after the devastating fire which gutted her on the morning of Sunday 27th April 1980.* Les Ring/PSPS Collection

paddle steamers are often members of the Society themselves, but this chapter concentrates on activity that has taken place officially on behalf of the Society.

Ever since the Society acquired *Kingswear Castle* and

Waverley it has provided money to support their operational preservation. From time to time it has also made donations in support of other British paddle steamers, most notably to *Maid of the Loch* and *Medway Queen*. These funds have variously been sourced from surpluses on the Society's general account, from bequests (some for a specific ship, others for general purposes), and from appeals launched in response to specific needs.

Decisions on financial support for ships have generally been taken in response to specific requests and the Council of Management (and its predecessor Central Committee) has always taken the view that the Society's own two ships should take top priority but that modest support should also be given to ships owned by other voluntary societies.

Clyde favourite, *Jeanie Deans*, a 1931 product of Fairfield Shipbuilding & Engineering Company at Govan, Glasgow, was withdrawn from commercial service in 1964 and purchased by a PSPS Member, Don Rose, with some assistance from the Society in the negotiations. She was renamed *Queen of the South* and offered for service on the Thames in the 1966 and 1967 seasons. A number of PSPS members sailed with her as crew on the voyage south, and appeals were made for volunteer assistance from Society members during her winter refit. Ultimately, poor reliability and lack of experience led to her failing to complete either season, and she met her end at Belgian shipbreakers. Nevertheless, important lessons were learned that proved of value when the Society took on the preservation and operation of *Waverley*.

Another Clyde favourite, *Caledonia*, was, for a while, more fortunate. She was completed in 1934 by William Denny and Brothers of Dumbarton. In 1969 she was withdrawn from service and PSPS members attempted to save her, including trying to secure the steamer as a Scottish operating vessel. In the event, she was sold for scrap, but, with further

Medway Queen *in use as the Medway Queen Club at Binfield, Isle of Wight, on 3rd August 1967.* Richard Clammer

A tragic sight. Medway Queen, *having been replaced at the Binfield marina and club on the Isle of Wight by the larger* Ryde, *was moved out of the millpond and into the river where she subsequently sank. She is seen here with decks awash at high water on 30th August 1980, with* Ryde Queen *behind.* PSPS Collection

encouragement from the PSPS, she was sold on to Bass Charrington and she served as a floating pub and restaurant named *Old Caledonia* on the Victoria Embankment in London from 1972 until 1980, when she suffered a serious fire. She was assessed by Waverley Steam Navigation as a potential

operational support vessel for *Waverley*, but was deemed beyond economic repair. *Caledonia* was scrapped near Sittingbourne, in Kent but her engine was saved, and is now in the care of the Hollycombe Steam in the Country Museum, near Liphook. Although it is housed in a purpose-built building, at present it is not operational or open to the public.

High on the list of worthy candidates is *Medway Queen*. She was built by the Ailsa Ship Building Company of Troon and launched in 1924 for service on the Thames estuary. She was used as a minesweeper in WWII and is famous for her seven trips to Dunkirk to rescue troops in 1940. After the war she returned to her old route until she was withdrawn in 1963, and the fledgling PSPS took steps to save her from the breakers - finding a home for her under new private ownership, on the Isle of Wight as a clubhouse. The Society made a loan to assist with this, and appointed a representative to liaise with the new owners. Eventually, she was replaced in the role by the former Southern Railway paddle steamer *Ryde*, and she eventually sank near her former berth on the river Medina. In 1984, she was acquired by the Medway Queen Trust, who brought her back to the River Medway on a pontoon and planned to restore her. Those plans came to nothing, and she was removed from the pontoon to become a sunken wreck alongside St. Mary's Island. The Medway Queen Preservation Society (MQPS) was formed in 1985, and eventually re-floated the ship, albeit temporarily, and moved her to Damhead Creek. Once the MQPS was formed, their roadshow was invited on board

Heading home. The rebuilt Medway Queen *is pictured leaving Bristol's Floating Harbour on 31st October 2013, on her way home to the River Medway. She is now berthed at Gillingham Pier where the Medway Queen Preservation Society is working hard to complete her restoration.* R. Clammer

Ryde Queen, *with* Medway Queen *in the background, at Binfield.*

The full extent of Ryde's *dereliction is painfully evident in this close-up view taken on 14th April 2019. The bridge structure had collapsed during the previous winter.*

John Hendy

Waverley on the Clyde. Whenever *Waverley* passed *Medway Queen* on the Medway, MQPS was given a plug and *Medway Queen* reports became a regular feature in *Paddle Wheels*. In 1991, a liaison committee was set up between the Medway Queen Preservation Society and the Paddle Steamer Preservation Society, at around the time the ship was finally re-floated at Damhead Creek. As a result, MQPS distributed *Waverley*, *Balmoral* and *Kingswear Castle* publicity material at events which they attended and MQPS display boards were placed on board *Waverley* and *Balmoral*, together with membership leaflets. Letters of support by PSPS were written whenever requested, joint raffles were held on *Kingswear Castle* whenever she visited Damhead Creek, and, eventually a PSPS representative was appointed to attend the MQPS Committee with an invitation for MQPS to send a representative to PSPS Council of Management. Waverley Excursions Ltd were contracted by MQPS to prepare a part of their application to the Heritage Lottery Fund to restore *Medway Queen* to operation and fund-raising leaflets were circulated with *Paddle Wheels*. In 2008, MQPS awarded a contract, with the aid of a Heritage Lottery Fund grant to Abels of Bristol to build a fully riveted hull for *Medway Queen*. In 2009 PSPS agreed funding of £20,000 to restore the *Medway Queen's* condenser. The Society archive holds a collection of material relating to the *Medway Queen,* including the house flag flown on her final sailing in September 1963.

Ryde was built in 1937 by Wm. Denny & Bros. at Dumbarton, Scotland, for the Southern Railway's ferry service from Portsmouth to Ryde. After withdrawal after the 1969 season, she effectively replaced *Medway Queen* as the Marina clubhouse and discotheque at Binfield Marina, Isle of Wight, by then renamed Ryde Queen, eventually becoming a nightclub. In 1991, following news that the developers of Binfield Marina wished to dispose of the *Ryde*, the Society formed a Ryde Project Sub-Committee. In the event, the *Ryde* changed hands, and the Society worked closely with the new owner to establish plans for her future. An appeal was launched for pledges, the Society offered a loan, and work was carried out for the first time in over two decades. Areas of new plating were completed and the engine room was cleaned up. Sadly, after initial work had been carried out to get the ship reliably afloat again, all further offers were turned down. The Society has maintained contact with the different owners and their representatives over the years.

The ship was visited by PSPS representatives in 2006 to explore the options for the ship at a meeting with the representative of the owners. The amounts expected as a selling price (just for the engines) were unrealistically high. According to the representative there were several offers for the ship abroad. PSPS offered to provide assistance to them as it was more important to preserve the paddler than see her remain in a poor state in the UK. Despite the written offer, there was no response from the owners or their representatives. The Society actively encouraged the PS Ryde Trust, which was set up to

Tattershall Castle in her current role as a pub on the Thames Embankment, seen from the London Eye in August 2010. David Haddleton

Wingfield Castle *at Hartlepool, September 2018.*

David Haddleton

restore the vessel in 2009, offering them the chance to put an appeal in Paddle Wheels. Despite this, news was received that the ship was being broken up without the knowledge of the Trust, who had put in a firm offer to purchase the ship and were awaiting a reply from the brokers. PSPS contacted the Isle of Wight Council, National Historic Ships, and the Environment Agency, and an order to stop work was received from the Environment Agency in conjunction with the Health and Safety Executive. This bought another reprieve but, in the end, the Trust could not conclude a deal to save the vessel and the ship continued to deteriorate.

In 2018, it was reported that *Ryde* had been sold to a charitable trust and that funding applications for the restoration would be made. Unsurprisingly, an inspection revealed that the remains of the bridge and much of the decking had collapsed, attempts to remove the vessel would be environmentally hazardous and the only remaining option is to dismantle the vessel. Money raised from an on-line appeal will, instead, be used to fund work on the *Medway Queen*. Nevertheless, preservation of her *Rydes's* engines and other artefacts would be desirable and this is being investigated. Fortunately, the engine console and one ventilator from the ship are already in the Society's archive collection, and her aft capstan still operates on *Waverley* as a replacement for the one originally fitted. Less fortunately, her steering engine was removed from the ship and ultimately scrapped.

Tattershall Castle was launched in 1934 by Wm. Gray at

Hartlepool for the LNER Railway's Hull to New Holland ferry service. She was the first of the three *Castles* to be withdrawn in 1972, and, with encouragement from the PSPS, was sold to serve on the Embankment in London as an art gallery from 1975 to 1981. A year later she was sold and opened as a Chef & Brewer group pub and night club. She has changed hands several times since then and has been extensively altered over the years, but although her paddles have been removed, her engine remains intact and in situ. It would be wrong to mention *Tattershall Castle* without mentioning her devoted Chief Engineer, Terry Prudames, a PSPS member who assessed the viability of *PS Tattershall Castle* for private ownership after her withdrawal on the Humber, accepted the post of Chief Engineer in 1973, and brought the vessel to London. He retained his position right up to his death in 2008. Terry ensured that the ship was always well presented, and kept the steam engines in working order, always happy to give guided tours and turn the engines over for any enthusiast who knocked on his door. The ship played host to PSPS events through his generosity.

Wingfield Castle was launched in 1934 by Wm. Gray at Hartlepool for the LNER Hull to New Holland ferry service. Withdrawn in 1974, she changed hands several times before being purchased by Hartlepool Borough Council for restoration as an exhibit of Hartlepool Museum. Unfortunately she is currently closed to visitors. The Society keeps an eye on her, and discussions have been held with her local authority

Lincoln Castle *in Alexandra Dock, Grimsby, July 2009.*   David Haddleton

owner to see if it can help with volunteer support to maintain the ship's standard of presentation and these discussions are ongoing.

One of the saddest stories concerns *Lincoln Castle* which was built in 1940 by A. & J. Inglis, Pointhouse, Glasgow and entered service on the LNER's Hull-New Holland ferry service in 1941. She was the last of the *Castles* to be withdrawn, in February 1978. The Society assisted with the formation of the 'Save PS Lincoln Castle' Campaign, with a view to securing her for operational preservation, but in the event, she was opened as a pub at Hessle close to the Humber Bridge, eventually changing hands and moving to Grimsby as a bar and restaurant at the Heritage Centre at Alexandra Dock. She was closed to the public in late 2006, and moved along the dock, beached on limestone tipped into the corner of the dock to avoid sinking. Following an approach from the owner, PSPS commenced discussions with a view to securing a long-term future for her. A letter was written to all members to determine support for PSPS ownership of the paddler. The response was remarkably good, the vast majority being in favour of taking on the ship, albeit with the proviso that she must not affect the operation of the ships we currently support. A survey was commissioned, but after much debate PSPS Council decided not to proceed with acquisition of the ship. One of the major reasons was the risk to our existing operating ships. Recent poor seasons saw Society reserves severely depleted by the need to keep *Waverley* and *Balmoral* sailing. Nevertheless, the Society worked hard behind the scenes to assist potential buyers for the ship. The Lincoln Castle Preservation Society was established at the end

of May 2010 to buy the ship for restoration and eventual return to service, but in the end the owner refused to sell or give the ship to another body and started to scrap the ship. There were several buyers for the engine and other machinery, including a museum that had cleared some space to take the items, and PSPS were actively involved in facilitating this. However destruction continued in spite of those interested parties.

All that remained of Lincoln Castle *on 15th October 2010.*
John & Myra Allen

The paddle tug John H Amos *sunk at her berth at Chatham on 7th May 1994, seen from* Kingswear Castle. R. Clammer

The 12-passenger Monarch *off Cowes on 27th June 2009 during her period based on the Isle of Wight. On this occasion she had ventured out of the River Medina to greet* Balmoral *which was celebrating her 60th Anniversary with a special cruise from Southampton* R. Clammer

John H. Amos is a paddle tug built in 1931 by Bow, McLachlan & Company at Paisley and used as a tug/tender on the River Tees until withdrawal in 1967. She was purchased on behalf of Teeside County Borough Council and some renovation was carried out in Middlesbrough, but eventually was put up for sale. Renamed *Hero*, she became part of the fleet of International Towing Ltd, based at Chatham Dockyard. In 2001 ownership was transferred to the Medway Maritime Trust. Eventually she was holed and sank at her mooring, resulting in being moved to a slipway, and in 2009 she was lifted onto a pontoon where she remains today. The Society has been approached for assistance and has agreed in principle to assist the setting up of a separate body to take on the ship if possible. Further discussions with the owner are intended.

Apart from *Waverley* and *Kingswear Castle*, *Monarch* is the only other active paddle steamer in the UK. She was designed and built by PSPS member Brian Waters. Construction started in 1984, and she finally entered commercial service in 2003. She changed hands, and was based at Island Harbour Marina on the Isle of Wight for three seasons from 2008 until 2010, offering excursions for up to 12 passengers in the River Medina. After a spell on the River Tamar she changed hands again, and now operates from Wareham on the River Frome, Dorset,

Sightseers watch from Wareham Bridge as Monarch *turns in the River Frome before setting off on a cruise downstream during August 2015.*
Mike Tedstone

although she is, once again, up for sale. In the meantime, members of the Society's Wessex and Dart Branch can often be found amongst her crew when she is sailing.

The *Maid of the Loch* was mentioned at the start of this chapter and the years of dedication put in by her own Trust, with the support of the PSPS, is described in the next chapter.

Monarch *alongside the beautiful quayside at Wareham in Dorset, preparing to embark passengers for a trip along the River Frome on 13th August 2014.*
Brian Jackson

Maid of the Loch *sits above her own reflection at Balloch Pier on 13th March 2018.*   John Beveridge

CHAPTER SIXTEEN

MAID OF THE LOCH
John Beveridge

MY interest in Clyde Steamers is probably down to a form of escapism and a love of the sea. To a schoolboy, they were big, beautiful, powerful vessels, each different, and could take you to places otherwise out of reach. In the days when there were few cars and bus journeys took hours, how else did you get to visit "exotic" places like Rothesay, Campbeltown, or Ailsa Craig? Even a trip to Millport was an expedition – my family of four with pram, changes of clothes and picnic on a steam train to Paisley, change trains to Largs, walk to the pier, and then onto the ferry (capacity 112) for a 30 minute crossing. It was lunch time by the time we arrived!

Paddlers were my favourite with their thrashing paddlewheels with the regular 8-beat thump of the floats hitting the water, and the open engine room watching huge pistons flashing round, or just to warm up from the heat of the machinery on a cold day! *Caledonia* was my absolute favourite, and I was devastated when she was withdrawn in 1969. While

she was laid up, I paid her a visit in February 1970 (no such thing as password protected security systems then) and "met" a young fellow with a similar idea. He also happened to "liberate" a lifebelt before introducing himself as Douglas McGowan, whose name I knew from the newspaper as one of the people trying to save the *Caledonia*. I am grateful for that fateful meeting as he & I have remained the best of friends ever since. In fact Douglas got me to join the PSPS which had just launched its Scottish Branch a few months earlier. Then he suggested I stand for the Branch Committee, and I served on it from 1972 to 1988, becoming Chairman in 1980-81. I also served three years as the Society's National Membership Secretary.

It was an exciting time. *Caledonia* was "saved" to become a successful floating pub on the Thames, but then *Waverley* was withdrawn at the end of 1973. The Branch delegated Douglas & myself to put the case for owning *Waverley* to the then Central Committee, in London. We were faced with (in my

Maid of the Loch approaching Tarbet, Loch Lomond, on 15th August 1968.

PSPS Collection

Maid of the Loch *steaming through the Balmaha Narrows during her last year in service, 1981.* John Beveridge

eyes) a group of old men in grey suits very sceptical of an offer to own a 693 ton, 1,350 passenger paddler, especially when the Society was still trying to get to grips with owning the 94 ton and 235 passenger *Kingswear Castle*, which it had bought seven years earlier. My recollections are that both Douglas and Terry Sylvester put up a strong case to gain the Society's backing to pursue the Caledonian MacBrayne offer, and we did narrowly persuade them in the end.

Douglas organised work parties to clean up the *Waverley* in August 1974, and I became a work party leader. As Chapter 10 has shown, he and others best know the "inside stories" of that fantastic campaign which saw her sailing again in May 1975. After that, given my career and studies, I helped where I could which included organising six major charters on her, on behalf of the Society. Then there was the purchase of the *Shanklin* (renamed *Prince Ivanhoe*) in 1980 and Society work parties to ready her for her first season in 1981. The withdrawal of the *Maid of the Loch* at the end of that year is where the story of the Society's, and my, real involvement with the *Maid* begins...

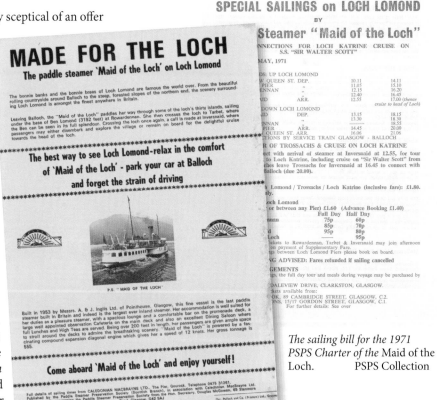

The sailing bill for the 1971 PSPS Charter of the Maid of the Loch. PSPS Collection

The publicity leaflet produced by the Scottish Branch of the PSPS in 1978 to promote increased use of the Maid's *Loch Lomond services.*
John Beveridge

It's probably a little known fact that the Society was associated with the *Maid of the Loch* from 1971 when it chartered her, with the fare for the full day of 95p! Two further charters followed, in 1974 and in 1976. 1976 was also the year the Scottish Branch produced a publicity leaflet entitled "Made for Loch Lomond", to publicise her as a paddle steamer.

For the *Maid's* 25th anniversary in 1978, PSPS persuaded Caledonian MacBrayne to have a special silver jubilee cruise where the Society would present the paddler with a commemorative plaque. John Whittle kindly offered special fares to PSPS members, and both he and Mona Moore (wife of Branch Chairman James Moore) unveiled it during the cruise. The Society's last charter of the *Maid* was an evening cruise in 1980.

By the end of 1981 it was accepted that the *Maid* would be withdrawn, so the Society convened a meeting with WSN/ WEL to discuss possible options about her future. WSN/ WEL were interested in becoming involved, but it was left to PSPS to take the interest forward. On 14th December my good friend Douglas McGowan and I met with Hele Weibye, an hotelier and businessman from Luss, as he had expressed an interest in purchasing the *Maid*.

Estimated operating costs were prepared by Terry Sylvester and we convinced Mr Weibye that operating her would be viable. The *Maid* was placed up for sale on 18th January 1982 and he agreed to submit a bid supported by PSPS to the brokers. Prior to the closing date of 17th February, I met with the brokers, but they proved distinctly unhelpful. Five offers had been received for the *Maid*, and on behalf of PSPS I contacted MPs and the media to gain support for the Hele Weibye/PSPS bid. This achieved good publicity, but in the event, the successful purchasers were Ind Coope Alloa Breweries and Verigen Ltd.

I then became the Society's "lead contact" for the *Maid*. Despite announcements to "renovate" the *Maid*, Alloa Breweries purchased the former *Countess of Breadalbane* and sailed her on the loch. No money was spent on the *Maid*. Repeated letters went unanswered. In January 1985 a reply was eventually received to such a letter and Terry Sylvester and I met with the company in February. Great plans were produced showing a children's play area, an open steak grille in the middle of the former cafeteria, (now the restaurant), and a new

Maid of the Loch *approaching Balloch, 1980*   Murray Patterson

colour scheme. Terry and I were impressed by their sincerity, and their assurance that the ship's refit was to start "soon", but were very sceptical of their plans to replace her steam propulsion with hydraulic machinery.

Months passed and we became increasingly concerned at her condition. Her decks were leaking badly, allowing rainwater to cause internal damage and accumulate in the bilges. We offered work parties to carry out "preventative" work to stop the rain coming in. A meeting with Alloa Breweries took place in August, but it took until November for them to agree the range of work to be done, and the following year to agree a budget. But on seven summer days in June and July 1986, Scottish Branch work parties laid a covering of protective plastic sheeting over her entire deck as a temporary measure until the refit could start.

Events then conspired against the promised investment. Ind Coope was bought by the conglomerate Allied Lyons, and in the company restructure Alloa Breweries were instructed to sell any non-core assets so both boats were placed on the market. In April 1989, Sea Management Corporation (from Australia) bought them and promised a multi-million pound investment, but they went into liquidation in 1990. Then the Francis Leisure Group from Newcastle bought them, with a promised £5 million investment. I made contact with each new owner, and was given assurances each time on their "big plans". The same year, I had taken up the position as a Director with Dumbarton District Council, which was to prove very fortuitous.

Then, on 10th February 1992, I wrote to the Francis Leisure Group that I had seen people with oxyacetylene cutting equipment on the ship, and I also informed the police. Fortunately the police put an end to the vandalism, because FLG's liquidation was announced some days later. With rainwater again accumulating in her hull, some smashed portholes, and the removal of her main discharge pipe from the engine room leaving a big hole for loch water to enter, she was in real danger of sinking at the pier. With the council's permission, on 4th March a team of council workers were dispatched to remove the risk of the *Maid* sinking at the pier by pumping her out.

A rusty and forlorn Maid of the Loch *at Balloch Pier in March 1993, shortly after her purchase by Dumbarton District Council, which was assisted by a donation from PSPS.*
John Beveridge

The *Maid* and *Countess* were put up for sale again. The council was persuaded to express an interest, but more to do with securing the land at Balloch pier than any philanthropic interest in saving a paddle steamer. To keep interest in the *Maid's* future to the fore, PSPS offered to contribute up to £5,000 to the council's bid. I discussed the sale with the seller's agent and understood that the council's offer was unlikely to be accepted. The Society then agreed to contribute up to £10,000 if the council would increase its bid to secure the sale, which it did, thanks to the support of the Provost, Patrick O'Neill, and Councillor William Mackechnie. On 3rd December, 1992 Dumbarton District Council became the *Maid's* new owners. In the event, the council would only accept £1,000 from the Society.

Owning the *Maid* and *Countess* became a real issue for the council, both politically and financially. My fellow Director in the council and good friend, Ian Fernie, (who later became a director of the Loch Lomond Steamship Company) was given the *Maid* to "look after" in his department's budget. With some hard work behind the scenes, I organised volunteer work parties from the Scottish Branch to carry out cleaning and painting in time to celebrate the 40th anniversary of her maiden voyage, in May 1993. From being rust-streaked, with moss growing out of her decks, and rubbish and debris everywhere, Society members had turned the "hulk" into a ship again. Such was the enthusiasm of the volunteers that work parties continued, with Michael Hughan agreeing to become leader. It was also decided to give the *Maid* a new colour scheme and her new red and black funnel, and black hull made newspaper headlines. The immediate danger to the *Maid* had been averted, but what of her future?

The following year, the council decided upon an independent study to determine the *Maid's* future. The Society contributed £1,000 to the report. Its findings came out in favour of her restoration, but the council had no interest in owning either vessel. I was involved in more behind the scenes discussions,

The first ever PSPS work party on board Maid of the Loch *on 22nd June 1986. Volunteers Stuart Mears, Leslie Brown and Peter Reid are laying Visqueen sheeting over the decks to stop the rain coming in.*
John Beveridge

Soon after Dumbarton District Council bought the Maid, *PSPS work parties began work again. This is the first such occasion, on 7th May 1993.*
John Beveridge

which resulted in the council agreeing to form a Trust to safeguard the *Maid*, with founding members being three representatives from the council (Provost O'Neill, Councillor Mackechnie, and myself); a rep from PSPS (Michael Hughan); and a rep from the Scottish Tourist Board (James Fraser). The wording of the Trust Deed did not allow the Trust to own the vessel, so a charity was created and on 19th September 1995, the Loch Lomond Steamship Company was established. Ownership of the *Maid* was transferred to the charity in March 1996, with charity members the same as on the Trust.

Since then, the PSPS has been one of the main supporters of the *Maid's* restoration project with grants, loans, publicity, advice, volunteers who were PSPS members, and regular articles in "Paddle Wheels". It even paid for her two new masts back in 2008. As a founder, and now Chairman, of the Loch Lomond Steamship Company, I know that the *Maid's* present condition as a static visitor attraction would not have been achieved without the backing she has received from the Society.

And so, 48 years since the Society first chartered the *Maid of the Loch*, the Society can be proud of its support and commitment to the on-going efforts to not only save and conserve the *Maid*, but to backing the aim of returning her to steam operation again for the nation and future generations. I look forward with confidence to the Society's *next* charter of the *Maid*!

During March 2018 John Beveridge, Chairman of the Loch Lomond Steamship Company and Jonathan McColl, Leader of West Dunbartonshire Council celebrate the award of £950,000 from the Scottish Government's Regeneration Capital Grant Fund. Despite the surprise refusal of HLF to grant an application which would have seen the Maid *return to service in 2020, this government funding has remained in place and is allowing much important restoration work to continue. The ship's owning charity remains determined to see her sail again.*
John Beveridge

Resplendent in her new colour scheme, Maid of the Loch *is pictured at Balloch Pier during 2013 with Ben Lomond looming large in the background.*
John Beveridge

Scottish Branch volunteers hard at work scraping and red-leading rust patches on Maid of the Loch's *hull, 22nd May 1993.*   John Beveridge

CHAPTER SEVENTEEN

VOLUNTEERS

With contributions from Nigel Coombes, Geoffrey Ryder, Terry Sylvester and Gordon Wilson

The operation and success of PSPS has, of course, always depended on volunteers. While many members are properly quite content to show their support by paying their subscriptions, donating to appeals, keeping up-to-date with the latest steamer news through their quarterly edition of "Paddle Wheels" and sailing on board the ships as often as possible, others choose to become more actively involved.

It is all too easy to overlook this quiet army of volunteers who, over the last 60 years, have brought their varied skills and enthusiasms to bear on a multitude of different tasks. Without them there would be no Society and our ships would not be sailing. The problem is how on earth to do them justice. **Terry Sylvester** sums up some of the key volunteering roles in his memories of people, sadly no longer with us, who influenced *Waverley's* success beginning with Directors, moving on to regional supporters, and then those involved in publicity who are not mentioned elsewhere in the book:

"Ian Burroughs came to the open day we held on board within days of taking ownership of *Waverley* & volunteered to play the vital role of Engineering Director... A few days after *Waverley's* first sailings, very tired Directors held a rather fraught board meeting (not really falling out – just rather exhausted). Ian exclaimed 'why can't we run *Waverley* without people' – but he really didn't mean it!

Donald Anderson, together with Norman Bird and John Brown, was a great White Funnel Fleet enthusiast before anyone knew what a steamer enthusiast was! John Collins lived at Rhoose, just three miles from where the majority of the work to promote and manage the marketing of *Waverley, Balmoral* and *Prince Ivanhoe* was carried out. John was a frequent visitor to the Barry offices to pack thousands of envelopes of *Waverley* publicity. In the early days Earnest Dumbleton, who had a deep

Reg and Bunty Collinson, Waverley's *original volunteer shopkeepers on board the steamer at Glasgow in 1979.*
G. Ryder

personal knowledge of the pre-war days of the Campbell fleet, did much to influence, guide and encourage younger members of the Society.

June Bushell was a graphic artist and drew... the very first artwork in late 1974. I used this on the front of thousands of envelopes and in all the newspaper advertisements for 1975 and 1976. John Easton was a reporter for the *Glasgow Herald* who approached me and said 'as a journalist I thought there must be another side to this fairy story, but now I have got to know you all I realise that you are a genuine bunch, what can I do to help?' I said publish a ship's newspaper and John produced *Waverley Times* for many years... completely free of cost.

Chris Collard became, probably the most prolific author of at least eight books on the White Funnel Fleet which have all played their part in promoting the operation of *Waverley* under the banner of the PSPS and when not engaged in his writing was souvenir shop salesman in the Bristol Channel."

Running the souvenir shops on board the two ships was one practical way in which members with a little time on their hands could actually get afloat and experience life on board for extended periods. A week or two of long sailings followed by cashing up, emptying the ship's post box, restocking and cleaning could be exhausting, but most came back for more. For many years the late Dr. Joe McKendrick was the mastermind behind the retail operation, sourcing and ordering a wide range of merchandise from confectionery through crested clothing, to souvenirs and books. He organised the shopkeepers' rotas for the Clyde and Western Isles, liaised with Pat Murrell, and Geoff Ryder to ensure that English sailings were covered, saw to all of the stock control and provided training where necessary.

Stories of shopkeepers' adventures and misadventures are

143

Geoffrey Ryder, with Derek Docherty and Ian Smiley in the shop on 29th April 2011. G.Ryder

Paul Semple and Joe Mc Kendrick in Waverley's *shop on 29th July 2010. Having served as a student steward and purser on both the paddler and* Balmoral *and played an active role in the Scottish Branch, Paul went on to serve as Chairman of the PSPS from 2017-19 and is currently General Manager of Waverley Excursions Ltd. The late Joe McKendrick, fondly remembered by all who knew him, was a superb shipping photographer, an avid supporter of* Waverley *and the key person behind the success of her souvenir shop.* G. Ryder

legion and most are probably best left untold. The hitherto unrevealed story of a donkey being smuggled on board late at night at Tilbury by one well-known shopkeeper will, no doubt be recognised by the person in question!

In recent years **Geoffrey Ryder** of the Wessex Branch has taken a particularly active role in organising the shops on both *Waverley* and *Balmoral*. He has a huge talent for spotting lines which will sell well, and constantly sets out to beat his own record for daily sales. It is a rare customer who, having called in to buy a postcard, manages to escape without a bag full of clothing, books and souvenirs they never realised they needed. Here he reflects on his own experiences of

Forty years volunteering in the souvenir shop.

Back in 1979 on *Waverley's* second visit to the south coast I helped with other Wessex Branch members to publicise the sailings. Terry Sylvester invited us to a press conference on Friday 13th April which was scheduled to be held on board but alas the weather intervened and *Waverley* was delayed so we met in a local hotel. At this event I met Bunty and Reg Collinson who looked after the shop in the early years of preservation and I volunteered to help them if required, not realising this would lead to forty years behind the shop counter.

Waverley duly arrived at Southampton and I had joined her as a passenger for a cruise round the Isle of Wight when shortly after departure Bunty invited me into the shop obviously to see if I could sell souvenirs. After a few days helping on the South Coast Bunty told me she was dreading the Thames sailings with the school cruise out of London and would I come and help her for a week. I said I would consider it. A few days after *Waverley* had left the south coast I received a letter stamped posted onboard with a note from Bunty saying "I have arranged everything with the captain and will expect you next Monday for the week". I quickly booked a week off work and duly arrived onboard on the 8th May for a baptism of fire with 1000 school children onboard and a never-ending queue stretching back to the Jeanie Deans lounge. We ended the day with several boxes full of 10p coins.

The following year, 1980, Jim Buchanan had taken over the management of the shop and asked me if I would help Bunty and Reg for six weekends in the spring so every Friday after work I travelled to *Waverley* for her sailings on the Thames, South Coast and her first visit to the Bristol Channel. The highlight was on one of the Thames sailings when we took over £1000 in a day and I remember Bunty and Reg doing a dance outside the shop. Another special day was on the 12th May 1980 when we sailed from Deal to the beaches off Dunkirk with many veterans onboard and a moving service was held over the location where the previous *Waverley* sank. I had the pleasure of having lunch at the officers' table with Captain Cameron, master of the old *Waverley* and first master of the present *Waverley* on this sailing. I also had the privilege of serving in the shop when *Waverley* sailed from Dover to escort the little ships across the channel for the 50th anniversary of the Dunkirk evacuation.

Sadly Bunty Collinson passed away in April 1981. Since then I have been involved with the *Waverley* mainly operating the shop on the South Coast and Thames, I have also spent time on the Clyde, Western Isles and Bristol Channel over the years and have sailed along the coast from the Western Isles to Great Yarmouth.

Over the years there have been many memorable sailings

including the day *HMS Invincible* returned from the Falklands war. *Waverley* was due to be off service that day alongside Ryde Pier but a special sailing was arranged and she sailed with a full complement. We followed the Royal Barge with the Queen and Duke of Edinburgh out of Portsmouth Harbour, and after meeting up with *HMS Invincible*, *Waverley* led the ships back into Portsmouth Harbour and tied up alongside the mooring point off Portsmouth Harbour Station while the naval ships sailed past before we then sailed round the harbour to view the ships. More recently in 1997 *Waverley* operated a special sailing from Southampton to escort the P&O passenger liner *Canberra* back from her final cruise and we sailed from Southampton at 6am with over 600 passengers picking up additional passengers at Ryde Pier. It was thick fog so our Portsmouth pick- up was cancelled and arrangements were made for the passengers to cross to Ryde by ferry to join *Waverley* there. Then *Canberra* appeared out of the mist and we escorted her in to Southampton, where we had to tie up at the Town Quay to allow the liner to berth. The Town Quay was crowded with people to view the arrival and we blocked their view so the initiative was taken to invite them to come onboard for £5 each and join us for a sail past *Canberra* after she had berthed. Many took up the offer and this helped boost the shop and dining room revenue.

The shop also becomes an information place for the passengers with the most frequent questions being "Where do I pay?" and "Is it possible to see the engine?" One of the most unusual questions to date was "Is there a souvenir shop onboard?! "

Over the years I have met many of our volunteer shopkeepers including Bunty and Reg Collinson, Jim and Betty Brackenridge, Peter Brackenridge, Pat Murrell, Lionel Vaughan, Ken Ryder, Basil Craggs, Betty Saunders, Beth Clammer, Allison Read, Paul Semple, Mike Tedstone, Deryk Docherty, Iain Smiley, Graeme Dunlop, Ian Hall, Robin Billings, Alan Bushell, Peter Bushell, Stephen Wilson and Brian Elliott. I remember one year Joe McKendrick could not find anyone to cover the Western Isles and I persuaded my father Ken to do it. Previously he had only ever been on as a passenger. He agreed and travelled up to Glasgow and Joe met him and took him to the ship. He obviously enjoyed the experience and over the years spent many more periods onboard.

In more recent years Peter Bushell has helped me during the busy periods on the Thames in addition to working in other areas. Peter always received a "Good morning Granville" when he came aboard from the Mate, David Howie. I guess that means I must have been Arkwright! I remember one morning coming up from my cabin and seeing the sign had been changed over the shop to ARKWRIGHTS EMPORIUM. I think this was the work of the then chief engineer who also played tricks on us, placing unusual items in the letter box. I remember Lionel Vaughan finding an X- rated magazine in the box one day when he was emptying it.

Back in 1981 I spent a weekend relieving Basil Craggs as

shopkeeper on *Prince Ivanhoe* on a sailing to Watchet and Minehead and the following day to Lundy Island. Over the years I have served on *MV Balmoral* becoming the Retail Manager for White Funnel and doing all the ordering of souvenirs for the three seasons she operated, as well as serving onboard and organising the volunteer shopkeepers."

Another enjoyable role on board, although not as part of the residential crew, has been selling raffle tickets and copies of the ship's newspaper *Waverley Times* around the decks. In addition to raising significant amounts of money for the cause, sellers act as important ambassadors for PSPS and the ships, chatting to passengers, explaining the aims of the Society, answering questions and generally making them feel welcome on board. Huge numbers of members have helped over the years but some particularly devoted and successful sellers must be mentioned. On the Clyde Derek Brown began selling *Waverley Times* on board in 1970 but took over as main raffle seller when the PSPS Grand Draws were introduced. It is estimated that he had raised over £200,000 for the cause before ill health forced him to hand over the role to Ken Darroch. On the Thames during the 1970s and 80s Ken Adams and Tim Wardley took the lead, often living on board and sleeping in the forward deck saloon, until they retired and were replaced by Peter and Allan Bushell. On the South Coast the two Dons – Drayton and Thompson – played a similar role during *Waverley's* visits, while on the Bristol Channel the amazing Betty Saunders, assisted by

Lunch break on board Balmoral *in the Albion Dry dock at Bristol, April 1997. Chief engineer Jim Bullen and Engineering Superintendant Ian MacMillan enjoy a break in the sunshine with two of the local volunteers.*
Nigel Coombes

Is there anywhere he didn't appear? Ray Eley marshalling the long queue of passengers waiting to board Balmoral *on her first visit to West Bay Harbour, Bridport, Dorset on 1st June 2009. Many other PSPS member have carried out similar tasks; taking lines, acting as pier hosts and distributing publicity, fetching stores and running errands as our steamers have visited piers and harbours all round the coast of the UK.* R. Clammer

Peter Tamblin, then Chairman of the Wessex Branch and periodic master of both Waverley *and* Balmoral, *makes a presentation to Don Drayton and Don Thompson on the day in 2011 when they retired from leading the raffle ticket sales during the steamer's annual South coast seasons. During 2010 and 2011 alone they raised £5,500 for the ship.* Geoff Ryder

her friend Barbara Brown, was almost a fixture on board and raised staggering sums of money. In June 1999 friends and crew were able to say a small thank you to Betty by arranging an 80th Birthday party for her on board *Waverley*, an event repeated ten years later for her 90th.

Winter work parties on board *Waverley* at Glasgow and *Balmoral* at Bristol have been another long-standing and important aspect of the Society's activities. Under the guidance of a member of the ships' permanent crews, groups of volunteers gather on a regular basis to carry out essential maintenance tasks and thereby save thousands of pounds in potential shipyard fees. Some of the volunteers are qualified electricians, engineers or ship repairers and are able to bring their professional skills to bear on various technical tasks, while others are happy to chip rust, clean, paint, varnish, caulk decks, make and store curtains or undertake any of the other essential jobs required on board a ship in refit. A great sense of camaraderie prevails and, as the start of the new sailing season approaches there is tremendous satisfaction in having helped to send the ship on her way looking thoroughly smart and shipshape.

While *Balmoral* was operating under the WEL flag she spent every winter laid up in Bristol and, until she was re-engined in the winter of 2002-03, regular work was required on her ageing Sirron diesels. Spares were hard to come by so often had to be manufactured and this task fell to volunteer Ray Eley. Hailing from the Midlands, Ray was a trained fitter and operated from a railway carriage which had been converted into a fully fitted workshop and which was shunted into position alongside the ship each winter. Within the cramped confines of "Ray's

146

Carriage" all sorts of minor miracles were performed. During the summer season Ray transformed into an apparently omnipresent line-handler, for whenever the ships called at obscure or unstaffed piers and jetties there he would be ready to assist with mooring and marshalling the queues of intending passengers.

During the dispiriting three years 2012-15 that *Balmoral* was laid up in Bristol following her withdrawal from WEL service, a loyal team of volunteers continued to maintain her in good condition and PSPS members were instrumental in setting up a new allied charity to raise funds to return her to service. This was successfully achieved and in April 2015 the ship was transferred from the ownership of MV Balmoral Fund Ltd and returned to passenger service for the seasons of 2015-17. At the time of writing lack of funds to meet new and tighter MCA requirements means she is laid up once again but the volunteers continue with their regular work while plans are laid for another renaissance. The PSPS Bristol Channel Branch works in close co-operation with the Balmoral Fund (which is a charity officially affiliated to PSPS) and holds regular winter meetings on board, while the *Balmoral* supporters are pledged to do everything possible to support *Waverley's* visits to the area. PSPS Vice President **Nigel Coombes** has shown great devotion to the motor ship over many years and, as one of the longest-serving volunteers, has become far-famed for his meticulous care of her varnish work. Regarding voluntary work parties, he recalls:

"The off season is a time of refurbishment and repair. Ian McMillan was a brilliant Chief Engineer supervising both ships; he knew each ship intimately and endured a deep affection for all the eccentricities both *Waverley* and *Balmoral* would throw up during the season, like a brace of naughty children. To back him up on both ships was a faithful crew of volunteers- not all of them members of the Society-all of them willing to give their utmost to keep their charges in good

Nigel Coombes sanding one of Balmoral's *window frames, 5th April 1996.*
R. Clammer

Tony Horn making one of two replacement windows for Waverley's *Jeanie Deans bar after the steamer had had a slight altercation with Helensborough Pier during 2010.*
Tony Horn

Ray Eley in his carriage-cum-workshop beside Balmoral *at Princes Wharf, Bristol.*
Andy Westmore

Two of the Society's longest-serving members, Pat Murrell (left) and Victor Gray, enjoying a day on board Waverley *on 18th June 1961. Pat has been an active member of both National and Branch Committees for 58 years, while between 1960 and 1980 Victor filled the roles of Secretary, Membership Secretary, Treasurer and Chairman.*
Pat Murrell

condition, like Mike Taylor, Bob Flook, John Holland, Chris Harvey and Neil Dee."

Sparkling varnish, of course, depends on sound woodwork and maintaining that is an extremely skilled and specialised job. A tour of *Waverley* quickly reveals how much there is. Wheelhouse, bridge wings, staircases, doors, saloon windows, hatchways and bars are all beautifully crafted from high-quality hardwood and almost all have been constructed, single-handedly, by PSPS volunteer Tony Horn who, quite apart from being a skilled model maker and marine artist, is a talented professional joiner. Tony was travelling back up Channel from Ilfracombe on board Balmoral one day in 1987 when he was introduced to Chief Engineer, the late Ian McMillan. Having mentioned that he'd like to help the ship, Tony was immediately asked if he could make two replacement windows and soon found himself in the forward saloon with Ian, hanging out through open windows to measure up their complex shapes. With two windows completed, Ian requested two or three more and over the next few years Tony finished up replacing every window in the ship. His then employers were most helpful allowing him to use their workshops after hours and supplying materials free or at cost.

With *Balmoral* completed, Tony's firm was asked to quote for replacing all of *Waverley's* windows. Sadly they became a victim of the recession before the job could be started and a now-unemployed Tony was asked to take the job on himself. Having agreed he began work in 1993 and gradually replaced all of the items mentioned above, along with glass screens in the aft deck saloon, deck seating and more. Most of the work was carried out in his garage/workshop and passing neighbours must have been amazed to see a full size ship's bridge and other nautical items taking shape beside a Worthing house. Even more amazing was the sight of teams of PSPS volunteers and crew members carrying finished doors and bridge wing parts along Worthing Pier to load on to one or other of the ships as they called in!

It is easy in this technological age to forget that communications were not so swift in the past– and occasionally still remain difficult. Internet ordering for supplies from large providers to were non-existent in the early days. This is where volunteers in each area come into their own for their local knowledge, and their apparent ability to drop everything and rush to solve a problem. Nigel Coombes recalls an early instance when, at Easter, *Waverley* was starting the season from Portishead, where she had locked in, Clevedon Pier having

Not what one expects to see in a suburban driveway! Waverley's new wheelhouse front taking shape at Tony Horn's Worthing home in the Spring of 1996.   Tony Horn

collapsed.

"Preparations were pretty frantic, making ready public rooms, Roddy McIsaac squeedgying the rails in time-honoured fashion..and leaving his mid-day pieces (sandwiches to non-Scots!), as any self- respecting bosun would, on any convenient girder on the ship... One particular morning a very worried Captain rang me on ship to shore. 'We're going down channel today and there is an evening cruise tonight. We have no potatoes, no bread, what can you do?' I went down the Gordeno Valley to all the farmers and small-holders for spuds and, being a Sunday, went to any supermarket open and cleaned them out of sliced white loaves. Thank God Capt. Neill didn't ask me for the fishes as well or I'd have been stumped."

As in any society, some of the least visible and glamorous task relate to administration. The members of the Society's National Council of Management (who are also the Society's trustees and company directors) are responsible for setting policy and ensuring good governance and financial probity. Much of this detailed work falls on the shoulders of the Chair, Secretary, Treasurer and other members of the executive committee some of whom have served for long periods and developed an invaluable long view. John Anderson recently retired as National Secretary after 37 years while Martin Longhurst has served as Treasurer since 1980.

Each of the Society's five regional branches also has a committee which is responsible for planning winter meetings, locating speakers, organising charters and fundraising events and liaising with the Council of Management. Before the advent of central mailing teams of "stuffers" would spend several days each quarter putting copies of *Paddle Wheels* into envelopes and mailing them; while others still pound the streets or drive hundreds of miles distributing timetables for the season ahead. In those area where one or other of the ships spends her lay-up, branches have also co-ordinated winter work parties and assisted the operating companies in any way they can. Many of these activities are described elsewhere in this book. Probably the longest-serving of all Branch Officers is the Bristol Channel Branch's remarkable Pat Murrell who has served for 58 years in every different committee role, as well as contributing a great deal to the national Council of Management. Not content with that he has also organised numerous charters, served long periods as purser or shop keeper on board *Balmoral* and *Waverley*, organised the shop keepers' rotas, and driven thousands of miles fetching and

Scottish Branch member Leslie Brown using an adze to trim off wooden plugs in newly-laid deck planking during a winter work party on board Waverley *at Glasgow during 1974.* Gordon Wilson

carrying spare parts and equipment for the ships.

Other members including Fraser McHaffie, Leslie Brown, Joe McKendrick, John Hollyoak, Richard Coton, Iain MacLeod and Mike Tedstone have contributed by researching and writing the popular handbooks and sailing guides which are sold on board and do so much to increase passengers' awareness of the historic importance of our ships. Jonathan Cohen, the well-known pianist, composer and presenter of BBC TV children's programmes including Jackanory and Play School performed at a number of fund-raising concerts and

Society events; while Richard Turner and Martin Oatway have spent years collecting and restoring valuable archive film for the PSPS collection, and producing a series of fascinating DVDs. Many members give promotional and historical talks to interested groups and Nigel Coombes describes over 30 years of giving river and coastal commentaries on *Waverley* and *Balmoral* as his most interesting job to help further the objects of PSPS. All around the coast PSPS members such as Jeremy Gold, Chris Warren and Iain Quinn do the same. In the archive David Green and his small team spend endless hours conserving, filing and cataloguing photographs and memorabilia from the Society's growing collection while others write funding bids or answer historical queries. Others attempt to drum up party bookings, some serve as pier hosts, welcoming passengers, distributing literature, answering questions and helping to resolve any problems which may arise from a delayed or cancelled sailing. The possibilities for volunteering are almost endless.

And then, of course, there is that equally large army of unsung partners who through their patience, advice and quiet skills allow all the rest to happen! To list every individual has been an impossibility, and to mention some and omit others always risks causing offence where none is intended. The best way out of this dilemma is to say to each and every volunteer who goes un-named: "You and your fellow enthusiasts know who you are, and your contribution is hugely appreciated. The Society gives you a heartfelt thank you".

Spreading the word. Many members in different parts of the country promote the Society and its ships by attending appropriate exhibitions and shows. In the South, Geoffrey Ryder and his trusty campervan has developed this into a fine art. The main event of his year is the Great Dorset Steam Fair which, conveniently, occurs just a few days before Waverley *opens her annual South Coast season. Geoffrey has attended for 35 years in succession and attracted countless passengers to sail on the ship.*
G. Ryder

As a reward for completing her log book a junior member visits Waverley's *bridge on 10 May 1988.*

R Clammer

CHAPTER EIGHTEEN

JUNIOR MEMBERS

With a contribution from Andrew Tedstone

FROM the earliest days of the PSPS, younger members were made extremely welcome and in 1962 the Society's rules were formalised to include Intermediate (age 15-21) and Junior (age under 15) categories, both of which proved remarkably popular. With hindsight this is perhaps not so very surprising as in the simpler, pre-computer world of the early sixties many boys (and, yes... it was mostly boys!) were interested in transport of all types, enjoyed train spotting and, if they lived by the coast, took a lively interest in the shipping movements in their local harbours. Some had been lucky enough to sail regularly on paddle steamers with their parents, and others developed a fascination simply because the paddlers were the most familiar and accessible of all local ships.

The newly-formed PSPS gave a focus to this interest. Winter meetings stirred an awareness of steamer history, summer excursions and visits provided the opportunity for new adventures on hitherto unfamiliar and exotic ships, and the campaigning aspect of the society lent an important sense of purpose. Strong and lasting friendships were formed and several of those early junior members are still active members of the society today.

Given understanding and patient parents who were willing to provide lifts or allow their offspring to disappear for long days by train to voyage on distant steamers, much fun was to be had. Your editor who grew up in Weymouth used to enjoy reciprocal visits with Peter Lamb in Southampton, sailed regularly on excursions and PSPS charters on board *Embassy, Ryde, Sandown, Balmoral, Consul*, while long day trips with friends on board *Princess Elizabeth* from Weymouth to Yarmouth during the school holidays were a regular occurrence.

Family trips to Weston and Ilfracombe allowed for occasional

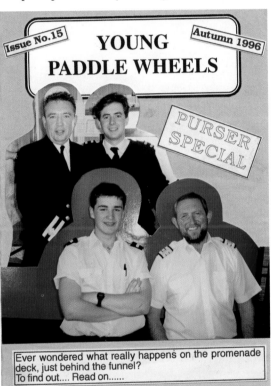

The front cover of Young Paddle Wheels *No 15, Autumn 1996, which focussed on the work of the ships' pursers. Pictured are Jim McFadzean and Chris Murray of* Waverley *and Neil O'Brien and Campbell Watt of* Balmoral.

sails on board *Bristol Queen* and *Cardiff Queen*, and he even persuaded his mother that a visit to Southend to take part in the final voyages of *Medway Queen* was absolutely essential! Along with fellow junior members Richard Green and John Megoran he was able to sail through Weymouth Town Bridge on *Princess Elizabeth's* last ever voyage in steam, while the ever-supportive Tony McGinnity allowed him almost free run of the *Consul* during her final seasons and arranged for him to sign on as a supernumerary member of the crew for the old ship's final voyage from Weymouth to Dartmouth. John Megoran was able to join *Jeanie Deans* for part of her 1965 voyage from the Clyde to the Thames, and others doubtless had equally memorable experiences.

As the number of operational paddle steamers dwindled the opportunity for these sorts of adventures also declined and so, quite gradually, did the number of junior members joining up. Some years later, however, as *Kingswear Castle* and *Waverley* established themselves in operational preservation, a new generation of Juniors began to emerge who were motivated not by nostalgia for what had been lost, but by the excitement of sailing on board the two surviving paddlers.

Conscious of the generally ageing profile of PSPS membership and the need to ensure a long-term future for the Society, Council of Management had always been acutely aware of the importance of encouraging more young members to become, and remain, members. Consequently, in the winter of 1991 a new initiative named "The Captain's Club" was launched. Special cruises were arranged on the Clyde, Bristol Channel and South Coast during which junior members could travel free, meet each other and visit the bridge and engine

Junior members visit Waverley's *bridge as she passes Hurst Castle, 5th September 1992.*

Junior members visit Waverley's *bridge at Weymouth, 16th September 1995.* R. Clammer

room. Painting and photographic competitions were held and *Paddle Wheels* now devoted a double page spread in each edition to junior members' articles, pictures and cruise reports. Regular early contributors included Chris Jones, Philip Camm, and Christopher Goodyear who, at five a half, was probably the Northern Branch's youngest ever member! Some of the older juniors such Paul Richards began to assist their parents as volunteers in the ships' souvenir shops and restaurants. "Teddy Bear Cruises" were also introduced to encourage more youngsters to travel on the ships with their families and hopefully to become PSPS members.

The Captain's Club initiative had the pleasing effect of doubling the number of junior members, but Chairman Nick James believed that even more effort was required. As he put it: "In the past junior membership has suffered from a chicken and egg scenario; we have done little to appeal to our Junior Members because we have few of them, and we have had few of them because we have offered them little." Determined to attract and keep more Juniors, who would represent the future of the Society, efforts were re-doubled.

During the winter of 1992 it was decided to discontinue the Captain's Club section within "Paddle Wheels" and replace it with a separate four page magazine with colour covers, which would be sent to all Juniors in the regular quarterly "PW" mailings. Named *Young Paddle Wheels* (or "YPW") it was edited by two Junior Members, Tom and Beth Clammer (aged 12 and 10 respectively) aided and abetted by their parents.

The new format allowed members' photographs and artwork to be reproduced in full colour, and the little magazine contained an entertaining mix of articles, letters, competitions and quizzes. A survey was sent out to all Juniors asking them what they'd like to see in print and what activities they would like to be provided. As a result of this some refinements were made to the successful Captain's Club formula.

Up to nine Captain's Club cruises were advertised each year involving all three ships and covering all of the main sailing areas. Junior members travelled free and one accompanying adult could claim a reduced fare as well. During the trips, circumstances permitting, visits were made to the bridge and

engine room, key crew members were introduced and the juniors were able to meet together for refreshments and a chat. In addition Captain's Club Log Books were introduced in which members could record dates and details of each trip taken and get it stamped by the purser. Once a full page of six trips had been completed the log book was signed and stamped by the ship's master and the member given a special reward such as taking a supervised period on the wheel or visiting a part of the ship not usually open to passengers. The idea proved so successful that senior members were soon getting jealous and asking for log books as well!

Junior winter parties were held on board *Balmoral* and *Waverley* during their winter lay-up periods, during which large numbers of juniors gathered to enjoy talks by Captains, engineers and volunteers, tours of the hidden parts of the ships, and some festive fun. Visits were also made to *Balmoral* in dry dock, the sailing ship *Matthew* and local museums. Particularly popular were the occasional bumper editions of "YPW" which included specials on engineers, pursers and deck crew explaining their roles and including interviews with key personnel. Enthusiastic contributors now included Sam Beaumont, Peter Weir, Jason Collins, Jonathon Westlake, Dominic McCall, Alex Collard, Ann Blackler. Scottish member Lorna Marshallsay built a wonderful model of *Waverley* while Philip Camm and friends raised £30 for the ship by doing a sponsored walk.

A membership pack was produced, containing welcome letters from the captains, a selection of books and souvenirs and a voucher for a further free trip and existing junior members were given guidance on how to organise group bookings for their schools or groups using the Charity Fundraising Tickets which were then available through WEL's Barry office. One member took a party of 500, which raised a considerable amount for both the ship and her school. The Northern Branch produced a series of cardboard cut-out kits which were sold on board but made available free to all juniors and made a considerable but ultimately unsuccessful effort to get an Airfix kit of *Waverley* produced.

Junior membership expanded to over 200 during this period

PW Editors Tom and Beth Clammer chatting with Nigel Coombes and National Chairman Nick James at the 1996 PSPS AGM held at the Norwegian Church in Cardiff Bay. Behind them is a display of artwork produced by junior members. R. Clammer

and it has to be said that much of the success of the initiative was due to the warm and friendly family atmosphere which existed on board the ships. *Waverley's* amazing purser Jim McFadzean and *Balmoral's* Neil O'Brien, along with most of the Masters and many of the crew seemed to know and greet every Junior by name, giving them a real sense of belonging and involvement. They were given every encouragement, under close parental supervision, to become involved in running the gift shops, helping with raffles, distributing leaflets and to develop a real understanding of the operation of the ships. They were also encouraged to join winter work parties and as teenagers many spent happy hours painting, varnishing and bilge-diving alongside parents and adult volunteers. This approach paid huge dividends as many still retain a keen interest in the ships. Some went on to work on board, others followed careers in the Merchant marine, Chris Jones is now a Harbourmaster, another, Ann Blackler, having spent many years as a ship's officer is currently a senior manager for a shipping company based in South Africa, while Dominic McCall is a First Officer with Swyres on the African Coast. Hopefully some of the others will read this book and make contact with the Society once again.

When Tom Clammer left home in 1998 his sister Beth continued to edit *YPW* alone for a further two years before she too headed for University. Between them they had produced 31 editions of the magazine over an eight year period, made many friends and derived a great deal of fun along the way.

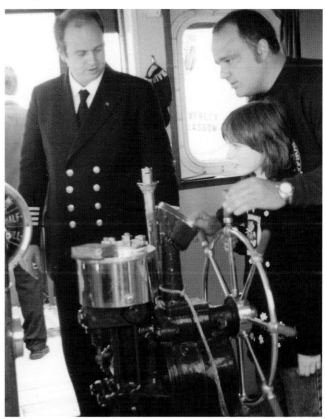

Having completed a page of her log book, Sophie Goodyear learns how to steer Waverley *under the watchful eye of Capt.* Graeme Gellatly

Despite following non-nautical careers in the Church and teaching respectively, both retain a deep affection for the ships, and Beth's own children now demand regular trips on board their local steamer, *Kingswear Castle*.

Responsibility for producing *Young Paddle Wheels* passed to junior Member **Andrew Tedstone** who takes up the story: "I took over the helm of YPW during Winter 2001 aged only 12. Whilst I almost certainly thought I was more than capable of running the whole show myself, it's clear now that the first year of editorship simply wouldn't have worked without significant behind-the-scenes input from Richard and my father Mike. Richard first gave me a thorough handover session, including which brand of sprayable glue to use for assembling printed sections of text and photos together to make the newsletter master for

Lorna Marshallsay with her model of Waverley, *1998.*

photocopying. I had different ideas having found the desktop-publishing software on the new family computer. The production became fully digital and included pestering Brian Whitmore, the membership secretary of the time, for up-to-date young members' lists so that I could mail-merge my own sticky mailing labels every quarter.

Young member numbers yo-yoed up and down over the next few years between around 50 and 100, including attracting members to join onboard *Waverley, Balmoral* and *Kingswear Castle* each summer by the lure of special young membership packs put together back in the winter on our living room floor in Wiltshire. Logbooks were an especially important part of this offer: get your logbook stamped by the Purser and every six trips you'd be entitled to a 'treat' such as a Bridge visit. If you felt one of the ships taking a zig-zag route up the Bristol Channel during the 2000s then it could have been my turn…

My YPW spell coincided with the start of widespread home adoption of the web, still mainly accessed by slow dialup at this time! During 2003, with a lot of support from John Megoran of *Kingswear Castle*, I put the first *YPW* website online. It was a steep learning curve and the site went through about four versions, culminating in 2005 with a new website complete with members-only features accessible by login. To compensate for the big increase in online effort we reduced the paper newsletter from four issues per year to two. GCSEs and other priorities then started to take over and so after 17 newsletter issues I handed over to Jack Woodham in 2007."

Sadly the junior membership bulge of the 1990s and early 2000s did not endure. Tighter maritime safety rules, the resultant regulations imposed by WEL regarding the role and qualifications of volunteers on board, plus changes of senior personnel all made it far harder to involve junior members in any significant way. With the much-lamented retirement of the inimitable Jim McFadzean in 2010 more of the "family atmosphere" on board *Waverley* was lost and with bridge and engine room visits removed from the offer, it proved increasingly difficult to attract juniors.

However, the PSPS Council of Management is still acutely aware of the importance of attracting young people into the organisation if it is to survive into the future. In 2017 a new category of Young Persons' Membership was introduced for anyone under the age of 26. Coupled with an improved website and a much-increased presence on social media, it is hoped that this will attract a whole new group of members who will want to become involved in all aspects of the Society and take it forward into the next 60 years. As we begin the Society's 60th Anniversary year the management team at WEL has made it clear that it values volunteers and wishes to strengthen its links with PSPS, so the omens are fair for a return to a warm and welcoming on-board experience and, hopefully, another boost to young people's membership.

Several teenage members were regular members of winter work parties. Here, Beth Clammer is seen painting Balmoral's *bilges on 18th March 2000.*   R. Clammer

Junior members and two parents enjoy a visit to Waverley *undergoing refit in Avonmouth Docks on 11th December 1999. Left to Right: Alex Collard, Alex Tedstone, unknown, Ann Blackler, Richard Clammer, Beth Clammer, Andrew Tedstone and Chris Collard.*   R. Clammer

Junior members enjoy a winter meeting on board Balmoral *on 18th March 2000. Capts. Ted Davis and Steve Colledge gave them a tour of the ship and answered questions before joining them for a party in the forward saloon.*   R. Clammer

Waverley departing from Ilfracombe on an afternoon cruise, 9th June 2007. R. Clammer.

CHAPTER NINETEEN

PADDLE WHEELS

John & Myra Allen

PADDLE *Wheels* is the journal of the Paddle Steamer Preservation Society which is provided for every member of the Society. It formally communicates Society news, such as the annual report and AGM notices, gives reports on Society activities including the archive, and it encourages volunteer and financial support. Nowadays it reports on 'our two ships', *Waverley* and *Kingswear Castle*, and other paddle steamers in the UK, such as *Maid of the Loch*, *Medway Queen* and *Monarch*. Reports on other paddlers worldwide, including occasional in-depth articles by local specialists, sit alongside historical research, sometimes featuring items from the Society Archives. Members can read about the operation of paddle steamers with occasional articles relating to their machinery, current operating principles, management and marketing.

Editors & Production

In March 1960 the very first issue of Paddle Wheels was published consisting of only four pages with no illustrations. The first Editor was Tony McGinnity, who took charge of the first four issues, suggested the name, and oversaw the production of the typed foolscap documents which were then laboriously duplicated and stapled. Subsequent issues were six pages which gradually increased over the years.

He was succeeded by Peter Ellis with assistance from Society Founder Alan Robinson and Assistant Editor John Stay, who in turn took over as Editor with the production of Issue 11. At this point photographs started to appear, usually on separate glossy covers. John Stay remained as Editor until issue 22, during which time the abortive acquisition of the *Alumchine* was covered, together with the more successful assistance in securing a future for *Medway Queen*. Dr Duncan Edgell took over in November 1965 for issues 23 to 26, covering the period when *Jeanie Deans* was purchased and transformed into *Queen of the South*.

Russell Plummer took on a lengthy Editorship role which lasted from1966 until 1992 initially assisted by William Pollard, and broken with a brief interval during 1979 and 1980 when he continued to look after the layout and design but Iain Macleod took on the editor's role.

During Russell's period of Editorship the production of Paddle Wheels evolved: until issue 36, the first to be seasonally dated as Spring 1969, each issue had been dated with the month

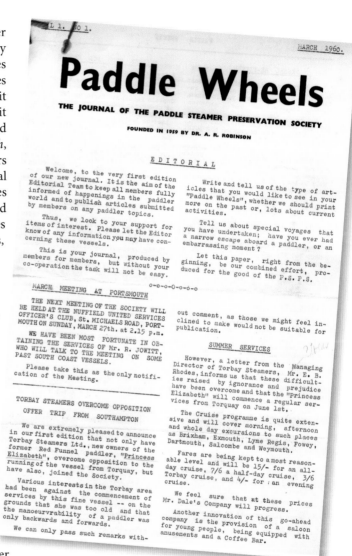

The front of the very first edition of Paddle Wheels, *March 1960.*

and year of publication, and then for some years a mix was used; It was only with issue 54 (Summer 1973) that seasonal dating became universal. The May 1970 – April 1972 issues were printed on A4 paper in magazine format, and a quarto size format was first seen in Issue 51. From Issue 107 (Spring 1987) onwards, Paddle Wheels changed to standard A5 format and it remained the same until Issue 229 in the Autumn of 2017.

Although he arranged the printing of the next three editions, Russell Plummer handed over to the current editor, Myra Allen, in the summer of 1992 with issue 128 which was the last to be produced wholly using traditional paste-up methods. From Issue 131 onwards, typesetting was carried out using Pagemaker® commercial software, with photographs scanned by the printers and added to the camera-ready text. Issues 129 and 130 were hybrids, with some pages traditionally pasted up, whilst others used the software.

As more material has been received electronically, more has been done in-house, and it is now all done electronically, using Pageplus® commercial software, with.pdf files sent directly to the printers. The software is installed on the editor's home computer, as are the flatbed and slide scanners used on the rare occasions when traditional photographs are used.

Gradually, as technology moved on and costs came down, the amount of colour pages increased, and the journal became full colour from issue 188 in the summer of 2007.

Many different printers have been used over the years to produce the journal. These have included Alderson Print Group, Anglebury Press, Anglia County Press, Blue Group, Dramrite Ltd, First Impressions, Halligans Ltd., HenDi Group, Howard Hunt (City) Ltd., Nene Lithographics, Newby Printing Services Ltd., Penshurst Press London Ltd., Premier Print and Mail Group, Pureprint Group, Showcase Design and Print, and SMAC Associates.

There were, of course, a few inconsistencies and oddities to challenge the avid collector, and a few production issues have kept the collectors guessing: for example there was no Summer 1974 issue, issue 56 being dated Spring 1974, and issue 57 being Autumn 1974; issue 65/66 was a combined edition for Autumn and Winter 1976; and Summer 1980, (issue 80) was also published as a Waverley Souvenir Issue for 50p, but with a different front cover, inside and out, and a different centrespread!

Distribution

Distribution arrangements have varied over the years. When the membership was small, it was done centrally, sometimes by the Society Secretary. In more recent years, prior to the move to A4, distribution was carried out by other PSPS

The twin funnelled paddle tug moving a hefty rake of barges is a sight that has now disappeared from even the great rivers of Europe. This view of the DDSG tug Suppen (1921-1967) was captured a few years back by Gustl Gloss of Passau, Germany.

PADDLE WHEELS

NUMBER 44 41   MAY 1970
THE JOURNAL OF THE PADDLE STEAMER PRESERVATION SOCIETY

Edition 41, May 1970, the first of nine produced in an A4 magazine format.

volunteers in the branches. Once printed, the copies were dispatched to the Branch distributors, with further copies sent to those who dealt with new members, late renewals and other recipients such as the British Library. The Branch distributors collated all the inserts, some of them specific to the Branches, stuffed the envelopes and mailed them.

With the move to A4, the opportunity was taken to use a specialist distribution house. This required a rationalisation of the inserts, but the resulting simplification, and use of discounted postal rates, has resulted in an overall reduction in cost, and a shortening of timescales.

Paddle Wheels is currently produced 4 times each year, for dispatch in March, June, September and December.

Content

Over the years Paddle Wheels has always contained a mix of articles, including some of a historical nature, featuring ships and operating companies of the past, and some of them educational, including technical articles and those explaining the operation aspects of ships.

During the 1960s, articles often focussed on the remaining operating paddlers, at home and abroad, with frequent reports of PSPS charters and, sadly, reports of their withdrawal from service. There were frequent questions about the future of the Society, the merits of steam versus diesel propulsion, and whether the Society should support screw steamers and motor vessels. Ship modelling was also featured.

Although foreign paddlers had been featured occasionally beforehand, it was Russell Plummer who covered them on a regular basis. Issue 27, Russell Plummer's first, featured the paddlers of Lake Luzern and later issues reported the building of the new paddle steamer cruise ship *Mississippi Queen*. Sadly, she did not last, being scrapped in 2011.

The back cover of Issue 94 featured a colour photograph of the magnificent Hudson River side-wheeler *Alexander Hamilton*. The loss of this vessel by fire and subsequent sinking in 1977 is perhaps one of the greatest tragedies in the last 50 years of paddle steamer preservation. The back cover of Issue 155 featured the Luzern paddle steamer *Stadt Luzern* complete with a bulbous bow!

As the commercial operation of the last paddlers in the UK ceased in the 1960s and 1970s, Paddle Wheels chronicled the acquisition, restoration and subsequent operation of *Kingswear Castle* and *Waverley*. Almost half of Issue 71 is devoted to Captain David Neill's story, including his involvement with attempts to save *Caledonia* for operational preservation, and the grounding of *Waverley* on the Gantocks in 1977. It makes a fascinating read.

The 1980s included the motor ships *Prince Ivanhoe* and *Balmoral*, which both operated in conjunction with *Waverley*, together with the ongoing attempts to rescue and restore the *Medway Queen* and *Maid of the Loch*, and the ongoing status of the other statically preserved paddle steamers which still survived. The news pages also shifted focus and featured car ferries and other coastal and inland cruising vessels. This attracted occasional criticism from the paddle steamer purists. Issue 140 announced the formation of The Paddle Steamer Cruise Line and its plans to build a fleet of paddle steamers in tourist areas throughout the world. The first ship was to be named *New Caledonia*. Sadly, the plans eventually came to nothing.

The Captain's Club was introduced in Issue 125, Autumn 1991, as part of an initiative to encourage more young members. Issue 126 onwards, a Junior Section of *Paddle Wheels*, initially edited by Jane Jones, was a regular feature until, from issue 131 onwards, a separate publication was produced, edited by Junior members themselves

More recently, the journal has concentrated on paddle propelled vessels, and as the Society's archive has developed, regular reports have been included, featuring acquisitions of special interest. Periodically, articles relating to the finances of *Waverley*, *Balmoral* and *Kingswear Castle* have appeared, as have articles on piers, without which, it is very hard to operate paddle steamers.

It is difficult to highlight notable issues, but a few deserve a special mention.

Celebratory articles have appeared regularly. The front cover of Issue 58, 1974, featured the famous 'Paddler for a Pound' photograph, whilst *Waverley's* triumphant

return to service was covered in Issue 60 and a gold front cover to celebrate the 50th anniversary of *Waverley* featured in 147. Likewise Issues 94 and 95 reported *Kingswear Castle's* return to steam after her 10-year restoration.

Issue 185, 2006, was more upbeat than most, reporting the trial slipping of *Maid of the Loch* following the restoration of the Balloch Steam Slipway, the successful approval of Heritage Lottery Funding for *Medway Queen's* new hull and the celebration of three significant birthdays; Jim McFadzean, *Waverley's* long serving and ever popular purser's 60th, Alan Bruce, well-known London Branch Member's 80th, and the 100th birthday of Jane Hughan, mother of Michael Hughan (Loch Lomond Steam Packet Company)!

Of course, PSPS patrons Timothy West CBE and Prunella Scales CBE have featured in various issues from time to time notably issue 174 which pictured Ronnie Barker with catering manager Craig Peacock and purser Jim McFadzean on the charter of *Waverley* to celebrate their Ruby Wedding.

Other VIPs and celebrities have featured occasionally. Royal appearances could definitely not be missed: Issue 153 pictured HRH Prince Edward on *Kingswear Castle* whilst filming a TV series called *Crown and Country*; HRH Princess Anne, the Princess Royal, was shown aboard *MV Balmoral* on a Missions to Seafarers Charity Charter in issue 178 and again in 187 on board *Maid of the Loch* for the formal re-opening of the restored steam slipway at Balloch.

The Autumn 1987 journal, reported on two VIP visitors for *Kingswear Castle*, Prime Minister Margaret Thatcher, who took a trip from Thunderbolt Pier to Gillingham, and Harry Secombe, who featured the steamer on the TV series *Highway*. Writer Peter Ackroyd on board *Kingswear Castle* (Issue 193) was pictured whilst filming for television and also Michael Portillo on *Waverley*, (Issue 218)

Cardiff Queen *pictured on the cover of the Spring 1987 edition, the first A5 issue.*

The Swiss diesel-electric paddler Italie, *back in service after a major rebuilt, was the cover choice for the final A5 edition in the Autumn of 2017.*

filming one of his *Great British Railway Journeys*.

Musicians too made their appearances: Issue 72 features Radio 1 disc jockeys Kid Jensen, Paul Burnett, Dave Lee Travis and Tony Blackburn on board *Waverley* as part of Radio 1 Scottish Week; folk legend Jimmy McGregor appeared in issue 142 at the launch of the appeal to purchase *Maid of the Loch* from Dumbarton District Council; and Issue 161 showed well-known guitarist Gordon Giltrap making his first performance afloat on *Kingswear Castle*. Slightly less well known for being a musician but more for his political role as Tony Blair's Press Secretary, Alastair Campbell, was shown playing bagpipes on board *Waverley*!

Stunning photographs of *Waverley* in heavy seas off Douglas Head appeared on the front and back covers of issue 100 and two journals later there was a picture of *Waverley's* Captain, Andy O'Brian, being winched off the ship by the Coastguard helicopter in an innovative means of avoiding pilotage fees!

Perhaps the quirkiest news item, way back in Issue 7

Winter 2017 saw the publication of the first edition of Paddle Wheels *in its new, full-colour, A4 format.*

Paddle Wheels

Winter 2017 • Issue 230

Waverley Study Group Report of 1971 published for the first time
Maid of the Loch - On the verge of steaming again!
Recalling Waverley's first Mersey Adventure
New Chairman's Welcome

A ship which featured regularly in the early editions of Paddle Wheels, Princess Elizabeth *is pictured on a hot afternoon in September 1964 loading passengers for an afternoon cruise from Wemouth Pleasure Pier.*

Jim Fraser/PSPS Collection

featured a six week old donkey, Cuddly, who travelled from Weston to Cardiff on *Cardiff Queen*. Mum Judy was deemed too large, so was left behind by Captain Leo Virgo!

Moving Forward

Electronic copies can potentially be produced if it is thought desirable, and if a means of distribution can be established to ensure that only paid-up members can access it. But the reduced likelihood of critical information being absorbed and acted upon needs to be acknowledged. It is worth noting that at the last consultation of the membership on this topic, only 37% of the members who responded said they would want to receive Paddle Wheels on line, and almost half said they would not.

Finally, it would be wrong to end a feature on *Paddle Wheels* without acknowledging the contributions made by all those who have written the articles and supplied the photographs, whether regularly or occasionally. Without them, there would be no journal.

Since she took over as editor in 1992 Myra Allen has worked incredibly hard behind the scenes to ensure that Paddle Wheels *has maintained the highest standards of content and presentation. Together with her husband John she has travelled all over the world sailing on and photographing almost every surviving paddle steamer. She is pictured here on board the paddler* Vltava *at Melnik in the Czech Republic.*　　　　　　　　　　　　　　John Allen

Dressed overall and sounding her whistle in greeting Waverley *makes a dramatic sight for passengers on board* Balmoral *as the two ships meet off Penarth on a choppy day, 16th June 2009*
Chris Jones

THE PSPS COLLECTION
David Green

Sixty years ago when PSPS was formed the concept of a comprehensive, readily-available archive with computer access could only have been a dream. Many individual members had personal collections and with the formation of Branches additional material began to accumulate. In the early '60s donations to the Society began to arrive, two of the first being a lifeboat plaque from *Golden Eagle* and *Monarch's* bell from 1888. Photographs and press cuttings began to accumulate and were looked after by a succession of willing members.

During these early years a founder member of the London and Home Counties Branch (L&HC) was amassing his own personal Collection in East Bergholt, Suffolk. His name was Harold Collard Stone. Collard, as he was known, always wanted to assure his maritime collection's preservation for posterity, so it was in March 1969 that The Pleasure Steamer Historical Trust (PSHT) was formed. It consisted of three trustees, Collard, C.

David Green, the current PSPS Archivist, hard at work cataloguing postcards in the Chatham office. Heather Green.

P. G. Taylor and E. H. Wingfield, all PSPS members. It was at their inaugural meeting on the 1st March 1969 that he donated his entire maritime collection "comprising of steamship relics, models, photographs, books and manuscripts and the like... to the Trust for preservation and its maintenance for the public benefit and public exhibition." It is his collection together with the artefacts that were held by the PSPS branches that now form the core of the archive that PSPS owns and manages today.

As a boy Collard lived in Southend-on-Sea, Essex, and together with his brother made crude models of the steamers they'd either sailed aboard or had seen sailing to and from Southend Pier. In adulthood he refined his modelling skills and together with photographs and sailing bills his collection began to grow. In 1963 he was able to acquire 'The Ladywell Relics.' These had belonged to the late Ted Groom of Ladywell Rd, Lewisham and were being disposed of by his daughter. He wrote that they were to be disposed of "to someone who could preserve them in the interest of posterity." Collard was to be that person. In the period 1920 -1929 Ted Groom was an agent for The Royal Sovereign and Belle Steamer companies and when *Royal Sovereign*, *London Belle* and *Clacton Belle* were scrapped he visited the ship breakers in Holland and brought back various "relics" which the Society still owns today.

For two summers an exhibition was put together from Collard's "relics" and items belonging to the L&HC Branch which were to be displayed in local libraries, first at Margate and then Folkestone. This was followed by the formation of a small museum on board *Medway Queen* but his letters show that it was Collard's wish to find a home "on a permanent central site... in or around London." He feared that this was unlikely,so, when the Maritime Museum of East Anglia first opened at Great Yarmouth in 1967, "the opportunity of procuring one of its rooms for the Collection was seized" and the majority of Collard's collection together with that of L&HC Branch was to remain there until 1976.

During 1975 the Maritime Museum at Great Yarmouth came under the auspices of Norfolk Museums Service and it was decided by the powers that be that henceforth they only wanted to display artefacts directly associated with Great Yarmouth. Unfortunately this meant that much of the Trust's material was irrelevant. The Trust was reluctant to break up the Collection so the decision was taken to terminate the contract and seek a new location. Several sites were discussed including, when her restoration was complete, on board *Kingswear Castle*, but for one reason or another they all proved to be unsuitable. By this time the situation was becoming urgent and an approach was made to The Harwich Society which was setting up a museum in the Harwich Redoubt. An agreement was reached and, as recorded in the Trust's minutes, the collection was "lying in the Harwich Redoubt now waiting rebuilding completely". There is no record of what happened in the intervening years but in 1979 the Trust minutes record: "As it has been impossible to set up the Collection in the Harwich Redoubt, due to the dampness of the structure, it was set up as a temporary expedient in the Studio at 6 Quintons Corner, East Bergholt." However this secured only part of the Collection, the rest going to Trust and PSPS members for safe keeping.

H. Collard Stone, a founder member of the London Branch and the Paddle Steamer Historical Trust, pictured at Frinton in 1979. Peter Morley

From the very early days of the Collection and throughout the existence of PSHT there was a desire to make it available for viewing by the public and to create a museum in which to do so. With that in mind Collard had a plan whereby "many interested persons might care to avail themselves of the opportunity of viewing (it) at leisure during their convenience". A suitable building "equipped for the purpose" was constructed adjoining his residence at East Bergholt. It was to be known as "The Thames Estuary Maritime Museum". This part of the Collection remained at East Bergholt until 1981 when Collard and his daughter Margaret decided that due to his advancing years it should be moved to a new location. For the Trust finding a new home wasn't easy and after vetting several places they eventually decided on the Training Ship *Orwell* at Ipswich. It remained there until the mid-'90s and then moved to the newly formed Felixstowe Museum to be housed in their Paddle Steamer Room. Not all the items went to Felixstowe: some were displayed at Ramsgate and Margate museums and the surplus was once again entrusted to various Trust and PSPS members "until a suitable display site can be provided via the Central Committee" of the Society. Apparently this seemed to become the norm whenever storage difficulties arose, probably with the hope that eventually a suitable site could be found to create a permanent PSPS Museum.

One of the oldest and rarest items in the PSPS Collection, the bell of the paddle steamer Prince *built by John Scott Russell in 1852.* Prince *was the first custom-built Cosens steamer, the first pleasure steamer to be based at Torquay, and was closely involved with the development of Bournemouth and Swanage as resorts.* R. Clammer

Both having similar aims, the Trust and the PSPS always tried to work closely together. By 1979 the PSHT, had become increasingly concerned about its own lack of resources to meet its objectives and, believing that the Society could provide these, put forward a proposal to integrate the two. Much discussion then followed resulting in the PSHT becoming an integral part of PSPS and changing its name to The Paddle and Pleasure Steamer Historical Trust (P&PSHT). Thus, after 28 years almost to the day from its formation, the Trust ceased to exist and transferred all its property to the ownership and care of PSPS.

Until the appointment of a PSPS member Andrew Gladwell in 1995, the running of the Society Archive had been ably overseen by a number of volunteers including Bernard Cox, Richard Howarth, R. Hodge, Peter Lamb, Iain McLeod and Bernard See. Although Andrew was a volunteer at that time he was working in the museum sector. On his appointment, with concerns over ownership and location and with items spread far and wide, he set about locating artefacts and putting the archive on a more professional footing. Using his museum knowledge, giving each artefact an accession number and description, he transformed the previously written inventory into a searchable computerised professional catalogue which is still used today. He reorganised paper and computer records to meet museum standards and catalogued donations using museum criteria.

Both the Trust and the PSPS had always wanted its 'reserve' collection, (i.e. that not on loan to a museum), to be housed securely under one roof, so in 1995 premises in London were sought and the parts of the collection in members' custodianship were retrieved and stored at Nine Elms. However, that was not to be its final home. In the years that followed it was on the move again, firstly to Swanley and then to its current much larger and more appropriate premises in the Royal Historic Dockyard at Chatham. Today it welcomes visitors, enquiries and researchers by prior arrangement with Council of Management Archive Trustee David Green, contactable via the Society's website.

Since the original Trust was formed 50 years ago it has in some ways come a full circle. It is still fully owned by the PSPS

A fire bucket from La Marguerite. PSPS Collection

This fragile memorial card is a reminder of the tragic loss of life when the Thames steamer Princess Alice *collided with the collier Bywell Castle in Galleon's Reach on 3rd September 1878. The PSPS collection also includes a rather macabre souvenir in the form of a small wooden box made from timber recovered from the wreck.* PSPS Collection

A brass plaque from the dining saloon of the famous La Marguerite *of 1894, which at 2,205 gross tons was one of largest British paddle steamers ever built.* PSPS Collection

but now benefits from agreed dedicated funding, the lack of which was so often a problem in the past. It is currently overseen by a committee of three: PSPS Council of Management appointed Trustees, David Green and Richard Clammer and PSPS member Peter Box who work within agreed policies and procedures and hope one day to achieve national accreditation for the archive. As well as purchases it continues to welcome and receive legacies and donations, big and small, one recent addition being further items from the 'Ladywell Relics' donated by Ted Groom's grandaughter. A significant purchase has been the collection of Sydney Clifton Smith-Cox, the last Managing Director of P & Campbell Ltd., which consists of handbills dating been back to the 19th century, company records and photographs. Over the years the

This postcard-sized painting of Cosens' Monarch *of 1888 is one of over 4000 cards within the George Thomas collection which was added to the archive in 2016. The artist was A.H. White of Bournemouth who painted a large number of images, large and small, of local paddle steamers. The bell of* Monarch *was the first item acquired by the PSPS when it was donated by Cosens in 1960.* PSPS Collection

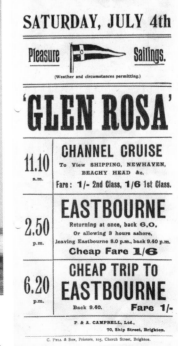

An example of one of the thousands of postcards from the George Thomas Collection within the PSPS Archive. This view shows the Hastings, St. Leonards & Eastbourne Steamboat Co.'s Cynthia arriving at Hastings pier between 1905 and 1907.

An example of one of the many crested or official company cards in the PSPS collection. This one depicts the Southampton, Isle of Wight & South of England Royal Mail Steam Packet Company's Lorna Doone and dates from 1898.

P&A Campbell's first Bristol Channel steamer, Waverley, which came from the Clyde in 1887. She is seen here leaving Cardiff Pier Head with the Mountstuart Dry Dock and a local pilot cutter in the background.

The River Dart Steamboat Company's Totnes Castle *on moorings in the River Dart during December 1963. Following an unfavourable survey, she had been withdrawn from service at the end of the previous summer and a replacement motor vessel ordered from Bolsons of Poole. Named* Cardiff Castle, *she was fitted with the paddler's wheelhouse and boat, which are missing in this atmospheric photograph.* Totnes Castle *was subsequently sold and converted into an accommodation ship for a local sailing school, but the venture failed to thrive. Sold for breaking up at Plymouth she sank while under tow in Bigbury Bay on 9th November 1967. This fine slide is from one of the many collections donated to the PSPS Archive.*

Jim Fraser / PSPS Collection

Archive has increased to over 50,000 artefacts covering the development of paddle steamers up to the 1960s, as well as items relating to *Waverley*, *Kingswear Castle* and *MV Balmoral*. The collection is wide-ranging, including ships' bells, telegraphs, lifebelts, chairs and plans, models, photographs, postcards and film, handbills and ephemera. The slide and negative collection is currently being scanned and digitised by a dedicated member living on the Isle of Man.

Margate Museum (housed in the Old Town Hall) and Felixstowe Museum at Landguard Fort continue to display the original Trust and PSPS collections in their Paddle Steamer Rooms. Southend Pier museum also has items on display and although not available for public viewing, and *HMS Wellington*, moored on the Victoria Embankment in London, displays a model of *Golden Eagle*.

One of the aims of the Society through its Archive is to "educate the public in the historical significance of paddle steamers in the Nation's maritime and industrial heritage". As it continues to develop and expand it plans to further that aim, one not dissimilar to the Trust all those years ago, by displaying part of its Archive on the Society's website, thus bringing the pleasure of Paddle Steamers to a 21st Century audience.

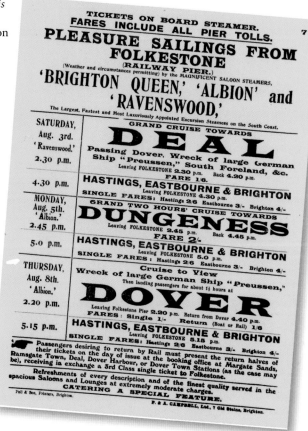

Waverley *departing from Swanage Pier on 3rd September 2010*   Chris Phillips (Swanage)

CHAPTER TWENTY ONE

DEVELOPING TO SUCCEED

Paul Semple (PSPS Chairman 2017-2019 and currently General Manager of Waverley Excursions Ltd)

As will be clear from the preceding chapters, the achievements of the Paddle Steamer Preservation Society and its associated owning and operating companies over the past 60 years have been truly astonishing. But what lies ahead?

In 2018 the Society published an ambitious three-year Development Plan. Ambitious in that it contained several Key Priorities, but all linked to one key component: to increase the membership against a year-on-year membership decline since 2004. Following the implementation of some actions points contained in the Development Plan the membership saw a small increase in 2018.

The Society is a group of members who have a common interest in wanting to help preserve paddle steamers, whether that be in terms of operating vessels or retaining materials and artefacts. However, it is through sailing on *Waverley* and *Kingswear Castle* that we attract the vast majority of members in support of our ships' continued operation.

When *Waverley* was withdrawn from service at the end of the 1973 season it could have been the end of paddle steamers on the Clyde for good. Caledonian MacBrayne couldn't have simply given her away to a couple of enthusiasts that had shown interest, but they could and indeed did gift her to an organisation whose purpose was to preserve paddle steamers. That organisation was of course our Society. The Paddle Steamer Preservation Society is the organisation that saved *Waverley*. – Does anyone need any other reason to join?

The story of a paddler for a £1 has captivated the public's imagination ever since and it is a story we must never tire of telling. The legal transfer of ownership of *Waverley* and her return to service is at the core of the PSPS. It was the Society's members who started the work parties, who approached local authorities, private companies and individuals for help and funding. It was PSPS members who formed a Board of directors to take official ownership of *Waverley*. For 45 years *Waverley* has been owned and operated by companies where

Kingswear Castle *heads downstream towards the castles at the mouth of Dartmouth Harbour at the start of an afternoon cruise on 2nd June 2018.*

R. Clammer

With her passengers safely landed at the end of a day trip around the Isle of Wight, Waverley *rests in her overnight berth at Southampton on 14th September 2013.*

R. Clammer

one of the conditions of being a director is to be an active member of the PSPS.

With *Waverley's* operational preservation came an opportunity for the Society to gain true respect by proving that a group of enthusiasts could indeed own and, more importantly, run a paddle steamer. Of course, this wasn't just a small, part-time affair where the ship steamed for a few days each summer. It was a full-time operation, often seven days a week in the peak season. The operating company was relatively small in terms of shipping but large in terms of public profile and remains so to this day.

It was the success of *Waverley* which attracted new members to join the PSPS, knowing that by doing so each one of them would become a small part of the *Waverley* story. The Society's membership hit a peak of over 4,000 members shortly after *Waverley's* rebuild in the early 2000s. On reflection the PSPS saved *Waverley* and *Waverley* saved the PSPS!

By early 2019 the total level of the PSPS's financial support for *Waverley* had reached just short of £3 million, a mighty achievement. On several occasions urgent PSPS funding has been essential to help ensure *Waverley's* continued operation. Today the PSPS holds reserves as an emergency fund for *Waverley* should she need it for an unexpected repair or to cover the cost of a winter refit should a season not generate sufficient income to make it through the winter. Put simply - the PSPS is needed to help safeguard the operation of *Waverley*.

While the full restoration and return to service of *Kingswear Castle* took longer than *Waverley's* and was achieved in a very different way, there is little doubt that a growing PSPS membership linked to *Waverley's* high profile helped to generate the funds which made the whole project possible. PSPS funding support for *Kingswear Castle* now stands at over £600,000 including a ring-fenced sum which was passed to *KC's* owning charity a few years ago.

For many years now, PSPS funding has helped to protect the operation of two cash-thirsty paddle steamers which will require on-going support if they are to continue in passenger service into the future. The strength of the Society and its ability to provide that funding comes from the membership, so it is imperative that we continue to increases our membership. We need the next generation to be recruited or our past achievements will be put at risk.

Some may ponder how much longer can we continue to operate paddle steamers. However, given that we are able to retain the "grandfather rights" which currently apply to historic ships, both steamers should continue for many years to come provided they are maintained and repaired as necessary. Both ships will, in the next give years, need to undergo substantial

While her passengers enjoy time ashore, Waverley *manoeuvres alongside the pier at Lundy Island on 9th June 2013.*   Ashley Gill

work. *Kingswear Castle* is likely to have a partial rebuild after the 2020 season, before her centenary in 2024. *Waverley* will require new boilers and other substantial investment shortly after. We have saved two ships which have outlived their fleet mates twice over. We should pause and consider the enormity of what has been achieved but never be complacent.

So how do we attract new members?

The Development Plan has many suggestions, but communication is key. We need to refine our approaches. A newly restyled Society magazine, refreshed publicity materials, vibrant social media platforms, greater presence in the media and across the shipping industry, a growing YouTube channel, incentives to join and a closer association with the steamers we saved will all form part of the strategy.

The Society must change and develop to survive. The generations which remember the post war era of paddle steamers around the U.K. are diminishing. Those under fifty today don't have personal experience of paddlers much beyond *Waverley* and *Kingswear Castle*, but we are now observing the emergence of a new group who harbour fond and nostalgic memories of the early years of our own steamers' preservation careers. A marked shift! We must therefore capitalise on the fact we have three operational paddle steamers in the U.K. – *Waverley, Kingswear Castle* and the little privately-owned

Monarch down in Dorset - and a fourth when *Maid of the Loch* steams again.

The ships are our best recruitment tool. We must engage future members through their experience of sailing on *KC* and *Waverley*. By sharing the stories of the past, giving the ships a personality, and making the passenger experience the best it can possibly be we will attract increased support. Passengers become supporters when they know they can make a difference. When they know how their fare helped cover the operating costs or their donation paid for a coat of paint, a new deck or refurbished paddles. We will retain members if we are honest with them, ensure they are the first to hear important news, and are offered clear explanations of any problems which arise and the solutions that were found.

For some, getting more deeply involved will help capture their interest. The Society and ships' companies will always require new directors and future Chairmen prepared to make them work, and both Branches and winter work parties always welcome new recruits.

In *Waverley* and *Kingswear Castle* we have two magnificent survivors from a world long since passed and two unique and priceless pieces of Britain's maritime heritage. Their future and that of the Society is reliant on new supporters. If you have yet to join, please do so and become part of the story – our Paddle Steamers need YOU!

Visit paddlesteamers.org and join now.

NATIONAL POSTHOLDERS

POSITION	DATE	NAME
PRESIDENT	1962-present	Alan Robinson
VICE PRESIDENT	1968-1969	Nick Knight
	1976-present	WG Prynne
	1988-present	Nigel Coombes
	1999-present	J T Sylvester
	2004-present	Nick James
	2004-present	Douglas McGowan *MBE*
	2017-present	John Anderson
CHAIRMAN	1959-Nov 1962	Professor A R Robinson
	Nov 1962-May 1963	J D Potter
	May 1963-Nov 1963	Bill Prynne
	Nov 1963-1967	Nick Knight
	1967-1976	Bill Prynne
	1976-?	Alan Peake
	1976-1980	Victor Gray
	1980-1982	Douglas McGowan
	1982-1988	Nigel Coombes
	1988-1991	Jeremy Gold
	1991-2004	Nick James
	2004-2012	Myra Allen
	2012-2013	Douglas McGowan
	2013-2017	Iain Dewar
	2017-2019	Paul Semple
	2019	Peter Morley
VICE CHAIR	1959-1962	Captn LGH Thomas
	1962-May 63	P Southcombe
	1964-65 Act.	Victor Gray
MEMBERSHIP SECRETARY	1962-1965	Victor Gray
	1965-1967	D V Wainwright
	1967-1976	John Millar
	1976-1980	Douglas McGowan
	1980-1981	Victor Gray
	1981-1982	Nigel Coombes
	1982-1991	Douglas McGowan
	1991-1994	Jeremy Gold
	1994-2001	Graham Hand
	2001-2004	Myra Allen
	2004-2007	Alex Lewis
	2008-2012	David Haddleton
	2013-2016	Jeremy Gold
	2016-2017	Paul Semple
	2017-present	Gordon Wilson
NATIONAL SEC	1959	Tony McGinnity
	1959-1960(Acting)	Bernard Cox
	1960-1962	Victor Grey
	1962-May 1964	T G Cadman
	1962-1968 Ass't. Sec	V F Burrell
	1964-1968	W Blakeney
	1968-1972	Chris Phillips
	1968-? Ass't. Sec	D K Jones
	1972-1975	Iain MacLeod
	1975-1979	Mike Hodges
	1979-2017	John Anderson
	2017-present	Angela Johnston

POSITION	DATE	NAME
TREASURER	1959-1959 (Acting)	Tony McGinnity
	1960-1961	ETY Randle also *Secretary & Editor*
	1961-1962	V F Burrell
	1962-1964	D L Dougan
	1965-1975	Victor Gray
	1975-1980	Iain McLeod
	1980-present	Martin Longhurst
SUBSCRIPTIONS SECRETARY	1959-1961	Tony McGinnity
	1965-1969	A P Clark
	1969-1980	David Swaffield
	1980-1983	John Beveridge
	1983	A W McRobb
	1983-1993?	Clem Robb
	1988-89	Leslie Brown
	1989?-2000	Mrs G Anderson
	2000-2009	Brian Whitmore
	2009	John Anderson
	2009-Temp	John Anderson
	2009-2013	Jon Joliffe
	2013-2015	Vacant
	2015-2018	Jon Joliffe
	2018-present	Gordon Wilson
SUBSCRIPTIONS OFFICER	1975-1976	Victor Gray
	1976-1980	G A Lewis
	1980-1988	P M Reid
SECRETARY & TREASURER	1961-1962	J H P Ellis
	1963-1965	J H Stay
	1965-1966	Dr Duncan Edgell
	1966-1978	Russell Plummer
	1979-1980	Iain McLeod
PADDLEWHEELS EDITOR	1960-1961	Tony McGinnity
	1961-1962	Peter Ellis
	1962-1965	John Stay
	1965-1966	Duncan Edgell
	1966-1979	Russell Plummer
	1979-1980	Iain Macleod
	1980-1992	Russell Plummer
	1992-present	Myra Allen
CURATOR	1961-1980s?	Bernard Cox
	1981-1995	R.Hodge, R.Howarth, I. Macleod, B. See.
MUSEUM OFF.	1995-2014	Andrew Gladwell
ARCHIVIST	2014-present	Richard Green
DATA CONTROLLER	2014-present	Richard Green
PATRONS	1960-1984	Sir John Betjeman
	1916-present	Timothy West CBE
	1916-present	Prunella Scales CBE

Source: PSPS website (with some simplifications)

THE PADDLE STEAMER PRESERVATION SOCIETY AND THE OWNERSHIP AND MANAGEMENT OF PS *WAVERLEY*, PS *KINGSWEAR CASTLE* AND PS *MAID OF THE LOCH*

THIS NOTE explains the relationship between the different charities and companies.

This legal structure has been developed to create managerial and financial separation between the various companies. This creates clarity about the respective responsibilities of each constituent part and minimises the possibility of any difficulties incurred by one impacting on the others.

Paddle Steamer Preservation Society (PSPS) is a charity and a limited company which exists to: preserve one or more paddle steamers, preferably in sailing condition; to educate the public in the historic importance of paddle steamers; and to create, manage and display items associated with these ships. Its members pay their subscriptions to belong. The PSPS is run by the Council of Management (in effect its Board of Directors) of up to 17 members. There are five geographical branches, each run by a Branch Committee. The members and the Branch Committees appoint most of the Council of Management. Although PSPS has provided substantial funding for Waverley and Kingswear Castle, usually for specified purposes, it does not as a matter of policy involve itself in their management.

Waverley Steam Navigation Co Limited (WSN) is the legal owner of *P.S. Waverley*. It is also a charity and a limited company. The PSPS holds 65% of its shares (a controlling interest) and has the right to appoint two directors. To maintain links, WSN may appoint one member of the PSPS Council. As

a matter of policy, PSPS will not normally exercise its controlling interest. *P.S. Waverley* is operated by **Waverley Excursions Limited (WEL)**, which is a wholly owned subsidiary of WSN. The PSPS has the right to appoint two Directors of WEL.

Paddle Steamer Kingswear Castle Trust Limited (PSKCT) is the legal owner of *P.S. Kingswear Castle*. It is also a charity and a limited company. The PSPS holds 83% of its shares (a controlling interest) and has the right to appoint two directors. To maintain links, PSKCT may appoint one member of the PSPS Council. As a matter of policy, PSPS will not normally exercise its controlling interest. *P.S. Kingswear Castle* has been placed on a long-term charter expiring in 2027 to Dart Pleasure Craft Limited (DPC) which is operating the steamer at Dartmouth. DPC is a wholly owned subsidiary of Dart Valley Railway Limited (DVR). The PSPS has a nominal shareholding in DVR. No single shareholder controls DVR. DVR and DPC use the trading name of Dartmouth Steam Railway and River Boat Company (DSRRB) and are commonly referred to as 'the Dart Company'.

P.S. Maid of the Loch is owned by **Loch Lomond Steamship Company (LLSC)** which again is a charity and a limited company. As the initial major funding came from local government, the PSPS has no control over LLSC but has contributed funds over many years. LLSC may appoint a PSPS director to PSPS Council.

Waverley *steaming into Oban Bay on 5th May 2013.*

Ashley Gill.

FURTHER READING

As a history of the PSPS, this book has constantly referred to the Society's two ships, *Waverley* and *Kingswear Castle*. It has not, however, attempted to provide a full and detailed history of either vessel, as this has already been done in a number of other excellent publications. Readers who would like to learn more are recommended to read:

Waverley

Waverley. Paddler for a Pound Douglas Mc Gowan, Tempus Publishing, 2003.

P.S. Waverley, The First Sixty Years, Alistair Deyton & Iain Quinn, Tempus Publications, 2010.

Waverley Steam Navigation Company, Compiled by Alistair Deyton & Iain Quinn, Amberley 2014.

Waverley: The Story of the World's last Seagoing Paddle Steamer. Waverley Excursions Ltd., updated regularly and available on board the ship or from the Waverley office.

General contact details: Waverley Excursions Ltd,
36 Lancefield Quay, Glasgow, G3 8HA,
Telephone 0141 243 2224,
Email info@waverleyexcursions.co.uk.
Website: www.waverleyexcursions.co.uk

Kingswear Castle

Paddle Steamer Kingswear Castle & The Steamers of the River Dart, Richard Clammer & Alan Kittridge, Twelveheads Press, 2013.

P.S. Kingswear Castle, A Personal Tribute, John Megoran, Amberley, 2017.

Both are available from book sellers, on board the ship or from her operators, The Dartmouth Steam Railway & Riverboat Company, from whom full details of sailings may also be obtained: Kingswear Station Office, Kingswear Signal Box, The Square, Kingswear, TQ6 0AA.
Telephone: 01803 555872.
Email: enquiries@dsrrb.co.uk
Website: www.paddlesteamerkc.co.uk

Other paddle steamers and coastal excursion steamers associated with or supported by the PSPS and currently undergoing restoration are:

Maid of the Loch

Maid for the Future *Maid of the Loch* souvenir brochure. £5 + p&p.

On Landlocked Seas: Ships of Loch Lomond, Loch Katrine and nearby lochs, Brian Patton £10+ p&p.

The Maid Story. A pack containing a *Voyage of the Maid* DVD and a copy of *On Landlocked Seas*.

The above available, with other merchandise from maid-of-the-loch.myshopify.com and on board the ship during her regular opening hours. Or from: Loch Lomond Steamship Company, The Pier, Pier Road, Balloch, G83 8QX. Telephone 01389 711865.
Email: mail@maidoftheloch.org

Loch Lomond Passenger Steamers, 1818-1989, Alan Brown, Alan T Condie Publications, 2000.

Scottish Loch & Canal Steamers, Alistair Deyton. Both out of print but available from on-line book sellers.

Medway Queen

The Medway Queen, Richard Halton, MQPS / Noodle Books, 2013.

The Medway Queen - Rebuilding the Hull, Richard Halton & Bob Stokes, MQPS / Noodle Books, 2014.

The Medway Queen Club, Richard Halton, MQPS / Noodle Books, 2016.

All available from Medway Queen Preservation Society's Website, www.medwayqueen.co.uk
or in person from the MQPS Visitor Centre, Gillingham Pier, Pier Approach Road, Gillingham, Kent, ME7 1RX.
Telephone 01634 575717.
Email info@medwayqueen.co.uk

Balmoral

Although no longer a member of the PSPS fleet, *Balmoral* has played an important part in the Society's story and, based in Bristol, is now owned by an associated charity.

Balmoral and the Bristol Channel, Mike Tedstone, Black Dwarf Publication, 2011.

The Honourable Balmoral: Her Piers and Peers, Richard Danielson, Maritime Publication, 1999.

MV Balmoral, The first 60 Years, Alisair Deayton, Iain Quinn & Patrick Murrell, Amberley, 2009.

Balmoral, Classic Coastal Cruise Ship, Mike Tedstone, MV Balmoral Fund Ltd/White Funnel Ltd. Most recent edition 2017.

General contact details: mvbalmoralfund.weebly.com
Many of the above books are available on board during the ship's open days or by post from the M.V. *Balmoral* shop at:
21-25 High Street Poole, Dorset BH15 1AB.
Email: shop@mvbalmoral.com

ACKNOWLEDGEMENTS

THE PRODUCTION OF THIS BOOK has only been possible because of the large number of friends and PSPS members and who have given freely of their time and knowledge, and allowed access to their collections of photographs and memorabilia. I thank them for their kindness and patience.

The Council of Management of the PSPS has been an enthusiastic advocate of marking the 60th Anniversary of the Society with a book, and several of its members have given valued advice and proof read the manuscript. John and Myra Allen, John Beveridge, Jeremy Gold, David Green, Guy Hundy, Nick James, John Megoran, Iain MacLeod, Douglas McGowan, Roddy McKee, Iain Quinn, Paul Semple and Gordon Wilson have all written chapters; while the memories of Nigel Coombes, Victor Gray, Peter Lamb, Pat Murrell, Chris Phillips, Geoff Ryder, Helen Stachan and Terry Sylvester have been incorporated into other chapters. In addition, Keith Adams, Brian Jackson, Angela Johnson, David Haddleton, Mike Tedstone, Martin Longhurst and Geoff Pritchard have all made valuable contributions. I am extremely grateful to David Green and his wife Heather who spent many hours selecting and delivering several crates-full of relevant documents from the Society Archive, which have helped to ensure the accuracy of the earlier chapters. Tremendous thanks are due to Margaret Hutchinson both for her meticulous proof-reading and for assembling invaluable notes on the memories of our founder, Professor Alan Robinson. Finally, a big thank you is due to our Patrons, Timothy West and Prunella Scales for contributing the forward.

Every effort has been made to establish and acknowledge the provenance of every photograph used in the book, each photographer has been acknowledged, and I apologise if any copyright has been inadvertently infringed. I owe an enormous debt of gratitude to Richard Danielson, of the Isle of Man, who for many months now has been patiently digitising and restoring the PSPS slide and negative collection and has drawn my attention to some outstanding images as he has gone along. Keith Abraham, Keith Adams, Tony Horn, Murray Paterson and Iain Quinn have all given me free access to their collections and a large number of individuals have supplied important, historic pictures. Thanks are due to Andrew Clark of the Clyde River Steamer Club, Richard Halton of the Medway Queen Preservation Society and Peter Lamb of the Coastal Cruising Association and for granting permission to use images from their respective organisations' archives. It has also been a huge privilege to include some outstanding photographs from the cameras of those superb, contemporary steamer photographers Ashley Gill, Chris Jones Chris Phillips of Swanage, Richard De Jong and Roy Tait.

Douglas and Jean McGowan have provided quiet encouragement throughout the project, which has been much appreciated. Finally, a huge thank you to my wife Carol who, despite some challenging circumstances of her own, has been her usual tower of strength; writing, editing, proof-reading, dispensing wise advice and offering unstinting support.